The Languages of Civil Society

EUROPEAN CIVIL SOCIETY
Editors: **Dieter Gosewinkel** and **Jürgen Kocka**, Wissenschaftszentrum, Berlin

Civil society represents one of the most ambitious projects and influential concepts relating to the study of modern societies. It encapsulates their structures and their gradual restructuring as well as their changing polities and cultures. Scholars working in this field aim to secure greater equality of opportunity, democratic participation, individual freedom, and societal self-organization against both the overbearing and overburdening powers of the modern state as well as the social deficits of globalizing neo-liberalism. This series deals with the multiple languages, different layers, and diverse practices of existing and emerging civil societies in Europe. Its leitmotif is to analyse whether and how far the renewed interest in the concept can contribute to the gradual evolution of a larger European civil society.

Volume 1
Languages of Civil Society
Peter Wagner

Volume 2
Civil Society: Berlin Perspectives
John Keane

THE LANGUAGES OF CIVIL SOCIETY

Edited by
Peter Wagner

Berghahn Books
New York • Oxford

First published in 2006 by

Berghahn Books

www.berghahnbooks.com

© 2006 Peter Wagner

All rights reserved.
Except for the quotation of short passages
for the purposes of criticism and review, no part of this book
may be reproduced in any form or by any means, electronic or
mechanical, including photocopying, recording, or any information
storage and retrieval system now known or to be invented,
without written permission of Berghahn Books.

Library of Congress Cataloging-in-Publication Data

The languages in civil society / edited by Peter Wagner.
p. cm. -- (European civil society ; vol. 1)
Includes bibliographical references and index.
ISBN 1-84545-118-X (hc) -- ISBN 1-84545-119-8 (pbk.)
1. Civil society. 2. Communication in politics. 3. Liberty.
4. Democracy. I. Wagner, Peter, 1956– II. Series

JC337.L35 2006
300--dc22

2006044451

British Library Cataloguing in Publication Data

A catalogue record for this book is available from
the British Library.

Printed in the United States on acid-free paper

ISBN 1–84545–118-X hardback

CONTENTS

EDITORS' PREFACE

Is there a 'European civil society' which cuts across national borders and spreads, though unevenly, through the continent? Does it help to form a European identity from below? Can it be seen as an answer to the obvious democratic deficit of the European Union?

For two and a half years, more than 40 political scientists, sociologists, historians and other scholars from 15 research institutions in 10 different countries have worked together on the project 'Towards a European Civil Society'. They were supported within the 5th Framework Programme of the EU. The network was coordinated by the Social Science Research Center Berlin. The results of the project are published in the volumes of this series which include studies by other authors as well.

'Civil society' means many things. The concept varies and oscillates. To give a working definition: 'civil society' refers (a) to the community of associations, initiatives, movements and networks in a social space related to, but distinguished from, government, business and the private sphere; (b) to a type of social action which takes place in the public sphere and is characterized by non-violence, discourse, self-organisation, recognition of plurality and orientation towards general goals and civility; (c) a project with socially and geographically limited origins and universalistic claims which changes while it tends to expand, socially and geographically.

Civil society is a deeply historical concept. For a quarter of a century, the concept of 'civil society' has experienced a remarkable career in several languages. Having a long tradition of many centuries, it had nearly disappeared during most of the twentieth century before being rediscovered and reinforced in the 1970s and 1980s when the concept became attractive again in the fight against dictatorship, particularly against communist rule in East Central Europe. But in non-dictatorial parts of the world the term and its promise responded to widely spread needs as well. Western Europe can be taken as an example.

Civil society as a political concept of our time has come to formulate critique of a broad variety of problems in contemporary society. To name three tendencies: first, the concept emphasizes social self-organisation as well as individual responsibilities, reflecting the wide-spread scepticism towards being spoon-fed by the state. Second, 'civil society', as demonstrated by the phrase's use by present-day anti-globalization movements, promises an alternative to the unbridled capitalism that has been developing so victoriously across the world. The term thus reflects a new kind of capitalist critique, since the logic of 'civil society', as determined by public discourse, conflict and agreement, promises solutions different from those of the logic of the market which is based on competition, exchange and the maximization of individual benefits. Thirdly, civic involvement and efforts to achieve common goals are specific to 'civil society', no matter how differently the goals may be defined. In the highly individualized and partly fragmented societies of the present time, 'civil society' promises an answer to the pressing question of what holds our societies together at all.

On the basis of broad empirical evidence, the project has analysed a large number of core problems of 'civil society', among them the complicated relation between markets and civil society; the impact of a European civil society on a European polity and vice versa; the importance of family and household for the ups and downs of civil society. The project has dealt with resources, dynamics and actors of civil society. It has dealt with questions of gender and other forms of inequality. It has compared developments in different European regions. It has begun to open up the perspective towards the non-European conditions, consequences and correlates of European civil society. It has reconstructed the language of civil society, including different semantic strategies in the context of tradition, ideology and power which explain the multiple uses of the concept for different practical purposes. These are some of the topics dealt with in the volumes of this series. The authors combine a long historical perspective with broad and systematic comparison.

What does it mean to speak of a 'European' civil society? It implies a certain common European development, a parallel or even convergent trend towards the emergence of civil society in Europe. Such a development may be based on the activities of civil society groups. From the eighteenth to the twentieth century, civil society circles, associations, networks and institutions largely evolved in local, regional and national frameworks. Trans-national variants, however, which might contribute to the emergence of trans-national coherence and similarities remained secondary. It is in the second half of the twentieth century that the quality of the process changed. In this phase, the development of civil society in Europe increasingly assumed trans-national, 'European' and sometimes global dimensions. This is a basic hypothesis of research in this series of studies. 'European Civil Society' will concentrate on trans-national dimensions of civil society in Europe by comparing and reconstructing interrelations.

The evolution of a European civil society in the process of trans-nationalization is based on actors as well as on mobile concepts. The ideas and practices of civil society have evolved in a very uneven way, starting to emerge mainly in Western Europe, where it was initially restricted to a few proponents and to specific circles. In the course of its development, civil society spread to other parts of Europe (and into other parts of the world) and gained support within broader social spheres. As they expanded into widening social and spatial environments, the ideas and realities of civil society changed. Thus, the potential of an approach is explored which takes civil society as a geographically and socially mobile phenomenon with a good deal of travelling potential and with the propensity to become a European-wide concept.

'European Civil Society' focuses on Europe in a broad, not merely geographical, sense. This includes comparing European developments with developments in other parts of the world, as well as analyzing processes of (mutual) transfer and entanglement. Europe in this sense transcends the institutional and spatial realm of the European Union. Yet, studying the emergence and dynamics, the perspectives and problems, of civil society in Europe may produce insights into the historical process of European integration, a process which is underway, but far from complete, and presently in crisis.

'European Civil Society' is a common endeavour of European and non-European scholars. It centres around a topic which is both the object of scientific analysis and political efforts. The political success cannot be taken for granted. Scientific analysis, however, may help to work out the conditions under which the utopia of civil society in Europe has a chance of realization.

Dieter Gosewinkel
Jürgen Kocka

—

PART I

Beginnings

Chapter 1

CIVIL SOCIETY AND THE PROBLÉMATIQUE OF POLITICAL MODERNITY

Jean Terrier and Peter Wagner

Contemporary debates on civil society are usually based on a specific assumption about the historical trajectory of the concept. In its recognizably 'modern' form, the concept of civil society is said to have emerged in Europe in the late eighteenth century; it is taken to have lost most of its significance during the nineteenth and much of the twentieth century, and it revived in the late twentieth century. One of the purposes of this volume is to review this assumption. This task, however, will not be addressed here from a perspective of the history of concepts alone; we rather also see it as a work of retrieval of the significance of the concept for the understanding of contemporary societies and their political forms. In this sense, our discussion of conceptual history will aim to make two aspects of 'conceptual labour' (Wagner 2003a) particularly visible. First, it will set selected episodes in the history of the concept in the context of respective attempts at understanding society and politics; that is, it will see conceptual proposals as ways of linking a variety of otherwise highly different observations on the social world in such a way that common meaning and, in a second step, collective action upon the world become possible. Second, it will try to show how an analysis of the variety of such attempts across the history of Europe since antiquity, with a focus on developments since the late eighteenth century and with additional concept-broadening observations on East Asian and Latin American debates, can help resolve certain problématiques of political modernity in general. The concept of civil society is here discussed as one specific, historically varying way of addressing the requirements of the viability of modern polities.[1]

The current debate about civil society is in many respects a sophisticated version of 'tunnel history'. Rather than emphasizing either the gradual rise or the inevitable decline of a concept and of the phenomenon to which it refers, as affirmative and critical social theories and political philosophies of modernity do, it tends to claim that the concept arose promisingly during a certain period, fell into unjustified oblivion afterwards, to rise to new strength and, as it is hoped, to its full realization in the present. In a first step the background to this narrative, both historical and normative, is easy to grasp. The concept was first proposed to explore the possibility and limits of collective self-determination on the eve of the 'democratic revolutions'; it declined with the gradual normative acceptance and institutional consolidation of democracy; and it re-emerged at a moment of quest for a renewal of the democratic impetus, which was seen as threatened or emptied of substance in the face of the domination of political agency by bureaucratic or market-economic imperatives, variously underpinned by strong political doctrines. This first grasp at normative and historical contextualization demonstrates, in the first instance, the link of the concept of civil society to the idea of democracy, of collective self-determination. It thus justifies our proposal to set the analysis of the trajectory of the concept into the context of the problématiques of political modernity.

By *modernity*, to put it briefly, we refer to a situation in which human beings commit themselves to determine their own lives, their relations to others and their ways of being in the world. By *political modernity*, more specifically, we refer to the self-determination of the life in common with others, to the rules of the life in common. During the past two centuries, and in particular since the end of the Second World War, much of social and political theory has assumed that there is a single model of 'modern society', to which all societies will gradually converge because of the higher rationality of its institutional arrangements. Similarly, political modernity is then equated with a single institutional model based on representative democracy and a set of basic individual rights. Seen from a historical perspective, in contrast, the debate about civil society in its relation to political organization suggests that a commitment to political modernity does not lead unequivocally to a certain institutional form of the polity. Such commitment is not only open to interpretation, it is profoundly underdetermined and marked by deep tensions. Consequently, the existing polities that share this commitment are based on a variety of such interpretations. The following pages review some of these interpretations which are directly connected with the notion of civil society, both before and after the democratic revolutions.

Without doubt, the advent of the 'democratic revolutions', even though only moderately successful, spelt one major change in political form and was thus likely to have a strong impact on the way the concept 'civil society' was understood. On those grounds we start our observations in conceptual history with a short discussion of Adam Ferguson's *Essay on the History of Civil Society* (1767), possibly the most significant exploration of the term before those revolutions, to be followed by contrasting observations on Alexis de Tocqueville's *Democracy in America* (1835–40) as a deliberately post-revolutionary reassessment of the political situation of the time. Rather than starting out from G.W.F. Hegel's reasoning in *Elements of a Philosophy of Right*, as many contributions to the current debate on civil society do, we place Hegel's thinking as a rather specific one between the broader and more open conceptualizations offered by Ferguson and Tocqueville.

Adam Ferguson and the Possibility of Civil Society

Before the writings of Hegel (and those of Marx) who, as we shall see, introduced an important shift in the way in which the notion was typically understood, it is possible to identify two distinct usages of civil society. It is well known, as it has been well demonstrated by many historians of the term for authors as diverse as Hobbes, Harrington, Locke or Rousseau, that 'civil society' is used as a synonym for political community, and is opposed to the state of nature.[2] In the contemporary debate on civil society, this fact is often used to argue that there is no proper theory of civil society before the beginning of the nineteenth century – more specifically, before Hegel. In turn, this would be equivalent to saying that the problématique of civil society is not essentially connected to that of modernity – unless one adopts the notion, which is extremely reductive in our view, that modernity starts only with the democratic revolutions.

It seems, however, that there is another usage of the term 'civil society' before that date, in which civil society is not treated as a mere equivalent of the 'state', but receives a specific conceptual treatment. This usage seems to have been prevalent among the Scots and to have played quite an important role in the turn-of-the-century English and American discussion on the merits and demerits of the French Revolution.[3] In this other usage, 'civil society' is one of the main terms used in a debate about the transformation of social relations in modern times, and about the political consequence of such a transformation. In other words, it seems that it is possible to find debates in classical political thought in which 'civil society' does not refer to a liberal principle of limitation of state power,[4] but is rather connected, as it were, to a republican interrogation of the type of social individuals and social relations that are necessary to establish and maintain a free government.

In the 1740s approximately, David Hume started to publish the results of his long reflection on seventeenth-century political thought. From the point of view of the type of reasoning used in this context, one might argue that Hume paid great attention to certain themes that other philosophers with whom he engaged in discussion, such as James Harrington and John Locke, had left to a large extent untouched. These themes have something to do with the question of the form of social relations and the place of social individuals within them. Hume suggested that the image of human beings proposed by Harrington or Locke had no great correspondence with reality. The two thinkers, indeed, shared a perception of individuals as contributing actively to shape and transform the polity – for all its being implicit and underdeveloped when compared to the richness of Hume's study of human nature, their anthropology was clearly and distinctly a positive one. Hume, instead, emphasized the tendency of individuals to refrain from action because of contracted habits (that of obedience being particularly important).[5] In many cases this led individuals to prefer authority over liberty – or at least to accept the sacrifice of the 'strong passions' of liberty to 'the interests of peace and public order' ('Of the original contract', Hume 1964: 455):

> A great sacrifice of liberty must necessarily be made in every government; yet even the authority, which confines liberty, can never, and perhaps ought never, in any constitution, become quite entire and uncontroulable. ... In this sense, it must be owned, that liberty is the perfection of civil society; but still authority must be acknowledged essential to its very existence ('Of the origin of government', Hume 1964: 116)

Against the republican ideal of political involvement and the liberal appeal to explicit consent, thus Hume coolly argued that he 'shall always be more fond of promoting moderation than zeal' ('That politics may be reduced to a science', Hume 1964: 107); and that such a moderation in civil society would not necessarily make the polity unfree.

In another series of political essays, he turned his attention to a specific kind of social relations, namely *commercial* relations ('Of commerce', 'Of money', 'Of trade'). He welcomed the development of 'mechanical arts' as providing a greater well-being to most classes of the nation, thus diminishing the risk of political tensions and stabilizing the polity.[6] Hume's positive appreciation of commerce, combined with his other argument that political passivity can be a legitimate quality of the members of a 'civil government', is mirrored in the work of yet another important thinker of the Scottish Enlightenment, Adam Smith.[7]

According to the interpretation of J.G.A. Pocock, the line of reasoning of authors such as Hume and Smith was targeting the classical civic humanist insistence on the crucial importance of the political involvement of virtuous men for the survival of free governments (Pocock 1983). Against this republican perception Hume tended to question the very possibility of human beings to act virtuously, argued that grandeur and baseness were always relative ('Of the dignity or meanness of human nature'), and sustained that good institutions rather than virtuous individuals were crucial to the proper functioning of politics ('That politics may be reduced to a science').

In a certain way, one might argue that Adam Ferguson's *Essay on the History of Civil Society* constituted a reply to Hume by arguing that, while some kind of political virtue was indeed necessary to sustain a free polity, this virtue did not necessarily have to be purely individual, and could as well be collective. In this light one can understand better Ferguson's reflection on what he called the 'national spirit'.

Referring to the 'social disposition of man' (Ferguson 1995: 23), Ferguson's reasoning started from a reformulation of Aristotle's classic statement concerning the *zoon politikon* or, in the usual Latin translation, 'social animal'.[8] On the basis of historical evidence, Ferguson argued that individuals had a natural tendency to cohere in broad human associations in which they could enjoy the company of others. When trying to qualify the nature of the association formed by human beings, Ferguson insisted in particular upon the importance of the communicative dimension. He argued that linguistic exchange played a central role in cementing the association, insofar as the individual is 'inclined to communicate his own sentiments, and to be made acquainted with those of others' (p. 9). Thus, according to Ferguson, human beings belong to collectivities marked by linguistic interactions. These interactions could take various forms, including that of dispute: as he wrote, '[w]e are fond of distinctions; we place ourselves in opposition, and quarrel under the denominations of faction and party' (p. 26). This tendency of human beings to take part in public arguments explains why, in spite of the existence of some 'universal qualities in our nature' (p. 16), humankind is characterized by 'varieties' (p. 16). These varieties must be understood here as referring, on the one hand, to the differences existing between collectivities: Ferguson argued that '[t]he multiplicity of forms ... which different societies offer to our view, is almost infinite' (p. 65). On the other hand, a given collectivity is never completely homogeneous:

> Every nation is a motley assemblage of different characters, and contains, under any political form, some examples of that variety, which the humours, tempers, and apprehensions of men, so differently employed, are likely to furnish. Every profession has its point of honour, and its system of manners; the merchant his punctuality and fair dealing; the statesman his capacity and address; the man of society, his good-breeding and wit. Every station has a carriage, a dress, a ceremonial, by which it is distinguished, and by which it suppresses the national character under that of the rank, or of the individual. (p. 180)

The central tension in Ferguson's work emerges precisely from this insistence upon the diversity which marked any human association. His main concern, in the vein of classical republican thought (Oz-Salzberger 1995), is for the perpetuation of a collectivity of free citizens or, as we termed this issue above, for the viability of a polity in which its members handle their common affairs in collective self-determination. A free collectivity, however, is difficult to establish and even more difficult to maintain, insofar as it requires that an always precarious balance be found between two equally dangerous extremes: an excess of communication on the one hand, and a lack thereof on the other.

A free collectivity, Ferguson argued, requires that a set of institutions expressing the popular will be put in place:

> It is well known, that constitutions framed for the preservation of liberty, must consist of many parts; and that senates, popular assemblies, courts of justice, magistrates of different orders, must combine to balance each other, while they exercise, sustain, or check the executive power. If any part is struck out, the fabric must totter, or fall. (p. 252)

However, these institutions were not in itself sufficient to the preservation of liberty. One more thing was needed in this respect, which was a collective determination to obey just laws and to take part in their making:

> If forms of proceeding, written statutes, or other constituents of law, cease to be enforced by the very spirit from which they arose; they serve only to cover, not to restrain, the iniquities of power … And the influence of laws … is, in reality, the influence of men resolved to be free; of men, who, having adjusted in writing the terms on which they are to live with the state, and with their fellow-subjects, are determined, by their vigilance and spirit, to make these terms be observed. (p. 249)

This public-spiritedness, which Ferguson sometimes called 'the national spirit', (e.g. p. 77), is characterized by a twofold attitude: first, a respect for the diversity of opinions expressed by the various members of the collectivity:

> In assemblies constituted by men of different talents, habits, and apprehensions, it were something more than human that could make them agree in every point of importance; having different opinions and views, it were want of integrity to abstain from disputes: our very praise of unanimity, therefore, is to be considered as a danger to liberty…. if, in matters of controversy, the sense of any individual or party is invariably pursued, the cause of freedom is already betrayed. (p. 252)

Combined with this is a commitment to obey the laws which are the output of free deliberation: 'The love of the public, and respect to its laws, are the points in which mankind are bound to agree' (p. 252).

According to Ferguson, two things could undermine the cohesion of society, guaranteed by public-spiritedness. In some cases the divergences of opinions, if unaccompanied by a willingness to respect the popular will, could turn into a 'civil discord' (p. 26). Such tensions could render necessary 'secessions and actual separations' (p. 26). In some cases, only the emergence of a common external enemy and the threat of a war could reunite the members of society into an integrated whole. Ferguson, however, thought that the opposite danger – that of a lack of civil communication – was more serious, and more likely to occur. Very differently from Hume, he witnessed the rise of commercial states, as he called them, with the suspicion that they could become a threat to freedom. The development of commerce, indeed, took society into the spiral of the division of labour, which in the same time specialized and separated individuals, thus threatening to undermine the cohesion of the whole:

> Under the *distinction* of callings, by which the members of polished society are separated from each other, every individual is supposed to possess his species of talent, or his peculiar skill, in which the others are confessedly ignorant; and society is made to consist of parts, of which none is animated with the spirit of society itself. (p. 207)

Ferguson believed that commerce could transform the collectivity into a loose aggregate of 'detached' and 'solitary' beings (p. 24) suffering from the 'competition with … [their] fellow-creatures' (p. 24) and remaining together only for the material advantages ('external conveniencies' [p. 23], in Ferguson's terms) which belonging to the collectivity provides. Ferguson's conclusion was straightforward:

> The members of a community may, in this manner, be made to lose the sense of every connection, but that of kindred or neighbourhood; and have no common affairs to transact, but those of trade: connections, indeed, or transactions, in which probity and friendship may still take place; but in which the national spirit, whose ebbs and flows we are now considering, cannot be exerted. (p. 208)[9]

In the terminology proposed above, Ferguson develops a view of the configuration of social relations that starts out from the assumption of a diversity of orientations among members of a polity. This assumption resonates with the liberal approach for which this diversity is precisely the origin of the political problématique of modernity, to be addressed in this tradition by the idea of the social contract. In contrast to individualist predecessors such as Hobbes or Locke, however, Ferguson did not think that political philosophy can disregard, or abstract from, the substantive nature of the social relations entertained by the members of a polity.

These relations are rich and manifold in substance, and some forms of them are more conducive to support a modern polity than others.

At this point, Ferguson introduces the distinction between communicative and commercial relations that should remain central to much of nineteenth- and twentieth-century social and political theory and especially, even though often in a different guise, for the conceptualization of civil society. Drawing a sharp line between the two modes of relating to the other, he emphasizes that the presence of a *communicative flux* between *diverse* individuals is the condition of the existence of a free society, whereas a situation in which members of a polity relate to each other predominantly by *trade* tends to undermine the possibility of collective freedom. Importantly, the political significance of communication in his view does not stem from its capacity to produce consensus, unlike some Enlightenment contemporaries of his thought (and, much later, Jürgen Habermas). On the contrary, he went as far as to assert that 'the noise of dissension ... generally accompany the exercise of freedom' (p. 242); rather than the search for agreement as such, it is the communicative engagement with the other in common matters that sustains the polity. With regard to commercial relations, he was in turn unwilling to believe that the interest in peaceful relations that tradespeople would show was on its own sufficient to make a modern polity possible. The problem of the engagement with the other through trade was, in his view, that 'no common affairs' were transacted; and therefore the concern for collective freedom was not likely to be strongly on the mind of tradespeople.

If thus the concern for 'common affairs' is the centre of Ferguson's exploration of the viability of a modern polity, this finds its empirical-historical expression in the identification of the 'spirit' that prevails in a polity, often more precisely defined as a 'national spirit'. Importantly, this 'spirit' is not seen as a property that members of a polity share before they engage in political interaction, in contrast to all communitarian thinking. 'Habits and apprehensions' as well as 'opinions and views' are diverse among the members of a free polity, and 'praise of unanimity' is considered a problem rather than a precondition for a free polity. Rather, the republican spirit, since this is what Ferguson describes here in its most modern articulation, expresses itself through, first, engagement with common matters, 'love of the public', and, second, through obedience to the laws that are arrived at in common deliberation, 'respect to its laws'.

Two elements of this conceptualization are important to retain for further discussion. First, Ferguson introduces distinctions between types of social relations in the way in which they should become central in later discussions. In contrast to later debates, however, in which types of relations were taken to constitute separate spheres of society, or even social subsystems, he insists that he is referring in the first place to 'connections' or 'transactions' only. In the terminology of late twentieth-century social theory, we may say that he retained a constitution theory of society, starting out from interactions between human beings, rather than moving towards a differentiation theory of society (the terminology draws on Giddens 1984 and Joas 1992), in which logics of development unfold 'behind the backs' of the human actors. Furthermore, even though he places an emphasis on those types of interaction the recent development of which he sees as crucial – supportive or detrimental – for the modern polity, Ferguson does not lose sight of other significant ways of relating to the other, such as 'probity and friendship'.

Secondly, in the light of later debates, it is significant that Ferguson studiously avoids making assumptions about prior commonality among the members of a polity. His concept of 'spirit' should in all likelihood not be seen as a moral commitment external to political matters as such – as, for instance, Weber's spirit of capitalism as a non-economic, religious commitment that precedes the actual engagement in economic practices – but as that 'love of the public' that arises when engaging in common matters. The notion of 'national spirit', then, as much as it seems at first sight to anticipate the later cultural-linguistic theory of the polity that underpinned nineteenth-century nationalism, with its emphasis on obedience to self-set laws, is closer to 'constitutional patriotism' than to any form of communitarianism. As we shall see later, this position progressively declined in the course of the nineteenth century.

G.W.F. Hegel and the Moment of the Democratic Revolutions

The time at which Ferguson wrote, we tend to think today, was a culminating moment in the history of both European political thought and institutional development in the state systems of Europe and North America. In the latter regard, it was the moment shortly before the 'democratic revolutions' that would transform the centre of politico-institutional contention for more than a century by placing the question of collective self-determination and fully inclusive democracy at the top of the domestic agenda. In Europe, it is now often seen as the moment at which republicanism declined from its key position in European political thought, to only find its last strong expression for the next two centuries in the North American constitutional debates, and in which individualist liberalism, prepared during the seventeenth and eighteenth centuries, started to rise to its current status as the pivotal theory of political modernity.

The reasons for this coincidence have been little explored. For many liberal political theorists of later years, the history of liberal thinking proceeds hand in glove with the history of democratic institutions, and the moment of revolution is nothing but a move from thinking about possibilities towards carrying them out. For those who try to revive republican thinking in our time, in turn, the fall into oblivion of this mode of political thought is enigmatic to the degree that it must be deplored because of the loss of normative possibilities, but it cannot be explained. After all, republican institutions had stayed alive since the times of the Florentine and Venetian republics, most importantly perhaps in the Dutch republic, but also in city self-government, even though they became increasingly marginal due to the rise of the territorial state; and the normative demands of liberal-democratic thinkers on the absolutist regimes should have been compatible with the republican concern for common affairs.

Elsewhere, we have tried to advance the understanding of this enigma by referring to the difficulty of reconciling the quest for greater inclusiveness, increasing both the number and the diversity of participants in the debate, with the demanding concept of liberty that republican thought embraces. More specifically, this tension became a historic reality in the double context of the *territorial* enlargement of the polity into what we now call the modern European state, and the emergence of the 'social question' as a political question due to the *social* enlargement of the polity that comes with the acceptance of the doctrine of popular sovereignty (Wagner 2001a: chap. 2). In the current context we want to show that one of the expressions that this tension finds is precisely the introduction of a sharp distinction between 'civil society' and 'state' in the aftermath of the democratic revolutions. To do so in all due brevity, we can compare G.W.F. Hegel's conceptualization of civil society, as proposed in his *Elements of the philosophy of right* (1821), with Adam Ferguson's reasoning as presented above. In this light, three features of Hegel's view stand out.

First, Hegel shares with Ferguson and many of his contemporaries – whom we now consider as 'modern' for precisely this reason – the view that social and political thought needs to accept individual liberty as (one of) its starting assumptions. In contrast to liberal Enlightenment thought, however, he insists that 'abstract liberty' is also insufficient as a basis for a moral and political philosophy, that it needs to be complemented by other assumptions. While this view is as such fully compatible with the Aristotelian and republican view that the human being is constitutively a *zoon politikon*, Hegel proposes a different solution. For him, the advent of the abstract conception of the individual is a historical fact that further political theorizing needs to take into account. Thus, as the architecture of *Elements* shows, he aims at confining the impact of this view by proposing other components of society as complementing and balancing elements. The price to pay for this conceptual move is the separation of the freedom of the individual from other societal institutions. Thus, strangely, Hegel appears to be an individualist liberal on the one hand, because he accepts abstract freedom, but on the other hand also a conservative who reacts to the rise of individualist thinking by advocating non-liberally constituted institutions as a counterpart to the freedom of the individuals.[10]

This can only be understood in relation to the eighteenth-century debate itself, which Hegel tried to supersede. As we have argued above, the Scottish debate about the kind of social relations that are necessary to sustain a free and peaceful polity opposed authors such as Ferguson and to a lesser extent the social contractualists, who insisted on the importance of political involvement either as permanent participation or as explicit consent, to those such as Hume, who argued that a certain quality of political institutions, not of individual conduct, was the best guarantee for collective freedom. We know that Hegel, like Kant before him, was an attentive reader of the Scots – for instance, we know that he had read Ferguson and Smith, and there are reasons to think that his conceptualization of civil society is a reinterpretation of their contribution to political thought. Hegel, however, reformulated the terms of the debate about the conditions of liberty. For him, *both* institutions *and* individual conduct were necessary to maintain a free and peaceful polity: individuals needed to have a sense of the common good, and thus to avoid acting in a purely self-interested manner; but this public-spiritedness could not and should not be understood as mere virtue (that is, as deriving only from individual effort). On the contrary, it was the product of an institutional setting in which individuals were brought to realize their interdependence and their need for a strong state. Hegel's theory of the opposition between state and civil society, which is at the core of his theory of ethical life and represents a major shift in the history of the reflection on civil society, must be understood in this light.

The concept of civil society itself, second, is introduced by Hegel as part of a general distinction between spheres of morality, all intended to counteract the damaging impact of the rise of purely individualist thinking, that is, of precisely the kind of thinking that intends to derive societal institutions from the aggregated will of the individual. As such, it remains an inspiration for *social* philosophy, for instance in Axel Honneth's recent attempt to distinguish a variety of modes for recognizing the other, only one of which is based on a conception of the individual human being as a holder of rights (Honneth 1992; 2001). Arguably, however, Hegel's approach bears fruit for *political* philosophy predominantly in a negative way, namely by supporting arguments for the insufficiency of individualist liberalism. In a constructive way, he limits the reach of his approach by first partially accepting individualist liberalism and by then explicating the partial nature of this acceptance by the separation of spheres. The precise delineation of spheres, including 'civil society', though, has little conceptual ground to stand on and has appeared to later readers as rooted too strongly in the context of the Prussian state and society of the time.[11] Ferguson, in comparison, by starting out from diversity of orientations, but not from atomized individuals as the units of political life, avoids this issue and refines his analysis by a 'history', rather than a philosophy, of civil society instead.[12]

As a consequence, thirdly, Hegel cannot but be seen as ultimately abandoning the commitment to political modernity shown by earlier political thought. Due to the separation of spheres, which is an essential element of the detailed analysis, there is no idea of the self-institution of society in the *Elements*. The state, rather than presenting the instituted form of the ways of dealing with common matters, as it does in Ferguson, is external to other walks of social life and always already precedes them.[13] This description certainly mirrors important features of the history of political modernity in continental Europe, where demands for popular sovereignty arose from within given state structures. It does not, however, provide an adequate conceptualization of political modernity, since precisely the institutional core of the common is thus conceptualized as 'non-political', not open to deliberation itself.[14]

For Hegel, therefore, the conceptual pair 'state/civil society' was employed as a means to deal with the radicalization of the political problématique that was provoked by the democratic revolution. Since he could not believe that a viable political arrangement could be created and upheld in communication between the members of a polity, as republicans did, nor that the basic institutional questions could be dealt with once and for all in a social contract that not only instituted the polity but also clearly separated the public from the private, as liberals did, he solved the question by separating the state from civil society and considering the former as external to the working of the latter. This enabled Hegel to both have a theory of social relations in modernity (marked in particular, within the sphere of civil society, by the division of labour and the exchange of goods) and escape the very modern political question of self-determination and self-rule. In other words, Hegel did not satisfyingly answer the question of the relationship between social relations and political institutions, how they affect each other, and how each should take the other into account.

Hegel's conceptualization may throw some light on the ways in which the Prussian state during the first half of the nineteenth century tried to deal with the double challenge of the call for the liberalization of economic action, on the one hand, and the gradual emergence of socio-political movements that demanded both more inclusive participation and, in response to liberal practices, more state action against rising social inequality, on the other. Because of its incomplete appreciation of the challenge posed by the idea of collective self-determination, however, it seems hardly convincing as an answer to the problématique of political modernity. This objection, specifically, also throws doubt on the ways in which the term civil society came to be employed in the search for such an answer. Rather than accepting the state–civil society distinction as an achievement of modern political theory, as much later commentary has done, it seems important to keep open the question of the relation between configurations of social relations and forms of the polity. In the light of this observation, we now turn to Alexis de Tocqueville's analysis of democracy in America.

Alexis de Tocqueville and the Question of Representation

In his *Essay on the History of Civil Society*, Ferguson left one aspect, that of the institutionalization of civil society, largely untouched. While he insisted that a free polity should be made of communicative interactions, and that each law needed the scrutiny and approval of all, he did not propose a full-fledged theory of how these interactive fluxes can crystallize into political institutions and collective decisions – how, in our vocabulary, social relations relate to the forms of the polity. On premises very similar to those proposed by Ferguson, Tocqueville tried to furnish exactly this.

The significance of Tocqueville's *Democracy in America* (1994) resides not least in the fact that it provides a first full-scale analysis of a configuration of social relations in which the commitment to collective self-determination – all limitations notwithstanding – is key part of the imaginary signification of society. (Among recent reappraisals see, in particular, the work of Claude Lefort, e.g., 1992, and Pierre Manent, e.g., 2001.) As a society that constitutes itself in the democratic revolution (Arendt 1965; Derrida 1986; Honig 1991), the United States had to squarely face the question of the institution of democracy as part of the self-constitution of society. More broadly speaking, and accepting that his interest was less in America than in the conditions of possibility of democracy, Tocqueville addresses the political situation after the democratic revolution: in contrast to Ferguson's time of writing, an experience of the realization of democracy was now available for inspection.

Tocqueville's discussion of the vibrancy of associative life in North America and the significance of such activities for making democracy normatively viable, that is, helping to avoid the risks of conformism and the tyranny of the majority, is too well-known to be repeated here. Without the author himself giving much importance to the term, his analysis has often been re-interpreted as an analysis of civil society in the U.S. and has thus been used as support for the equation of civil society with associative life. As in our view this conceptual connection tends to unduly neglect the question of the linkage between social relations and the form of the polity (as discussed in more detail in chapter 10 below), the emphasis of our discussion is on that notion in Tocqueville that directly provides for such a linkage, the concept of *representation*.

A link between civil society activities – whatever form they may precisely take – and democracy exists whenever the deliberations in civil society concretely translate into the transformation or establishment of institutions endowed with political legitimacy. A typical form of such a realisation process in Western polities is the passing of law by a *representative* body to respond to publicly formulated demands. From this angle, Tocqueville's reflections on representation are extremely informative of the logic of civil society.[15]

Two apparently contradictory Tocquevillian sentences can be taken here as a starting point. On the one hand, Tocqueville argued that in America (the place in which democracy has reached its highest development), 'it is not only one section of the people that undertakes to better the state of society, for the whole nation is concerned therewith' (Tocqueville 1994: 242).[16] This quote a priori seems to pave the way for a theory of direct democracy ruling out any representative mechanism; this was not, however, Tocqueville's position. Indeed, he asserted, on the contrary, that in America, 'In New England the majority works through the representatives when it is dealing with the general affairs of the state. It was necessary that it should be so' (p. 64). It is our contention that there is no contradiction between these two statements, if Tocqueville's thought is more fully reconstructed.

First, he explained that an almost universal interest in public affairs existed in America; this interest was fostered by the presence of a set of intermediary institutions (whose existence constituted, as it were, a first mitigation of the principle of representation). Indeed, most American citizens were called to exert public functions, such as those of local counsellor or jury member. The effect of this system of participation was to arouse the political interest of Americans in the first place. 'It is hard to explain the place filled by political concerns in the life of an American. To take a hand in the government of society and to talk about it is his most important business and, so to say, the only pleasure he knows' (p. 243). In turn, this political interest resolved itself in a vibrant public opinion manifested in a very diverse, widely read, and extremely influential press.[17] Moreover, America's representative institutions were organised in such a way as to ensure a permanent turnover of their members. In such a context, argued Tocqueville, the citizens sitting on representative bodies were put under constant pressure. This translated into a situation in which *public opinion eventually dictated the representatives' decisions*, as Tocqueville unequivocally sustained:

> Direction really comes from the people, and though the form of government is representative, it is clear that opinions, prejudices, interests, and even passions of the people can find no lasting obstacles preventing them from being manifest in the daily conduct of society. (p. 173)

According to Tocqueville, American democracy rested on two fundamental pillars. On the one hand, it enabled the direct participation of citizens to political affairs. At the level of communes (townships), individuals could actually take part directly in collective decisions, gathered into deliberative assemblies: 'in the township, where both legal and administrative action are closer to the governed, the representative system is not allowed; there is no municipal council; the body of the electors, when it has chosen the officials, directs them in everything beyond the simple ordinary execution of the laws of the state' (p. 64). Hence, in Tocqueville's system, direct participation is allowed at least at the communal level. As Larry Siedentop has rightly argued, there are Rousseauian undertones in Tocqueville's appreciation of the township system: 'The American townships enabled Tocqueville to "save" part of Rousseau's defence of participation and its moralizing effects' (Siedentop 1994: 67–68).[18]

However, as we have seen, Tocqueville recognized on the other hand the necessity of representation, since no deliberative assembly could be put in place beyond the local, communal level. Tocqueville's conception of representation was very specific. He did not envisage it as a completely independent body: quite on the contrary, it was constantly kept under the direct influence of the popular will. This is because, while no physical gathering of citizens in deliberative assemblies is thinkable at the general level of the state, their *virtual* gathering remains possible, *under the form of the public sphere*, taking up the idea of communicative exchange as a necessary type of social relation for the realization of a free polity.

Civil Society, Social Relations, Political Forms

In most current usages, the relation between 'civil society' (as a specific configuration of social relations) and 'democracy' is conceptualized in such a way that the former is seen as a necessary social underpinning of the latter. We discuss below the validity of this distinction in more detail; what needs to be emphasized here is that such a conceptualization has the merit of introducing a distinction between, on the one hand, a configuration of social relations, for which 'civil society' becomes the shorthand, and a political form, a set of institutions, on the other, for which the term 'democracy', it seems, is used as a term for that form that is seen as normatively desirable.[19]

Building on this distinction, we can now say that the reconstruction of the debate on civil society as proposed above suggests, in our view, that the issue of the configuration of social relations has often been discussed in connection with the questions of *what types of social relations* are more or less conducive to support the viability of a modern polity. Such types were often specified by the nature of the exchange between human beings. Most prominently, but not exclusively, a distinction has been made between relations of *communication* and relations of *commerce*. Significantly, the rise of either of those forms during what we now call early modernity has been interpreted as permitting the rise of political modernity.

Albert Hirschman (1977), for instance, has demonstrated how the idea of 'doux commerce', of the pacification of social relations through extending commercial exchange, provided 'political arguments for capitalism before its triumph' and supported the notion that domestic and international peace could be durably achieved by shifting the centre of human life on 'interests' rather than 'passions'. In turn, other strands of eighteenth-century thought underlined the formation of 'public opinion' through communicative exchange and saw precisely this phenomenon as a necessary precondition for the exercise of popular sovereignty, a precondition that fortunately – from the normative viewpoint of numerous authors – started to be fulfilled. During this process, as Keith Michael Baker (1990) has shown, the term 'public opinion' radically shifted meaning. From referring to the diversity of popularly-held views, often ungrounded, it moved to signifying the aggregate result of a polity-wide process of free, and therefore rational, opinion formation, the outcome of which could and should guide political decision–making.[20]

The question that we need to pursue in this regard is that of the relation between abstraction and concreteness in conceptual terminology. That is why we propose to speak of *configurations of social relations* and *political forms* in the broadest, most encompassing sense, and to use these terms to understand how concepts such as 'civil society', 'state' and 'democracy' are developed in relation to those most general concepts as expressions for specific historical or normative examples of the most general concepts. In short, therefore, the concept 'civil society' refers here to a way of answering the question of how a configuration of social relations can find its adequate expression in a political form under conditions of political modernity, that is, of a commitment to collective self-determination, in a given historical context.

Notes

1. If our historico-conceptual reasoning in the following proceeds by discussing selected authors in their contexts, this is not meant as a 'great thinkers' approach to the history of ideas. Rather, it marks our own compromise between the need to on the one hand discuss in detail some conceptualizations of civil society and the political problématique to which they refer and, on the other, to give some idea of the long-term socio-political transformations towards which the politico-conceptual work addresses itself.
2. E.g. Bobbio (1976), Colas (1991), Keane (1998).
3. We have in mind here the contributions of Price, Burke, Paine, Wollstonecraft, to name but a few, all of whom made an intense use of the term 'civil', including in relation to 'society'.
4. We are here referring, specifically, to the following assertion by John Keane (1988: 32–33): 'The conventional Marxian understanding of the distinction between civil society and the state forgets that the term civil society *pre-dated* the emergence of the bourgeoisie, being well-developed, for instance, in classical and medieval political thought; and, most importantly, that the distinction has a *variety* of early modern meanings, all of which are concerned however with the *political* problem of how, and under which circumstances, state power can be controlled and rendered legitimate.'
5. See in particular the essay 'On the origin of government' in Hume 1964.
6. On Hume and commerce see Robertson 1983; for the general argument about commerce, see Hirschman 1977.
7. While Smith did not use the term 'civil society' very systematically, related notions – in particular 'civilized nation' or 'civilized society' – were recurrent in his prose. Another author that we cannot mention here in full detail, but who also offer an argument against the republican insistence on virtue and an advocacy of commercial society, is Mandeville. His reflection can be interpreted as a response to some authors defending a more active perception of citizenship, John Locke *inter primis*. His *Second Treatise of Government* can indeed be read as a description of the way to set up the various institutions that are necessary to restore some kind of social order once society has reached the critical stage at which its size is too large for mere local self-organisation to prevail. As is well-known, the state of nature in Locke is not characterized by anarchy; its actual order depends upon its being contained within strict territorial limitations. The discovery of money is a cause of disorder insofar as it multiplies the possibility of individuals to act from a distance and thus gives rise to social configurations of unusual expansion. In such a context, face-to-face interactions are not sufficient to allow for an acceptable coordination of action. From this moment on, continues Locke, central institutions need to be established to set up binding rules for an enlarged society, enforce social order, and allow for collective decision-taking. Mandeville's contention, arguably, consists precisely in denying the fact that any qualitative change in the way in which social order needs to be established occurs as an effect of the enlargement of society. For Mandeville, the self-organising power that prevailed in small communities before the advent of money persists in the new social situation of generalized commerce.
8. The history of the translation of Aristotle's *Politics* from Greek to Latin is discussed in chapter 2. We only point out here that the shift from a politics-oriented terminology to a society-oriented one, which initiated in the fifteenth century and was then still framed by republican thinking, should become a key element of a much more profound reorientation of social and political philosophy in the late eighteenth century. Very broadly speaking, Aristotelian conceptions of politics prevailed in the history of European political ideas until the late eighteenth century and did not

suddenly wither away immediately after either. The recent debate on republicanism, inspired by J.G.A. Pocock's *Machiavellian moment* (1975), does not fully capture this continuity and the reasons for the subsequent rise of liberal orientations. See Maier (1965) and Hennis (1987) for analyses of Aristotelian thinking and the challenges to it in the eighteenth and nineteenth centuries.

9. This view, we may underline already at this point, stands in striking opposition to the perspective Emile Durkheim would develop more than a century later: the view, namely, that the division of social labour provides the ground for a new form of social cohesion and sense of the common. He called this 'organic solidarity' and linked it to a concept of modern 'society' that offered a completely different response to the political problématique of modernity from that of the earlier debate on 'civil society' – even though similar thoughts on the division of labour can already be found in Hegel, albeit in much less prominent role (see the brief discussion of Hegel's *Philosophy of Right* in this chapter).

10. The interpretation of Hegel's work has always been torn between such radically different views of his political position. A separation of the young, radical and liberal Hegel from the older man who supported the institutions of the non-liberal Prussian state is of no help, as the co-existence of both modes of thinking in the *Elements* shows.

11. Later attempts to revitalize the approach of *Elements*, such as most notably Jürgen Habermas's *Theory of Communicative Action* (1981), have suffered from the same problem. Even though the emphasis on communication as a primary way of relating to others marks a (implicit) return to Ferguson and Enlightenment thought, the distinction of spheres in Habermas's work appears too closely tied to socio-political the situation of the 1970s, the zenith of the democratic Keynesian welfare state.

12. Throughout our reasoning, the relation between historicization and conceptualization will be an implicit central theme (for some discussion of the issues at stake, see Wagner 2001a, prologue).

13. In this respect, Hegel's *Elements* prefigure later conceptualizations in the social sciences, in which the search for non–chosen social regularities became one way of limiting the range of viable answers to the problématique of political modernity. We return to this aspect in the following step of our historical reconstruction.

14. Such conceptualization in particular fails to comprehend any significant restructurings of the polity, as for instance nowadays the process of constituting a European polity, a question addressed in later chapters of this volume.

15. One of the most authoritative interpreters of Tocquevillian thought, Jean-Claude Lamberti, asserts that Tocqueville's concept of sovereignty is 'confusing' and 'inconsistent' (Lamberti 1989: 73). We are far from sharing this judgement, but we agree that Tocqueville's idea of representation is somewhat difficult to grasp – but for reasons of complexity and not of vagueness.

16. Cf. the more explicit French original: 'ce n'est plus une portion du peuple qui entreprend d'améliorer la situation de la société; le peuple entier se charge de ce soin'.

17. Consider, for instance, the following quote: 'The power of the American press is immense. It makes political life circulate in every corner of that vast land. Its eyes are never shut, and it lays bare the secret shifts of politics, forcing public figures to appear before the tribunal of opinion. The press rallies interests around certain doctrines and gives shape to party slogans; though the press the parties, without actually meeting, listen and argue with one another. When many organs of the press do care to take the same line, their influence in the long run is almost irresistible' (p. 186).

18. Discussing the 'difference in political climate between America and Germany', even Theodor Adorno noted in 1951 that 'the American state' is 'never experienced by its citizens as an authority that floats above the individuals, as commanding them in any absolute way'. In the U.S., according to the returned exile, large parts of the population do not have 'the feeling that the state is anything different than they themselves', and

Adorno goes as far as claiming that this nuance of difference between MacCarthyite U.S. and post-Nazi Germany entails 'a more happy relation between the supreme form of societal organization and its citizens' in the former (Adorno 1986: 290–91). Such comparative observations resonate again today in the claim that republican thinking remained vibrant in the U.S. while it withered away in Europe. While they are hardly convincing as such, they point to different possible articulations between 'civil society' and 'democracy'.

19. As we discussed in chapter 10, such distinction is in several crucial aspects different from another, apparently similar one – namely the historical conceptual differentiation in which the 'state' emerged as distinct from 'civil society' and which significantly prevailed in the aftermath of the democratic revolution.

20. Below (chapter 4) we discuss these two ways of thinking as giving rise to economic liberalism on the one hand, and to republicanism and political liberalism on the other.

Chapter 2

FROM *KOINONÌA POLITIKÈ* TO *SOCIETAS CIVILIS*: BIRTH, DISAPPEARANCE AND FIRST RENAISSANCE OF THE CONCEPT

Peter Hallberg and Björn Wittrock

Introduction

Reflections on the 'origins' of civil society often lead back to Aristotle and his invocation of *koinonìa politikè*, subsequently translated into Latin as *societas civilis* and into vernacular languages as 'bürgerliche Gesellschaft', 'société civile', and 'civil society'.[1] As the object of analysis moves from origins to dissemination conceptual clarity in civil society research is notably scarce. The proliferation of the term as a philosophical label, it is often claimed, has emptied it of any stable and analytically useful meaning. Moreover, usage of 'civil society' is said to indicate conventional assumptions about its positive value, and hence obscure its relations with Eurocentric and colonial modes of discourse, theories and practices of masculine domination, and ideologies of both neo-liberalism and neo-conservatism (Kaviraj and Khilnani 2001).[2] As Sunil Khilnani puts it, the concept 'embodies the epic of Western modernity', a narrative organized around consecutive intellectual responses to a particular set of cognitive and socio-political challenges in Western Europe and America (Khilnani 2001: 14). Couched in a more encompassing critique of European paradigms of social thought, warnings against the casual use of 'civil society' suggest that mistaking the context-sensitive particularity of these historical responses for analytical universals disables creative analysis of varying conditions of social change, both in Western and non-Western politics.

From the viewpoint of conceptual and intellectual history, the different and shifting meanings of 'civil society' are neither surprising nor problematic. As some leading exponents of conceptual history write, sets of concepts are always liable to 'become worn and frayed' (Ball, Farr and Hanson 1989: 1). From a perspective that stresses conceptual innovation and change, problems of indeterminacy provide opportunities to rethink and critically evaluate established modes of political thought. Besides testifying to the historical fate of most key social and political concepts, the problem of indeterminacy in civil society research constitutes a research task: to enquire into the development, uses and transmission of languages of civil society across time and space. Such an endeavour may prove helpful in efforts to clarify current uses of the term around the globe, to resolve the problem of indeterminacy and hence restore 'civil society' as a meaningful descriptive and/or critical term in the human sciences.[3] It is possible but far from obvious, we believe, that such benefits can be gained from conceptual history, but enquiries into the ways in which the concept has acquired new meanings and lent itself to different uses throughout history, within and between traditions and polities, constitute a field of research within the larger field of the history of political thought where 'civil society' is a key term.[4]

The general purpose of this chapter is to initiate a discussion that can shed light on the various strands of the conceptual web that is 'civil society'. Our purpose is not to rescue or clarify the term, but to trace the opacity of civil society in order to think it anew. This implies looking not only at what texts say, but how they were received and altered in various contexts, and how those alterations then played out in further diffusion within and between European polities. Put another way, we set out to recover the ways in which concepts of civil society were used by individuals and groups in the past, chiefly by looking at the transmission of a vocabulary or political lexicon that provide the backbone of languages of politics.[5] Thus phrased, the result will bear upon the imaginary institution of civil society rather than its actual realization or defeat.[6] This chapter, then, focuses on the 'origins' and subsequent translations of the concept civil society, whereas Chapter 3 analyses some aspects of its transmission in a national context. With regard to historical period, the present chapter focuses on the thirteenth century, at which time classical vocabularies of political community became available through the introduction in Christian Europe of Aristotelian political thought. Of particular importance, beyond the proliferation of key terms in theological discourse, were conceptions of the origins and mechanisms of political community and the nature of political agency and citizenship.

More specifically, this chapter treats the 'origins' of discourses on civil society, although the language of definitive origins and foundations should be approached with scepticism. Keeping with the conventional wisdom that posits Aristotle's *Politics* (*c*.335–323 BC) as providing the early vocabulary of civil society theorizing, this chapter attempts to ascertain how the Aristotelian language of political community passed through different intellectual and linguistic contexts, from medieval to early renaissance political thought (*c*.1250–1450). Most existing conceptual overviews tend to focus on the eighteenth century since it was around 1750 that a distinction of crucial importance to *contemporary* efforts undertaken in the name of civil society, namely the state–civil society distinction, which had been implicit in some writings since the late sixteenth century, began to be explicitly articulated. A fuller account, which takes into consideration the history *before* the emergence of the state–civil society distinction, requires a longer time frame. Of particular interest in this regard is a series of conceptual reconfigurations that start with the Catholic theologian Thomas Aquinas in the mid-thirteenth century and are reconfigured again by the civic humanist Leonardo Bruni in the early fifteenth. Aquinas's importance lies in his incorporation of Aristotelian philosophy into Catholic thought, while Bruni's lies in completing a definitive Latin translation that would form the basis for numerous vernacular translations. It was Bruni's Latin term for Aristotle's *koinonia politikè*, that is, *societas civilis*, that formed the basis of the vernacular discourses on civil society that emerged during the course of the sixteenth century and contributed to a gradual, if highly uneven, replacement in favour of *societas* of a series of earlier terms such as 'communitas', 'communio' and 'communicatio'.

The Aristotelian Vocabulary of Politics

Even if we agree with Stephen Everson in his recent Cambridge edition of the *Politics* that Aristotle's economical prose in the *Politics* means 'that the details of the argument are to be seen without a distorting polish', translators and commentators have hardly hesitated to embellish, amplify or even change the order of presentation of Aristotle's original text (Everson 1996: x). Passing from one interpretative context to another, transforming the key concepts to better fit the debates, projects and general moral vocabularies of their own time was the first duty of translators and commentators. With specific audiences and purposes in mind, some of which are known to us and some of which are not, the transmission of Aristotelian philosophy was thus shaped through the ages and across space; from one language to another; from one tradition of thought to another; and from one set of cosmic certainties to another. A systematic analysis of the changing meaning of Aristotle's key political terms – for our purposes here *koinonia politikè* and *polis* – would accordingly require us to familiarize ourselves with multiple contexts of translation and reception, most importantly the available political vocabularies of the time as well as the more general intellectual and cultural contexts of social thought. In what follows, we are only able to reconstruct a thin layer and a partial history of the transmission and transformation of Aristotle's political vocabulary in Europe.

The lasting importance of Aristotle's ethical and political texts has to do with his ability to bring into a systematic whole an analysis of existing and ideal institutions such as state, society and citizenship and values such as equality and justice. His reflections on the relationship between active citizenship and political community and the ways in which this relationship is affected by different constitutions, governments or forms of rule have been enormously influential and account for the majority of contemporary scholarship on Aristotle's political philosophy. According to Aristotle, the best form of active citizenship involves not merely distinguished members assuming real responsibility in public affairs, but the 'multitude' participating in the life of the *polis* with a constant eye to the common good. Thus, a good constitution, or *politea*, is defined both by the procedural aspects of governance (for example rotating office) and by the most basic motives of the governors (that is, advancing the good of the people). Integral to this view of active citizenship and good government is the notion that humans are naturally disposed to live in communities, the *polis* being the highest developed form of the family, which is conceived of as the organizational result of innate human inclinations of sociability. As Aristotle puts it, in Everson's edition: '[H]e who is unable to live in society, or who has no need because he is sufficient for himself, must be either a beast or a god: he is no part of a state [or *polis*]' (Aristotle 1996: 1253 a26–9). The innate disposition to forge communities on part of (civilized and terrestrial) individuals is what makes the *polis* 'natural'. By similar logic, the actual qualities of active citizens define the character of a *polis* and different types of government. Thus,

> He who would inquire into the essence and attributions of various types of government must first of all determine what a *polis* is … But a *polis* is composite, like any other whole made up of many parts – these are the citizens who compose it. It is evident, therefore, that we must begin by asking, Who is the citizen, and what is the meaning of that term? (Aristotle 1996, 1274b32–4, 1274b38–1275a2)

Whether Aristotle provides an analytical and transhistoric (or decontextualized) account of key political institutions and values, or if his account is limited to an empirically specific form of human community, that is, the Greek city-states or *poleis* of his own time, has been a continual subject of debate in the study of classical political philosophy. In his introduction to the *Politics*, Stephen Everson engages in the debate by arguing for the conceptual affinity between 'the state' in a modern, or at least early-modern sense, and 'the *polis*' in its classical sense. The actual closeness of the terms, he believes, determines Aristotle's relevance to readers of the twenty-first century. If the analysis is confined historically and geographically to the Greek city-states of Aristotle's own time, which were of course small in size and founded on specific mechanisms of exclusion, this would suggest that the *Politics* does not engage with 'perennial' problems in political philosophy and that it would hence be of limited interest and practical use in the twenty-first century.[7] If, however, Aristotle by 'the *polis*' actually refers to an institutional arrangement that we today recognize in 'the state', his work will, in Everson's view, continue to shed light on human community and the exercise of public power.

Although we are prone to question the immediate practical uses of classical thought but agree that it, like many other systematically worked out theories of political life, can provide useful analytical tools, the debate between analytical and contextual approaches to the study of political thought is not addressed in this chapter.[8] It does, nonetheless, call our attention to the question of the extent to which the act of translation should be considered a sort of speech-act in its own right. In fact, the history of nineteenth- and twentieth-century vernacular translations of the *Politics* reveals that the translation of *polis* has been indeterminate and oscillated between 'city' and 'state', for example, *cité* (1824, 1962, 1990) and *Etat* (1803, 1837) in French; *Staat* (1872) in German; *città* (1918) in Catalan; and *city* (1984) and *state* (1946, 1996) in English. Clearly, translating 'the *polis*' into 'the state', which is Everson's choice, reflects a commitment to social theorizing that goes beyond 'mere' translation, in his case an approach to past thinking that asserts its contemporary relevance. The question is whether a science of the state and a science of the city amount to the same thing? Can, for example, institutional prescriptions for a city be applied to a state as well? Surely, lexical choices that prioritize 'state' over 'city' will more easily lend themselves to notions of persistent and contemporary problems in political thought and history, whereas analyses of the city necessitate more context-sensitive approaches that treat comparisons with an eye to differences rather than writing long narratives with an eye for similarities.

This conceptual indeterminacy was inherited from previous centuries of vernacular translations, from the fifteenth century through to the eighteenth.[9] A similar history of conceptual indeterminacy can be told with regard to one of the other key concepts in the *Politics*, *koinonia politikè*, which has been identified as the first appearance of the term 'civil society'. As in the case of translations of *polis*, the history of the term *koinonia politikè* goes through a Latin transposition that brings it into existing and developing vocabularies of politics throughout Europe. It is a history that brings us first to medieval political thought, then to the political languages of the early Renaissance or civic humanism, and from there on to the emerging vernacular languages of politics of the later Renaissance, further on to the Enlightenment and up to present times.

Varieties of Interpretation, *c.*1250–1450

It is with the Florentine humanist Leonardo Bruni's 1416 translation of Aristotle's major work in the field of ethics, the *Nichomachean Ethics*, that the Latin translation of the Greek *koinonìa politikè* into *societas civilis* became the predominant, although by no means the exclusive, use; it replaced an earlier vacillating usage where *societas civilis* had appeared, but in single instances (first by Cicero and later by Thomas).[10] Bruni's translation of the *Politics* appeared in 1438, with the same lexical choices. In the previous medieval Latin translations of the thirteenth and fourteenth centuries *koinonìa politikè* had been referred to as *communicatio politica* or *civilis communitas.* The term *polis* became *civitas* in Bruni's translation. Although Bruni did not monopolize the Latin speaking market for Aristotle in the fifteenth century, his translation was soon held up as the ultimate.[11]

Importantly, Bruni's Renaissance translation replaced William of Moerbecke's until then definitive translation of 1265, an edition that was intimately related to the theological and political writings of Thomas Aquinas. At the insistence of Aquinas, Moerbecke, a Dutch Dominican bishop at Corinth, had created the most basic intellectual conditions for a medieval rediscovery of Aristotelian studies. Aquinas had set out his grand project to reconcile Christian metaphysics with Aristotle's philosophy, an undertaking that constituted the first serious encounter with classical philosophy in the Middle Ages. He wrote his twelve comments on the works of Aristotle, including the *Ethics* and *Politics*, between 1269 and 1272, while at the University of Paris. As James Blythe argues,

> It is largely through Aquinas that the ideas of man as a social and political animal, of the citizen as one who participates in government, of the classification of government by the number and quality of its rulers, of the mixed constitution, and many other concepts entered the medieval milieu; and future thought is as much shaped by his peculiar interpretations of these ancient principles as by Aristotle's ideas themselves.

Bracketing Blythe's rather linear notion of influence, as well as his assertion that Aquinas 'is certainly the most important for political theory as a whole,' (Blythe 1986: 547), it suffices to say that it was through Aquinas that the Aristotelian political vocabulary became available to medieval political thought.

Aquinas's engagement with Aristotle placed him at the centre of a new intellectual movement. While the political and ethical thought of Aristotle was unknown in the West until the late twelfth and early thirteenth centuries, Aristotelian studies were conducted in the Arab world by commentators like the physician and philosopher Ibn Sina (980–1037), better known under his Latin name Avicenna, and Ibn Rushd (1126–96), or Averroes. From the viewpoint of medieval Christianity, the rationalist tenets of Aristotle's work accounted for its radicalism and potential danger to belief. As J.G.A. Pocock writes, his 'assertions about the autonomy of reason and the rational direction of politics ... are potentially revolutionary because they call in question the extent to which grace and the channels of grace are necessary in the conduct of earthly affairs' (Pocock 1975: 67). In the Muslim world, Averroes waged a battle not unlike Aquinas's against the clerical authorities, arguing that the relationship between philosophical reflection and revealed Law need not be at cross-purposes (Butterworth 1996: 77–95). To the leaders of the Christian Church, who were suspicious of pagan political philosophy in general, 'the fact that Aristotle had been so much handled by Arab scholars was enough to infect him with the taint of Islam' (Dyson 2002: xxiii). Put another way, the fact that *Muslim* philosophers had been chiefly responsible for teaching the pagan thought that was now being imported to Europe made it especially suspicious.

The translation project initiated by Thomas Aquinas was a correction of, and an admission to, the inadequacy of existing knowledge of Aristotle in Christian Europe. Up until then, his works had been translated into Latin either by Italians from Greek or from Arabiv, the language that came to replace Greek (and Aramaic) as a general cultural medium in the Eastern Mediterranean area, Aquinas insisted that both these routes of transmission disabled any serious intellectual engagement with Aristotle's ideas in their 'original' or 'pure' form. Most fundamentally, the proper restoration and reassessment of classical philosophy required a new translation that bypassed not only the Arabic by going directly to the Greek editions, but also that surpassed translations made by individuals trained in the ill-reputed schools of Southern Italy. Indeed, Robert Grosseteste's translation of the *Ethics* from c.1246–47 – where *koinonia politikè* and *polis* were rendered, in Italianized fashion, *politica communicacio* and *police* – was the result of learning Greek at the hands of Italian teachers (Bolgar 1954: 227–28).[12] In the interest of medieval Aristotelian studies in general and Aquinas's project in particular, Moerbecke, who had studied the language in Greece at first hand, took it upon himself to return Aristotle to the state he was in before being revamped by Arabs and Italians. Greatly advanced by a considerable interest in Aquinas's Christian version of Aristotelian philosophy, Moerbecke's translation of the *Politics* became the definitive medieval edition. As we shall see, Aquinas's commentaries remained relevant throughout the Renaissance, not least for church Fathers who under the pressure of social change appreciated the Christian rendition of pagan political thought.[13] In Moerbecke's first new edition (1260–64) *koinonìa politikè* and *polis* were rendered *communitas politica* and *civitas*; in the revised edition (1265) the former became *communicatio politica* or *civilis communitas* while the latter remained the same (Riedel 1975: 727).

Two semantic innovations with direct bearing on the conceptual history of civil society can be observed in this first major transformation within medieval thought of the Aristotelian vocabulary of politics. First, the term *civitas* replaced the more Greek *police* as the Latin equivalent for *polis*. From here on it became the definitive Latin term to signify the institutions and life of the city-state, passing from the humanist translation of the early fifteenth century to the vernacular languages of civil society still in use today. The 1260s thus signal an important moment in the semantic history of 'civil society'. Secondly, we note for the first time the usage of a *civitas*-rooted word in conjunction with 'community', which was used as a synonym for *politica*. It is thus that the 'state-side' of the state–civil society relationship migrates to the 'society-side', emphasizing the confluence of modern conceptions of 'state' and 'society' in Aristotelian political thought and the traditions building upon it up until the eighteenth century, when the state–civil society distinction becomes explicit in civil society theorizing.

Semantic Relocations and the European Trajectory: Aquinas in Context

This brief semantic history of the emergence of a new vocabulary of civil society in medieval Europe is intimately interlinked with the social and political transformations during a period of deep-seated – and indeed hemispheric wide – cultural crystallizations in different parts of Eurasia. Thus the Aristotelian vocabulary is transposed into the political language of Western Europe at a time when the whole social fabric of political order and belonging is being reinterpreted. In the wake of what some scholars refer to as a confluence of a feudal and urban, a papal and an intellectual, perhaps even 'scientific', revolution, the whole social landscape of Europe gradually took on a new form.[14]

These developments in the Far Western periphery of the Eurasian hemisphere were mirrored by developments at the Far Eastern edge of this world, in Japan, where the old imperial order slowly gave way to an emerging feudal relationship. As a consequence, pressures mounted on 'a marginal and wandering population beyond the state's control', a population of fishermen, peddlers, storytellers, puppeteers, jugglers, magicians, prostitutes and iterant artists and artisans. This 'wandering world [*henreki no sekai*] – an almost nomadic population with no close ties to the land' was related to a pre-feudal social order of imperial rule and services of the court of the old order. It helped 'spread folk culture, throughout Japan, disseminated beliefs and fashions, and ultimately helped make the peoples who live on the archipelago a group more homogeneous than fragmented' (Souyri 1998: 14).[15]

In the far west of Europe there was no corresponding imperial order and an analogous translocal civil society. Such phenomena could only be found at the peripheries of Europe and at the fleeting borderlines between Church, monastic orders and heterodox sects. The new Aristotelian-inspired vocabulary of civil society was therefore part of a process of growth of a new kind of feudal and urban society. Increasingly regulated and with no imperial order, that in Japan – and even more so in China – exerts sufficient counter-pressure to allow for a more fleeting trans-local civil society beyond efficient control of feudal lords and urban councillors.

The new vocabulary should, as already pointed out, reflect both a conceptual and a social movement of the 'state-side' of the state-civil society relationship to the 'society-side'. This linguistic 'relocation' – to use a term suggested by Jan Assmann in another context (Assmann 2004: 131–54) – highlights the confluence of modern conceptions of 'state' and 'society' that were to remain a predominant, if increasingly problematic, feature of civil society theorizing until the end of the eighteenth century.

In this context, the diffusion of Moerbecke's new terms was greatly enabled by Aquinas's usage of them in his widely influential commentary on the *Politics*, dating from 1269 to 1272. The historian and philologist Nicolai Rubinstein has shown that the language of *politicus* was not eradicated with Moerbecke's translation, which treated words based respectively on the roots *politicus* and *civitas*, as interchangeable. What we have noted here is an early move towards the language of *civitas* without yet abandoning the language of *politicus*. More important, however, seems to us the decision to use both *politicus* and *civitas* in conjunction with *communitas*. The value of active citizenship has not yet made its way into the vocabulary at this point, a development that occurs with great determination in Florentine political thought in the period of early civic humanism in the first part of the fifteenth century (see below in this chapter). In the intellectual projects of both Christian and Muslim philosophers, theorizing about political communities and states was ultimately launched from the standpoint of revealed religion. As both the Catholic Aquinas and the Muslim Averroes claimed, speculating on 'the city of man' was the other and necessary side of safeguarding 'the city of God'.[16] Couched in vague processes that eventually became known as secularization, the acceptance of the existence of earthly political communities as places of human realization is the unintended result of the vehement determination to prove the opposite, or at least to moderate its consequences, by connecting them to biblical references and Christian morality. It is worth pointing out in this context that of all Aristotle's works, only the *Politics* was not translated into Arabic.

Thomas Aquinas's appropriation of Aristotelian philosophy in the *Summa Theologica* was rather straightforward and is clearly recognizable in his discussion of the sociability of humans and the origins of polities. Aristotle's arguments were frequently bolstered by biblical verses that any but the most pious twentieth-century scholar would find rather unconvincing. Justifying absolute but benevolent monarchy, Aquinas thus writes that although the common good is the ultimate goal of all legitimate communities, the proliferation of different interpretations of what is good requires superior guidance to forge a united community. Accordingly, there must be something 'that rules all the rest'. Relying on the corporate metaphor of the body politic, he then goes on to conclude: 'Among the members of the body there is one ruling part, either the heart or the head, which moves all the others.' The argument that the ruler must direct his efforts to the common good rather than his own private good is then fortified with quoting the word of God in Ezekiel 34:2 about how the first priority of the good shepherd is to feed not himself but his flock. (Aquinas 2002: 8). As an additional example of Aquinas's mixture of pagan philosophy and biblical verse in his Christian rendition of Aristotelian philosophy, consider the following statement in the *Summa Theologica* about monarchy as one type of government in Aristotle's famous discourse on the three good forms of government and their degenerate forms:

> And if just government belongs to one man alone, he is properly called a king. Hence the Lord, at Ezekiel 37:24, says: 'And David my servant shall be king over them, and they all shall have one shepherd.' It is clearly shown by this verse that it is the nature of kingship that there should be one who rules, and that he should be a shepherd who seeks the common good and not his own gains. (Aquinas 2002: 9)[17]

The fact that 'provinces or cities which are not ruled by one man toil under dissensions and are tossed about without peace' further suggests that the prophet Jeremiah's complaint that 'Many pastors have destroyed my vineyard' had been 'fulfilled', and that 'Hence the Lord promises His people through the prophets that, as a great gift, He will put them under one head and that there will be one prince in the midst of them' (Aquinas 2002: 11).

In this way, Aquinas in his defense of 'the good king' or moderate kingship produced a text where logical and revelatory exposition become mutually reinforcing, fusing, as it were, the voices of the pagan philosopher and God. To this mixture he added interlocutors such as

Augustine in *De civitate Dei*, Sallust in *Bellum Catilinae*, John of Salisbury in *Policraticus*, Cicero in *De re publica* and *De officiis*. Within a matter of only nine lines on the corrupting force of greed, Aquinas refers to the book of Job, to Cicero, and to Aristotle, or 'the Philosopher' with a capital P.

Its eclecticism notwithstanding, Aquinas's *Summa Theologica* is perhaps the unrivalled example of what Antony Black in his distinction between five different languages of political thought in Europe between 1250 and 1450 calls 'the Aristotelian language'. The other four major medieval and early humanist political languages identified by Black are: (1) the 'theological' language, which relied heavily on the Latin Vulgate translation of the Bible and the Church Fathers, especially St Augustine; (2) the 'native' language of communal, regional, national and civic laws that were supplemented by (3) an academic 'juristic' language developed by civil and canon jurists; and finally (4) the 'Ciceronian' language, based on the Roman rhetorician's exposition of Stoical ethics and civic education found in books like *De officiis* and *De republica* (Black 1992: 7).[18] As the previous comments about Aquinas's sources in his discussion of community and forms of government show, it is clear that his use of Aristotelian language was fused with theological language.

If Aquinas without hesitation took Aristotle's language of politics out of context and moulded it for his own purposes, the translation on which it relied – that is, Moerbecke's new standard edition from the 1260s – adhered to the literal method of translation. Positing word-for-word translation as his ideal, Moerbecke attempted to retain the Greek words and the original word order (Dunbabin 1982: 723). With regard to the political vocabulary Greek words were retained to the greatest extent possible. 'The method of translating', writes Bernard G. Dod, 'was born out of respect for authority; as with sacred texts, so with Aristotle it was important to preserve the actual words of an authoritative work. Hence the ideal was to present to the reader Aristotle's actual words, put together in just the way Aristotle had put them together, with minimum 'interference' from the translator' (Dod 1982: 66).

Civil Society and Florentine Humanism

When the time had come to replace Moerbecke's standard version of 'Aristoteles latinus' in the early fifteenth century, the method of translation was markedly different. The motive behind Leonardo Bruni's translation of Aristotle's works on ethics and politics was not one of disinterested scholarship, but ideology. Following Hans Baron's famous (but disputed) thesis of a clash in 1402 between republican Florence and absolutist Milan that gave rise to a 'crisis', Bruni's writings were ultimately the intellectual responses to it. The Aristotle that emerged from Bruni's translations became infused with a humanist political thought, and since language in and of itself became an object of study and admiration, the classical vocabulary of politics underwent significant changes as well. The semantic history of civil society and the state thus entered a new chapter in European political thought, where translators and commentators saw it as their duty to take ideas and concepts out of context to further the interests of their community or state.

A man of considerable learning, Bruni was a member of the Florentine chancery and a theorist and panegyrist of the city-republic. According to Baron, Bruni's importance lay in his contribution to the transition from intimations of republicanism in medieval political thought to its maturation in the 'civic humanism' of early fifteenth-century Florence (Baron 1996).[19] Baron's assertion that the translation signified a return of the 'echt griechischer Aristoteles' after long periods of supposed scholastic abuse greatly underestimates the liberties taken by the new translator (quoted in Moulakis 2000: 202). It was Bruni's firm conviction that the Florentine city-republic could justly be compared with those of Rome and Athens, a conviction that made careful study of the theories and practices of the Graeco-Roman world desirable (Bruni 1968: 217–63). In a world where revealed religion alone could not provide the comforts of cosmic certainties, the idea of a republican heritage provided a bedrock of secular beliefs that helped contemporaries cope with a tumultuous present. Working in this spirit, Bruni composed a laudatory treatise on the republican constitution of Florence and an attempt to apply Aristotle's theory of the mixed constitution to the Italian city-republic (Rubinstein 1990: 5).

A self-declared admirer of Aristotle's 'admirable power of analysis', (quoted in Hankins 2000b: 172n. 3 and 173), Bruni also issued a new translation of the *Politics* itself, a laborious task that formed an integral part in an ambitious project: making classical political thought on the one hand and humanist political thought on the other conceptually compatible and mutually reinforcing. His project was thus analogue to Aquinas's, with the obvious and notable difference that whereas Aquinas had put forth a Christian version of Aristotelian philosophy based on a literal Latin translation, Bruni presented a secular republican version of the same philosophy based on a freer translation. A key member of the Italian humanists of the fifteenth century, Bruni appropriated and transformed Aristotle's political vocabulary for his and his Florentine compatriots' own purposes. According to Richard Tuck, this move was of lasting importance in Western political thought, as it 'marked the breach between the Renaissance proper and the earlier 'humanism' of the twelfth century onwards' (Tuck 1993: 12–13). Ever since this time, the placement of the individual books that make up Aristotle's *Ethics* and *Politics* were rearranged in order to convey the author's argument in what contemporaries thought was the most logical and convincing way (Everson 1996: xxxiii). Bruni attempted to reshape available moral and political vocabularies for two related purposes: functional and aesthetic. He hoped to reinvent classical political theory to, on the one hand, enable discussions of republican government and, on the other, to make current vocabularies better reflect the urban political life of fifteenth-century Florence. Bruni truly believed that innovation by means of imitation held the key to improvement and eventual surpass the model.[20]

Bruni's reading of Aristotle was less concerned with the metaphysical aspects of terrestrial political communities, as it had been to Aristotelians working in the medieval Christian and Islamic traditions of theology and philosophy, and more about the mechanisms of city-states as such. The dichotomy between ecclesiastical and secular polities dropped from the horizon of political theorizing, a casualty of established secular thought. In Pocock's words, Bruni's generation approached Aristotle 'as the originator of a body of thought about the citizen and his relation to the republic, and about the republic (or polis) as a community of values', crucial notions to 'humanists and Italian thinkers in search of means of vindicating the universality and stability of the *vivere civile*' (Pocock 1975: 67). As Bruni concludes in his introduction to the new Latin edition of the *Politics*: 'no science is more useful ... than to know what a city is and what a commonwealth is, and to understand how civil society is maintained or destroyed' and further that 'man is a weak creature and draws from civil society the self-sufficiency and capacity for perfection he lacks on his own ....'[21]

The humanist reception and invocation of classical theories of citizenship and polity issued from two specific goals: (1) putting a sharper focus on the city-republic as both a source of and a space for values and (2) to overcome the perception of the secular world as particular and unstable, or at least develop a secular system of principles, not seldom in the form of ancient and universally applicable morality tales. Realizing both goals entailed a philosophical discourse where theological and religious considerations were removed from the centre of concerns. Bruni's exposition of classical political thought as the original locus of a descriptive and prescriptive science of republican government is registered in the new conceptual apparatus of the *Politics*. As Maurizio Viroli concludes, '*politia*-rooted words' were replaced by '*civitas*-rooted words'. Thus, the original Greek term in the *Politics* for the third undistorted form of government or constitution, *politeia*, signifying a government ruled by many in the common interest and limited by law and popular will – became *res publica* in Bruni's translation (Rubinstein 1990: 4).[22] Moreover, the study of politics and morality that the ancient Greeks referred to as *politica* should now be articulated with '*precepta circa rempublicam*'; and what Moerbecke in Greek/Italian-sounding vocabulary called *'politici intellectus et theoria'* now became *'civilis intelligentia et speculationis'* (Viroli 1990: 147). The decision to remain faithful to the conventional Latin rendition of the *polis* as *civitas* is not surprising considering that the entire translation formed part of a larger project of forging a language of *civitas* that laid out the moral and political foundation of the Italian city-republic.[23] Where Moerbecke had discussed the good constitution in terms of a *politia*, only marginally drifting from the original Greek, Bruni spoke of *civitas* and *civitatis*.[24]

In the political language of civic humanism, the life of the Hellenic *polis* became the life of the *civitas*, with Athens as 'an authoritative prefiguration' of republican Florence (Moulakis 2000: 219). The description was also a prescription and, in Viroli's summary, the Renaissance city 'is much more than a source of protection and a supplier of material needs, it is the humane community where the citizens have in common laws, magistracies, and religious and public ceremonies. In a true city the relationship between citizens are relationships of friendship and solidarity ... A well-ordered city is a self-governing community in which the populace has a place in public life ... and the citizens alternate in public office' (Viroli 1990: 147). In the context of Bruni's linguistic transformation of the classical Greek language of politics it seems only natural that he preferred to call Aristotle's book not by its conventional title *Aristotelis politicorum libri octo* but as *De republica*. As Richard Tuck points out, 'pure Ciceronians' continued to call it *De republica* during the following century (Tuck 1993: 13).[25] However, both titles were used throughout the fifteenth century and beyond.

The new humanist translation of the *Politics* into classical Ciceronian Latin itself symbolized the Florentine republic's rise as the ultimate *koinonìa politikè*. Cleansing the model *polis* from its medieval conceptual traces made the Greek and Latin heritage of Renaissance Florence all the more apparent and luminous (Riedel 1975: 727). The philological aspects of translating Greek political thought was equally ideological and made *societas civilis* one of a handful of key political concepts in a republican language of politics. As Dominique Colas writes: 'both philologically and ideologically the first civil society was that of fifteenth-century Florence as the humanists represented it to themselves at the time when Cosimo di Medici was settling into power' (Colas 1997: 27–30). Or as Nicolai Rubinstein concludes: 'The retranslated moral and political works of Aristotle, which they [the Florentine humanists of the early fifteenth century] studied with fresh interest, provided them with an authoritative confirmation of the all-importance of civic values.' In sociological terms, he continues, the vocabulary of *civitas* identified not only the structure of the Florentine government of the early fifteenth century, which in and of itself proved it a legitimate heir to Athens or Rome. In addition, the political class of Florence at this time, to which Bruni belonged, were honourable heirs to those active citizens, or political animals, described by Aristotle (Rubinstein 1987: 48).

After Bruni's humanist rendition of classical political thought, attempts were made to achieve even greater perfection. In 1542, the French humanist Joachim Périon embarked on a project that aimed at 'eliminating all the vestiges of medieval terminology' in the Bruni translation of the *Ethics*, a project that was further refined a few years later by Danys Lambin, a specialist of Ciceronian philosophy (Tuck 1993: 17). Their efforts notwithstanding, the 'medieval Aristotle' as Aquinas/Moerbecke had interpreted him and the 'humanist Aristotle' that emerged from fifteenth-century translations were not as clearly separated as for example Colas and Tuck have suggested. There were editions, for example, that combined a humanist translation with medieval Christian commentary. Thus, in 1492, a little less than fifty years after Bruni's death, readers could read his edition of Aristotle's text within what was actually a larger text, namely Aquinas medieval commentary, which as we have noted, was based on Moerbecke's 'barbarian' edition. According to the introduction to the 1492 edition – entitled *Politicorum libri VIII* – Bruni's translation of Aristotle remained flawless, but it had been severely distorted in the numerous printed editions that followed. Readers were, however, provided not only with a supposedly flawless translation, but also with Aquinas's commentary, which the editor felt had been marginalized by the humanists (Aristotle 1492: editor's introduction).[26]

The edition of the *Politics* thus combines two texts (a translation and a commentary) that concern the same work – Aristotle's *Politics* – but that were created in two radically different contexts: the world of medieval Europe of the mid-thirteenth century and the world of Italian humanism in the early fifteenth century. Readers of the 1492 edition were accordingly furnished with two major conceptual registers. In Bruni's translation, *koinonìa politikè* was, as we have already noted, translated into *civilis societas* whereas in Aquinas's parallel comments the older medieval usage remained, where *koinonìa politikè* was translated as *communitates* or *politica comunicatione*. With regard to *polis*, both men used *civitas*, directing our attention once again to Moerbecke's early introduction of *civitas*-rooted terms to Aristotle's political vocabulary (Aristotle 1492: 24 and 26).

Enabled by the nascent culture of print, the dissemination of the republicanized Aristotelian political vocabulary gained momentum in the sixteenth century. During the 125–year period stretching from 1475 (the year of the first *printed* edition of Bruni's translation at Strasbourg) to 1600 at least fifty different Latin editions were published in cities like Barcelona, Paris, Salamanca, Rome, Basel, and Leipzig (Colas 1997: 27–30). Medieval Latin editions of course survived the republican moment and they were used alongside the Bruni edition for instruction in universities. As R.R. Bolgar has pointed out, however, the relatively slow adaptation of the humanist Aristotle in the university does not testify to a lack of its diffusion, but to the contrary of a relatively wide dissemination *beyond* the confines of the academy. 'The translators', he writes, 'were popularizers. It lay in the very nature of their activity that they wrote less for the learned specialists than for the common mass of educated men. They addressed themselves perforce to all those who could read Latin; and we may suppose that they selected such authors as they thought would have a wide appeal' (Bolgar 1954: 277). The demand for Aristotle's works in the lingua franca of learned Europe was notable: during the fifteenth century, no other pagan author had as many translators (ibid.).

Diffusion and Vernacularization

Passing from its place of origin in Hellenistic culture via medieval political thought, Bruni's humanist Latin translation of the *Politics* and the *Ethics* constituted the master copy on which subsequent vernacular translations into European languages were based. As manuscript cultures were transformed into print cultures, the diffusion of Aristotelian philosophy increased dramatically, as did the exactness with which texts could be reproduced. Hence, identical political vocabularies could be dispersed like never before, a development that has not yet been sufficiently examined. Whereas copyists during the course of copying manuscripts by hand had unavoidably distorted the vocabulary of whatever they were translating, the mechanical perfection of the printing press ensured standardized political vocabularies. Judging from the number of translations of Aristotle's works from its original language into the major European vernaculars before 1600, the interest in his philosophy was notable in Italy and Spain. The *Politics* went through at least four Italian translations between the fifteenth century and 1600, and at least two Spanish editions. Interest in the *Ethics* was even greater, with five Italian translations and three or four Spanish ones. To the north, the *Ethics* was translated into German only once before 1600, but it was never printed. The *Politics* never appeared in a German language edition before 1600. The interest in Aristotle's philosophy of ethics in France and England can be culled from the early appearance of Oresme's French translation of the *Ethics* in c.1375, which was printed more than one hundred years later, and an English one from 1547. The *Politics* was translated into French and English much later, in 1568 and 1598 respectively. Before Leonardo Bruni's translations there had only been one vernacular edition of Aristotle's philosophy, the aforementioned

French manuscript edition from 1375, with the possible inclusion of the anonymous German translation from the fifteenth century, which was never printed either (Bolgar 1954: Appendix II, 506–11).

The *printed* vernacular editions of Aristotle's work on ethics and politics were all based on Bruni's work, which rehabilitated the Greek philosopher by means of phrasing his arguments in classical Ciceronian Latin, as distinct from the medieval Latin of past translations. It is thus that the Greek concept of *koinonìa politikè* remained in the emerging vernacular languages of politics, which branched out from its common roots in Latin to different national political vocabularies. As Reinhart Koselleck and Klaus Schreiner conclude: 'Since early modernity, there has been an unfolding of a common European conceptualization into a variety of national languages ...' (Koselleck and Schreiner 1994: 12–13).[27] To the extent that there was a common European Aristotelian vocabulary, made available through Bruni's Latin master copy, it consequently bore a humanist stamp. If, and if so to what extent, the different vernacularized classical political vocabularies retained the humanist tendency of Florentine political thought acquired in the first half of the fifteenth century is an interesting question.

These preliminary remarks on translation, reception and interpretation suggest that the intellectual and cultural contexts of Aristotle's political lexicon were numerous and overlapping already by the year 1500, as signalled by the appearance of the combination of Bruni's translation and Aquinas's commentary in a 1492 edition. When natural rights philosophers in the seventeenth century set out to explain the origins and mechanisms of 'civil society' not one but many Aristotelian languages of politics were available to them. Centuries of reception had produced a concoction of concepts and commentaries that had been reworked by a variety of groups and interests to respond to challenges that were experienced at once as particular and universal.

Stemming from Aristotelian moral and political philosophy, the term *societas civilis* was understood as a synonym for the *polis* or *civitas* as it would remain in the work of thinkers like Spinoza, Locke, Pufendorf, and Rousseau. Such a social formation was civilized in the sense that it was regulated by law and, ultimately, a constitution, the opposition of a state of nature. In Aristotle's terminology the *polis* was distinguished from the *ethne* (peoples), that is a population lacking political or legal institutions, and the sphere of public life (as opposed to the private nature of the *oikos*, or household). 'Civil society' emerges as synonymous to the English 'state' or 'polity' just as *koinonìa politikè* was previously used as synonymous to the *polis*.[28] As the first paragraph of the *Politics* reads in the 1954 Jowett translation:

Every state [*polis*] is a community [*koinonìa*] of some kind, and every community is established with a view to some good .... But, if all communities aim at some good, the state or political community [*koinonìa politikè*], which is the highest of all, and which embraces the rest, aims at good in a greater degree than any other, and at the highest good. (Aristotle 1996: 1252a)f

In Bruni's Latin translation, these lines were translated as:

Voniam uidemus omnen <u>civitatem</u> [i.e. *polis*] esse <u>societatem</u> [i.e. *koinonìa*] quandam: & omnem <u>societatem</u> boni alicuius gratia constitutā. Maxime uero principalissimu omnium que est principalissima & ceteras omnes complectitur. Est autem hec illa que <u>civitas</u> appellatur & <u>civilis societas</u> [*koinonìa politikè*]. (Aristotle 1492: 4)

Conceptually speaking, two distinctions or oppositions can be seen from the usage of the terms *civitas* and *civilis societas*: (1) the opposition between civil society and the state of nature, where the former simply denotes a community of individuals and groups living under the rule of law and political institutions, and (2) the opposition between a community supervised by a secular power and a community supervised by a religious power. Thus, civil society is conceptualized in the first case by recourse to the distinction between civility versus barbarism that is analogous to the distinction between Aristotle's social or political animals, who are capable of moral reasoning and discourse due to the power of speech, on the one hand, and those who linger below or above them, be they beast or God, on the other. In the second case, the opposition is conceptualized as a struggle and attempted imposition between worldly power on the one hand and spiritual power on the other. It could sometimes even be premised on a cosmological chasm between a mundane and a transcendental sphere with a divine society being constitutive of the latter and civil society of the former.

So far, we have not encountered a clear opposition between civil society and the state. It is rather the case that the world of Renaissance culture made such an opposition as unlikely as it had been in the explicitly theological forms of theorizing that had played such a pre-eminent role in the high Middle Ages. Indeed, the place in political thought of the city as a place of trade and economic exchange that, during the early Renaissance, came to the fore in the replacement of a conceptual field of *politics* with a field of *civility*, testifies to an early sensibility to the problems that Adam Ferguson would later contemplate from the horizon of the commercial society of the eighteenth century.

Reinterpreting Civil Society:
Natural Law and the Early Modern State

One may argue that 'Aristotelian' political philosophy has always been heterogeneous, and that tracing the emergence of 'civil society' through him reveals an archive of confused parchments that obscures as much as it reveals. Reading civil society, like reading Aristotle, yields a concept that does what its authors need it to do in particular circumstances. However, in the late sixteenth and seventeenth centuries, deep-seated transformations came to change these circumstances so as to force a reappraisal of key features of the earlier imaginary of thought about political order and civil society.

Whereas reformation theology did not entail a challenge to Aristotelian notions of civil society but rather their reaffirmation, events in the wake of reformation came to do so. One of the consequences of reformation – and subsequently counter-reformation – was that the powers of states grew. Confiscation of the lands of monasteries meant a strengthening of the fiscal basis of the state. New administrative chancelleries meant a more efficient management of state resources and there was a slow but irreversible build-up of the coercive powers of the state. The bloody religious civil wars of the sixteenth and seventeenth centuries were of course central events in this process.

It is in this context of an emerging absolutist state that it becomes necessary to refer to this new state and its coercive powers in new terms. A vocabulary slowly emerges that makes this possible. Central in this new vocabulary, which appears already with Jean Bodin, are notions of a society not only being civil but governed and ruled by a power that is ascribed sovereignty. This new vocabulary, however, does not so much replace the old vocabulary of *societas civilis* but rather changes the preconditions and conditions of usage. Civil society may now, as in the conceptualization of Bacon, be seen as held together either by laws or by force. These two moments may be operating separately and not necessarily in the same direction. Civil society still tends to be seen as having the household as its elementary building block in a hierarchy of relations. However, in addition to hierarchical relations of ordering there is also the idea of the mutual and equal interaction of human beings who jointly constitute a *societas civilis*.

In the new vocabulary, the state, even as the locus of sovereignty, is still understood as part of or relating to the communal life of a civil society, and this civil society is seen as both a historical and contemporary reality and as natural within an order of things that in the last instance is theologically guaranteed and that forms the mundane counterpart to the divine order of a transcendental sphere. In the course of the seventeenth century, however, this assumption is gradually being eroded.

The emergence of a new inquiry into nature and the positing of laws of nature, beyond the confines of the *lex naturalis* of medieval theology, that is, what is now often referred to as the scientific revolution, was of course a highly complex process filled with intricate practical, linguistic and ideational combinations and juxtapositions. However, for the different usages of the term civil society it meant that the concept of civil society could no longer, if in the last instance, be grounded in theologically sanctioned natural law.

It is against this background that different formulations of the concept of civil society are articulated within the new natural law theorizing of the seventeenth century. This occurs in a context where there was an urgency of finding ways of granting legitimacy and meaning to the new order that emerged in the wake of the Westphalian Peace Treaty and the provisional end of a century and a half of bloody civil wars in Europe. The concern with the constitution of political community becomes the central one in political thought from Hobbes and Pufendorf over Locke all the way to Rousseau. The wide range of answers given does not preclude a predominant thought figure from being that of some form of contractual reasoning. The existence of such a social contract was normally seen to entail an answer also to the question of which types of enforcement of the normative order that constitute the political community are the legitimate ones. More specifically, only those types of enforcement are sanctioned that, implicitly or explicitly, follow from the terms of the social contract itself.

Political theory from Hobbes onwards is centrally preoccupied with the nature and consequences of a transition from a state of nature, sometimes portrayed as an imaginary and sometimes as a quasi-historical account, to the contractually constituted political community. Ultimately, of course, all such forms of theorizing depend on a limited set of assumptions about human beings and the nature of their joining together in societies. One such set of assumptions refers to the assignment of some kind of human rights, that is, rights that accrue to human beings irrespective of their origins and other accidental traits and characteristics.

Furthermore, there is a set of assumptions that refers to the thought-experiment of society being created through a process that is normally described in terms of a contract, whereby human beings agree about their association in political form. Questions about enforcement, separate from an answer to the question of the constitution of a political order, based upon legitimately agreed contractual arrangements, were of subordinate and derivative importance relative to this overriding concern. This also means that the concept of civil society continued to be used in the old sense as a comprehensive term referring to public ordering and the state, while the social ontology behind this usage had been radically changed already in the seventeenth century and no longer posits a theologically guaranteed harmonious social whole, but rather individual components that must be brought to concur. Thus European political theory in this classical form emerged in a particular historical context both in European and world history. It also involved forms of theorizing that portrayed an imaginary contractual past as the point of constitution of polities. However, it was not in itself characterized by an effort to reflect on the history of political theory as an essential component of developing such a theory. This form of reflexive historical consciousness was to become a key characteristic of yet another major transformation in intellectual and political history, that of the late eighteenth and early nineteenth centuries.

Civil Society, Historicity and Modernity

In the political economy and moral philosophy of the Scottish Enlightenment, a view emerged of human beings as rational and deliberative individuals and of society as a compositional collective. This also made possible a new way of thinking about political community and its legitimacy. More precisely, it provided the possibility for thinking about political order as formed through the consent of individual human beings. However it was not, as in older contractual thinking, a consent that would have ushered in a distant and possibly hypothetical social contract but rather a consent that could be assessed and rationally evaluated in terms of its reasonableness in its present and historical context.

The contemporary form of socio-political order was also linked to a historical account of the evolution of human beings, normally in a four-stage evolutionary schema, which is sometimes cast as a history of civil society and its progress relative also to a wider process of the progress of civilising of humankind at large. In these accounts, the concept of civil society is also widened relative to older usage and comes to include economic interactions which are no longer seen as only or primarily part of the household and separate from the common concerns of a civil society. This opens up a new field of potential discursive contest, even if there is no final rupture in the older usage where state and civil society are seen as coterminous or partially overlapping.

It brings out an implicit tension in all the older usages, namely that civil society at one and the same time is the voluntary and mutually supportive form of human beings living together and regulating their common concerns and that it is constituted by the components, whether households and their masters or individuals, and their range of public interactions. In the late eighteenth and early nineteenth centuries, forms of economic exchange could no longer be conceptualized as belonging to the sphere of private households, nor as well-ordered components of a regulated mercantilist economy. In the world of the incipient industrial revolution, these interactions were both public and glaringly uneven. How could a civil society be possible in such a world?

The turn of the eighteenth century witnessed a range of different normative responses to this question. Most of these articulations allowed for debates about the relationship of the state to the range of interactions that formed part of a civil society. However, in hardly any of them was there a proposal to introduce a terminological rupture that would have irreversibly severed the link between the civil society of interactions and the political entity of the state. This is, in our reading, equally true of the very different conceptualisations of civil society even of Kant and Hegel. In Hegel, for instance, one important aspect of civil society is its embeddedness in a corporate ordering but also in a judicial ordering of the state. And even in Marx the crucial rupture is not between state and bourgeois civil society – since the state is of this society – but between the existing reality of bourgeois civil society and the emergent promise of the coming together of the proletariat in another form of mutual support and linking that will eventually overthrow it and replace it with a new state that will ultimately wither away in favour of a community that has all the characteristics of the core components of a civil society.

The turn of the eighteenth century also witnessed, however, a transition from political and moral philosophy to a science of society[29] – an intellectual change born of the experiences of the relative inability of the French Revolution to create stable institutions; of a new conception of human agency as formed and constrained by structural and systemic properties; and of a society conceived as an organic or systemic totality. Such a conception would in a conservative version lead to theories of the necessity to restore an organic political order, whether theologically sanctioned or not. In radical versions it could, however, also usher in demands for the overthrow of unnatural and illegitimate order and lend support to the idea that modern society was not an atomistic and distorted form of human community but could relate to an organic solidarity and a civil society compatible with the life of free citizens in a free republic.

Notes

1. The seminal conceptual history of 'civil society,' chiefly but not exclusively in the German language, is Riedel 1975. For the historical semantics of state and civil society, see also Kocka 1996 and Kocka 2004. The authoritative history of translations of Aristotle is Dod 1982.
2. The question of 'male-dominated' civil societies is discussed in Pateman 1998: 101–28.
3. This is how we read John Keane's observation that although the civil society–state distinction has experienced a resurgence in intellectual debates during the 1990s, and although it is both 'exciting' and 'controversial', 'it is hampered – and potentially

threatened – by widespread confusion about the *several* meanings and *various* implications of the distinction' (Keane 1988: 13). For the relationship between early modern political thought and contemporary concerns, with attention to how dialogues between scholars can lead to a better understanding of 'perennial problems' of political modernity and to shape viable normative theories of civil society, see ibid.: 28–29. See also the discussion of the contemporary relevance of conceptual history as a means of criticism in Ball, Farr and Hanson 1989 and Williams 1976.

4. We have in mind the approach to the history of political thought chiefly associated with J.G.A. Pocock and Quentin Skinner. See esp. Skinner's recent collection of his methodological writings over the past four decades in Skinner 2002.

5. Languages of politics is understood in the sense indicated by Pocock (1987: 21) 'When we speak of "languages" … we mean for the most part sub-languages: idioms, rhetorics, ways of talking about politics, distinguishable language games of which each may have its own vocabulary, rules, preconditions, tone and style.' See also the more communicative or action-oriented definition given by Ball, Farr and Hanson 1989: 1–2: '[A] moral or political language is a medium of shared understanding and an arena of action because the concepts embedded in it inform the beliefs and practices of political agents …. Our moral language maps political possibilities and impossibilities; it enables us to do certain things even as it discourages or disables us from doing others.' It is, of course, possible to examine the concept of 'civil society' without examining the words 'civil' and 'society', depending on one's definition of 'civil society' in the first place. Put another way, we can study how others have understood what we call civil society without requiring that they share with us the same vocabulary. See Skinner 2002: 159–60ff.

6. On this topic, see chapters 1 and 4 in the present volume.

7. From this perspective, we may add, the insertion of Thucydides' comments about 'democracy' from classical political thought into the 'Draft Treaty Establishing a Constitution for Europe' would require a modification. The statement that 'Our Constitution … is called a democracy because power is in the hands not of a minority but of the greatest number' (Draft Treaty 2003: 6) would at a minimum require adding that 'this fortunate condition is a reality to us because we have banished women and resident aliens from public life'. Although these preconditions may be shared by some, it is not likely the intention of the drafters of the constitution, who also seem unaware of the fact that, unmitigated, the word 'democracy' did not have the positive connotations to classical thinkers as it does to us, but rather refers to mob rule. Again, we can reasonably expect that members of a Union whose draft constitution basks in the rays of European civility – but blatantly ignores the barbarism that not only forms part of its history but also accounts for the very foundation of the early union – have something slightly different in mind.

8. See Skinner 1969. A revised version appears in Skinner 2002, 57–89. Our own view has to some extent been articulated in Hallberg 2003: 34–43 and Wittrock 1999.

9. See the list of translations mentioned in Colas 1997, app. B, pp. 365–67.

10. The classical Greek and Latin trajectories are analysed in Riedel 1975: 721–27.

11. During the fifteenth century, the *Ethics* was translated at least three more times: by Gregorio Tifernas (*c.*1450), G. Manetti (*c.*1459) and J. Argyropoulos (*c.*1440–80). The *Politics* was translated only once more, by J. Argyropoulos (*c.*1440–80; Bolgar 1954: 434).

12. Regarding the dating of Grosseteste's translation, see Callus 1947: 101–09.

13. It should be pointed out in passing that Aquinas's teachings still today form part of Roman Catholic doctrine.

14. For an elegant formulation of this view of the formation of the specific European trajectory, see Schluchter 1996: 179–243.

15. A brief history of the concept of feudalism in Japanese historiography and the interaction with German historiography is given in Shiro 1997: 75–85.
16. This is of course a core component of the hypothesis of the Axial Age, originally proposed by Max Weber and subsequently elaborated by his brother, Alfred, and also by Eric Voegelin, Karl Jaspers and in recent decades mainly by S.N. Eisenstadt. For a history of this concept see Arnason 2004: 19–48.
17. Aquinas also quotes e.g. Ecclesiastes 5:8, Ephesians 4:3, Jeremiah 12:10.
18. All of these languages were written in Latin, but were made up of 'separate vocabularies ... with their own concepts, prose styles, methods of argument and criteria of judgment, standard texts and authorities: distinct ways of articulating and presenting to their audiences political facts and ideas.' Black's understanding of 'political languages' is akin to Pocock's definition of political languages as 'sub-languages' in Pocock 1987: 21.
19. On Bruni's position in early civic humanism, see also Pocock 1975: 86. Baron's original German expression in *Historische Zeitschrift* from 1925 was 'Bürgerhumanismus' (Hankins 2000: 1). Baron has by now been roundly criticized for making a too sharp distinction between the 'pre-humanists' and the 'civic humanists'. A different account is presented in Seigel 1966: 3–48. Baron responds to some of his critics in the last chapter of Baron 1988.
20. On the methodology of imitation in the renaissance, see Cochrane 1981.
21. The original Latin, in the 1492 edition mentioned below, is: *nulla profecto convenientior disciplina homini esse potest quam quid sit* civitas: *et quid Respub. intelligere et per quae conservetur intereatque* civilis societas *non ignorare ... Cumque homo imbecillum sit animal et quam per seipsum non habet sufficientiam: perfectionemque ex* civili societate *reportet.*
22. In Everson's 1996 edition of the *Politics politeia* is rendered 'constitution' or 'constitutional government' (Aristotle 1996: 1279a38–9).
23. As Moulakis points out, Bruni used the word *politeia* to describe the emerging Florentine government and further claims that although it could be used to describe a form of rule, it could also be used to 'legitimize ... the established and recognized preponderance of a political class' (Moulakis 2000: 205). He does not, however, give any further details about this usage.
24. In his 1946 translation of the *Politics*, Ernest Barker remained faithful to the original Greek and spoke about the good constitution as 'a politeia' (Barker 1946: 1279a39).
25. The title was identical to one of Cicero's own works, *De re publica* (51 BC).
26. Dominique Colas notes a 1493 Leipzig edition that also combined Aquinas's commentary and Bruni's translation (Colas 1997: 377).
27. See further the other contributions in Koselleck and Schreiner's volume, as well as Riedel 1975.
28. For lexicographic reasons, *société civile* may have been preferable to many French authors due to the potential confusion raised by the fact that *cité* without the capital C means city and that *état* refers to 'state' as in a condition, e.g. state of mind (Colas 1997: 22–23).
29. For an analysis of this process see e.g. Heilbron 1995, Magnusson, Heilbron and Wittrock 1998/2001 and Wagner 2001.

PART II

Narrowing

Chapter 3

THE NATIONALIZATION AND POPULARIZATION OF POLITICAL LANGUAGE: THE CONCEPT OF 'CIVIL SOCIETY' IN SWEDISH

Peter Hallberg

This chapter thematically continues the line of inquiry of the preceding chapter on the national and transnational aspects of the languages of civil society.* It thus includes some reflections on Latin as the *transnational* political language of early modern Europe and its increasingly contentious relationship to *national* languages of politics. Emerging from a pan-European, but hardly non-contentious, discourse on politics that engaged small literate elites and was conducted chiefly in Latin, representatives from national political cultures began a quest to invent, refine or protect 'indigenous' political languages. Typically phrased as patriotic projects, the nationalization of political languages harboured democratic elements cast in the spirit of popular enlightenment that were posited against an elitist Latin cabal which was frequently likened to medieval clerics. In terms of research, our inquiry into languages of civil society entails an analysis into how a basic classical or republican vocabulary of politics still very much in vogue was reshaped as it was received in different cultural and political milieus. John Keane's notion of an '"emigration" of the language of civil society' is one way of bringing this phenomenon to our attention (Keane 2003: 35). Reflecting the ongoing 'globalization' of the concept, Keane writes about how 'civil society ideas and languages and institutions are spreading beyond their place of origin into new contexts, where they are in turn conceptualized or re-conceptualized in local contexts, from where the revisions, which are sometimes cast in very different terms, may and often do feed back into the original donor contexts' (ibid.: 36). The general aim of this chapter is to conduct such a study *historically* and in the context of the rise of the modern nation-state. Turning to the discourse in a peripheral country as an example of the larger processes at the contentious intersection of intellectual-linguistic Europeanization *and* nationalization, it analyses the invention of a national language of civil society in eighteenth-century Sweden.[1]

Languages of Politics: Latin versus the Vernaculars

When we speak of European *languages* of civil society, we propose to approach language not only as the conceptual register of an ideology or tradition of thought. In addition to such analyses, we suggest paying more attention than is usually the case to the history of national languages, or vernaculars, and their relationship to pan-European lingua franca such as Latin and French. This sub-history of political thought is of immediate relevance to civil society research. As Koselleck concludes: 'The common European theoretical tradition regarding the *societas civilis* was broken apart increasingly along national-linguistic lines in the early modern period' (Koselleck 2002: 215). During the course of the seventeenth and eighteenth century, the linguistic conventions of national languages emerged in the context of a Latin writing culture. Extending the usage of national languages from private or quotidian usage to public usage as the language of instruction and intellectual discourse entailed attempts at standardization. If national languages were to perform the functions traditionally performed by Latin, conventions regarding proper usage and meaning had to be standardized, a point of view that was often justified by recourse to patriotic rhetoric. In addition to standardizing spelling and conjugation, lexicographers sought to identify sets of words that together made up the national language in question. An integral part of these efforts was to invent new and to rehabilitate old words, and make recommendations on their proper usage in communication (Hannesdóttir 2002). We may refer to these efforts as the linguistic side of a de-Latinization or, alternatively, a nationalization of public culture and, consequently, of languages of politics. What, for example, happened to the republican heritage when the language with which it was communicated and extolled all but vanished from public discourse?

In the eighteenth century languages of politics, in the wide sense of the term incorporating both discourses of institution and dissent, emerged in the context of new public spheres and a politics of contestation (Baker 1990). Our hypothesis is that both the spheres and forms of political discourse during this period were nationalized and popularized on a scale and at a rate never experienced before. The formation of *languages* of politics thus became part of the *politics* of language. A previously common language of politics (Latin) with roots in Roman oratory, the manuscript culture of medieval scholarship, and the development of Renaissance discourse was challenged by new and differentiated languages that may or may not overlap, depending on the context of translation, reception and interpretation. Phrased as a hypothesis that has been verified at the macro-level, the notion of a nationalization of political discourse identifies opportunities for detailed comparative research into the history of political languages in Europe and beyond. A concept like *societas civilis* is an obvious candidate for such a project.

The preliminary remarks offered here about the relationship between transnational and national languages only concern its *cultural* aspects, understood in historical terms as the history of its uses or functions, including debates about its role as a means of communication. Reflections on the communicative function of transnational languages include both symbolic and social aspects of communication, such as its uses in religious and secular representation and its effects on social processes like exclusion and inclusion. The discussion here, which is at best preparatory, is undertaken in the spirit of clarifying the emergence of national languages of politics as they bear on the notion of a common European heritage that transnational languages helped shape and reproduce. This historical-semantic problematic corresponds to one of the questions with which contemporary civil society research grapples: can there be a civil society beyond the confines of the nation-state and, if so, what are the conditions for its existence? Bracketing pragmatic concerns about the feasibility of such a project, as well as the normative aspects pertaining to its desirability, the history of European civil society can certainly be studied on the level of intellection and language. In such a project, questions of meaning can be studied not only diachronically on the basis of individual and consecutive oeuvres, but also synchronically on the basis of different contexts of translation, reception, interpretation, and instrumentalization. A focus on the synchronic dimension of languages of civil society invites comparative analyses both within and between polities.[2]

As is the case of languages generally, political languages evolve through the more or less conscious actions of their users. Their existence is the result of conscious efforts by governments, organizations and social groups to master public discourse. The history of translations of Aristotle between 1250 and 1500 shows that Latin reigned supreme as the language of political reflection for the better part of the early modern period (see chapter 2). Following Richard Tuck's dating of the first record of Roman legal terminology to 450–400 BC, legal and political theorizing had been written in Latin for 2,100 years by the year 1700, at which time it was challenged (Tuck 1979: 7). As Tuck points out with specific reference to the concept *ius* (or 'right', 'Recht', 'droit'), but also with regard to the Latin language in general, the length of its history suggests that the *meaning* of key terms have remained far from stable. This has also been confirmed by the history of *Aristoteles latinus*. But the realization of contingency soon breeds a need for aesthetic and moral foundations. At least since the mid-eighteenth century, a common language has been seen as a means to forge community. Such projects have typically been legitimated as constituting necessary parts of patriotic, utilitarian and civilizing missions. What is important to note with regard to Latin is that it of course remained a scholarly and religious language well beyond the eighteenth century, thus lending credence to the conceptual affinity between the terms 'universal' and 'catholic'.

As has already been suggested with regard to the eighteenth century, standardization in practice meant nationalization: new 'national' words had to be invented or old ones had to be reinstated while foreign words had to be eliminated from the existent vocabulary. A truly free, modern and great polity, according to this notion of community and language, requires a language of its own. The nationalist quest for linguistic standardization in some instances harboured democratic tendencies in the sense of widening the circle of discourse by using the spoken (popular) language. It also meant that certain national languages of politics became inaccessible to large numbers of people, especially if that national language was spoken by a minority. Thus, the emergence of, for example, a Danish language of politics alienated French readers while Danish readers continued to read French.

The process under review was clearly one of slow transition rather than dramatic replacement. While, as we remarked before, many European universities remained bastions of Latin, scientific or learned academies increasingly adapted national languages for their procedures and publishing ventures. Reading publics perused works written in both native and foreign languages. Responding to these changes, publishing became organized according to two wide strains: one Latin and/or French strain of learned literature and one national strain with popularizing ambitions. Considering the fact that a number of the same key European thinkers were included in the university curricula in different nations, especially where scholastic methods of instruction prevailed, a Latin based pan-European intellectual culture continued, but during the course of the eighteenth century, this culture was increasingly confronted with a national variety.

As the lexicographer Howard Jackson has pointed out, modern English derives from three major sources or strata. The first of these is Anglo-Saxon, which developed around 500 AD during the invasion and colonization of England by Germanic tribes. The vocabulary of this language, Old English, derived from Germanic languages and to a lesser extent Celtic. In the wake of Augustine's mission in 597, ecclesiastic words were imported from Latin. The second stratum developed in the wake of the Norman conquest of 1066, at which time the language of government, administration and law became French in its Norman variety. The rising merchant class soon became fluent in both the language of politics (French) and of daily life (English). Some 10,000 French words entered English between the twelfth and fourteenth centuries. This development meant that English was Latinized via the French. As Jackson writes: 'Indeed, the [Anglo-Saxon] substratum suffered considerable erosion, with a large proportion of the Old English vocabulary being replaced by words from the Latinate superstratum' (Jackson 2002: 11). The third stratum emerged during the Renaissance, which brought further Latinization as the profound admiration for all things Greek and Roman inspired the addition of thousands more Latin, and also Greek, words to the English vocabulary. 'The Renaissance', writes Jackson, 'also saw the beginnings of exploration, which developed in the eighteenth and nineteenth centuries into colonization and empire; the contact with many different cultures and languages has enriched the vocabulary of English from a multitude of sources' (ibid.: 11).

In order to illustrate the relationship between language and politics, the following section considers the problem of standardization from the perspective of Swedish eighteenth-century lexicographers and in the specific context of inventing a Swedish political language.

The Language of Civil Society in Early Eighteenth-Century Sweden

At least since the late 1730s, eighteenth-century writers and printers recognized that the most basic strategy of publishing for a wider audience was to print books that were written in the vernacular. At the Swedish pantheon of practical enlightenment, the Academy of Sciences, vernacular printing projects would, from the time of its inception in 1739 and onwards, be considered a necessary means to fulfill its task of disseminating knowledge. Having delimited the subjects of the Academy and the basic condition of membership – 'love of useful sciences' – its statutes went on to outline the guidelines for diffusion. Since the Academy 'has only the public in view', its secretary was obliged to make sure that reliable results 'were printed in the Mother tongue without delay so that the public may soon enjoy their fruits' (*Kongl. maj:ts nådigste stadfästelse* 1741, chap. 1). The decision to publish only in Swedish was neither obvious nor unanimous in the eighteenth-century Republic of Letters. There were four major choices: one could publish in the old or the new international language, Latin and French respectively, in German, or in Swedish.[3]

Although some European academies used one of the international languages – the one at Berlin published in French, the one at Petersburg in Latin – the European trend in the eighteenth century was to communicate in one of the vernacular languages (Fay 1932: 263). The Academy of Sciences in Stockholm followed this trend. It also made language studies a prioritized area of investigation and declared that Swedish 'in manuscripts, print and at all public meetings should be used alone' (*Kongl. maj:ts nådigste stadfästelse* 1741, chap. 1, §5.).

A nationalist current is clearly perceptible in a number of contributions to the language question. Carl Gustaf Tessin commended the Academy's publications for their readability, the result of a conscious policy to avoid rhetorical expressions that clouded more than they illuminated and to keep the language 'pure and free of the contagion of alien words' (Tessin 1746: 5–9). Relaying the language issue retrospectively, Samuel Sandels discussed it in light of national honour or prestige. Printing in a foreign language, he claimed, was a courtesy that foreigners were not willing to return. Moreover, using foreign languages in scientific discourse reproduced the complacent habit in better Swedish homes to speak French (Sandels 1771: 16). Radical measures were proposed by the prominent academician and astronomer Christopher Polhem who, in a list of priorities in moral education, suggested that all sciences should be taught in Swedish, that visits abroad be closely monitored, that the free influx of foreign books be stopped and that the young should be protected from 'the thinking of foreigners' (Polhem 1745: 10; see also Ehrenpreus 1748: 3).

Prominent public figures, among them the historian and publicist Olof Dalin and his publisher, Lars Salvius, argued that more scholarly endeavours, including historical studies, should be published in Swedish instead of the literary Latin or German.[4] As Bo Bennich-Björkman has pointed out, the move towards national languages in scholarly publishing was part of a European trend that to a large extent was animated by the aforementioned ambition to spread knowledge – and thus sell more books – to larger segments of the population. This agenda had profound effects on the book market. What had previously constituted two distinct streams of publishing, one for learned readers and one for ordinary people, was amalgamated into one that favoured works that combined science and popular education, such as textbooks and manuals (Bennich-Björkman 1998: 51–55).

In his own works on history and geography Lars Salvius had pursued the explicit ambition to spread knowledge to a wider readership, paying particular attention to younger generations. Publishing was both a part of and a means to diffuse patriotism, a purpose that placed certain conditions on the endeavour of the scholar, especially on his or her choice of language and style (Legnér 2002: 53). During the debates on the relative merits of the ancients versus the moderns that preoccupied Renaissance writers, the idea that contemporaries write in the classical languages instead of in their vernaculars had been seen as having a crippling effect on present generations (Lowenthal 1997: 70–80). In the Age of Enlightenment, publishing in a language that very few could decipher became incompatible with the civilizational project. As the historian of ideas Sten Lindroth writes: '[T]he old Latin culture had had its day, and it was with easily understood essays on scientific and economic subjects that the Academy wanted to reach the Swedish public' (Lindroth 1978–81, vol. 3: 59)

There is a tendency in this testimony of eighteenth-century academicians that books on Sweden written by Swedish scholars were seen as a priori superior to those written by foreigners. At the same time, the pursuit of national honour that also dictated the quest for Swedish-made knowledge and books was motivated by the respect that foreigners would show the country if it became intellectually self-sufficient. Calls to increase the domestic production of knowledge and books can be seen as a corollary to another ambitious eighteenth-century project with roots in the antiquarian movement of the late seventeenth century: to present to domestic and foreign audiences a comprehensive and impressive cultural heritage (Legnér 2002: 48). Just as the civilizational influence of ancient Greece issued from its advances in the arts and sciences, Sweden could secure an elevated position in Europe if it followed in the footsteps of Greece (Elvius 1746: 13–4). To shoulder this responsibility, the means of social communication had to be standardized, a patriotic project that called attention to the work of lexicographers that in the year 1750 had been underway for about thirty-five years.

Taking his title from a word in the biblical Book of Judges – 'shibboleth' – the bishop and lexicographer Jesper Swedberg in 1716 published a book that outlined a political view of language and included a list of foreign words with suggested Swedish synonyms (Swedberg 1716). Chapter 12 of the Book of Judges tells the story about the great battle between two Semitic tribes, the Ephraimites and the Gileadites. Having won the battle, the Gileadites set up a blockade to catch the fleeing Ephraimites, asking each person to say the word 'shibboleth', which in ancient Hebrew dialects meant 'ear of grain'. The Ephraimites, who had no *sh*-sound in their language, pronounced the word with an *s* and were thereby unmasked as the enemy and slaughtered.[5] Taking this story as an analogue to the relationship between a well-developed vernacular language to national identity or character, Swedberg was chiefly concerned about the communicative aspects of language, as opposed to aesthetic aspects related to eloquence. Of paramount importance for the flourishing of a national language was the state's commitment to its standardization and subsequent usage in intellectual, administrative, religious and quotidian discourse. Citing Aristotle's notion of the human being as the speaking animal, Swedberg argued that language, or more precisely the forms of sociability enabled by language, was the perhaps most powerful means to build and fortify an 'intimate common Society'[6] (Swedberg 1716, preface §1).

Continuing the biblical imagery, the author compared the demise of ancient Hebrew and the concomitant break-up of God's nation to the demise of old Swedish and the possible break-up of that nation too. In this narrative of the corruption of linguistic communities, the Tower of Babel denoted not a singular incident, but an ongoing process with a history of its own. If the Bible supplied historical images as warning examples, it was Aristotle's notion that humans could use language both to make and break communities that captured the central argument of Swedberg's *Shibboleth*. '[T]he power of speech,' Aristotle had written, 'is intended to set forth the expedient and inexpedient, and therefore likewise the just and the unjust' (Aristotle 1996: 1253a8–18).[7]

The most damaging assault to linguistic communities, and hence to the very *idea* of communities, emanated from the inability among rulers and ruled to resist luxury, invariably spelled as foreign and artificial goods. Thus, the fall of the Tower of Babel is explained with the help of semi-secular arguments suggesting that it was the Jews' appetite for things foreign that caused God to turn away from the Hebrews and look instead to the Greeks, who had maintained their language intact. The eventual onslaught of sophism, which turned every question into quarrels about words, in turn destroyed this civilization (Swedberg 1716, preface §11). Convinced that the fall of the Greeks would inevitably be the result of the abuse of language in the city-states, God then turned west to the Romans, whose leaders clearly perceived the need for perfection. Their remarkable scientific and artistic creativity explained why the rest of the world yearned to 'learn the Latin language, before all other languages in the world'[8] (ibid.: §11). The well-known opulence of the later Romans passed the torch of communities united by language to Germany, at which stage Swedberg's otherwise cyclical history of rise and fall takes a distinct Protestant turn entailing a more linear narrative, the chief protagonists of which are Martin Luther and Charles the Great. Demanding that all public communication be written in German and ordering that linguists produce a standard book of grammar, the emperor paved the way to Luther's translation of the Bible, which was then turned into numerous 'mother tongues'.[9] What Leonardo Bruni's translation of Aristotle had done to release the tide of vernacular languages of politics (see chapter 2 of this volume) Luther had done for the vernacularisation of the Christianity vocabulary, spreading all the way to Eastern and Western India (ibid.: §12).

As an individual nation, Sweden was described by Swedberg as a now marginal one in the Protestant communication circuit, with its printing presses located in cities such as Lübeck, Wittenberg, Rostock, Riga, and Hamburg. The concentration of presses on the European continent, he concluded, had adversely effected the standing of the Swedish language by impoverishing the domestic book market. As in the rest of Swedberg's global history of language, it was corruption that spelled the demise of proper Swedish. This state of affairs, which had consecutively worsened since the mid-seventeenth century (the Peace of Westphalia to be precise), had in the second decade of the eighteenth century degenerated to a situation where 'The heart and the mind is nowadays completely beset with foreign languages and manners'[10] (ibid.: §29). Thus, in the wake of the creation of sovereign states at Westphalia, Swedes of some standing were curiously greeting one another in French and people liberally incorporated foreign words despite the fact that they were ruled by 'their own powerful and absolute Swedish king'[11] (ibid.: §30). The end result of this variety of the story of the Tower of Babel in early eighteenth-century Sweden was that its children were becoming strangers to themselves (ibid.: §32). For a country whose sixteenth- and seventeenth-century rulers[12] had driven out the Catholic church and revived the national language to a state of purity, Swedberg expressed uncompromising disappointment.

Latin culture was not the main target in *Shibboleth*. Swedberg's admiration of the Romans', and also the Greeks', efforts in linguistic refinement is apparent. Especially the efforts of their leaders to *institutionalize* language made them worthy of imitation. Swedberg certainly applauded King Gustavus Adolphus for his insistence that the young spend less time reading Latin and that the professors at Uppsala University should teach the arts and sciences in Swedish, but he did so in the spirit of the Romans and Greeks. Private and public teachers alike were encouraged by Swedberg to follow in Cicero's footsteps, who had composed *De officii* in Latin as a textbook for his son, who studied in Greece (ibid.: §34). According to representatives of the Swedish church, this book in particular and Greek and Roman learning in general could 'yield much fruit and benefit in young people through their pleasing morals and the splendid examples from the history of Greece and Rome which formed the contents of this book and which should be diligently recounted to young people to inspire in their minds desire and inclination to all forms of civil virtues'.[13] The political benefits of an offensive campaign for the vernacular were obvious: the recreation of a Swedish linguistic community would lead to a citizenry that showed equal piety to religious and civil government, to God and King. In fact, the civilization process enabled by a church armed with vernacular texts promised to make the machinery of the law superfluous (ibid.: §37). A civil society thus arose, with great ease, from the labour of religious instruction.

Fervent in his will to root out the proliferation of foreign languages in early eighteenth-century Sweden, Swedberg was more radical than one of his lexicographical predecessors, Haquin Spegel. In 1711, the year before he published his influential dictionary *Glossarium-sveo-gothicum eller Swensk-ordabook*, Spegel was appointed Archbishop of Sweden, the crowning of a successful career as preacher and rhetorician to magistrates and the royal court. In the preceding century, Sweden had grown into an empire that stretched over a large territory that incorporated different ethnic groups. One of Spegel's quests was to place the Lutheran religion in the service of a homogenizing, pacifying or civilizing state. Of central importance in his literary production was the politically motivated myth that Sweden was the early modern instantiation of Israel in the Old Testament. The Swedish people were accordingly God's people and their kings divinely appointed. In Spegel's view, religious sermons were instrumental to the creation of a common political ideology whose main function was to civilize or discipline a heterogeneous population (Ekedahl 1999).

His commitment to the promulgation of patriotic or proto-nationalist ideology is clearly visible in his work as a lexicographer. Firmly planted in the patriotic and puritan view of languages that has already been noted in the work of Jesper Swedberg, Spegel viewed foreign words, especially French ones, as imbued with the force of moral corruption. Within a patriotic framework, both Swedberg and Spegel approached languages pragmatically as a means to communication and, for that purpose, advocated a clear separation of different vernaculars (Hannesdóttir 1998). A mixing of languages spelled the break-up of nations, and since Sweden was the new Israel, the Tower of Babel was closer than many cared, or dared, to think. Spegel's view of the history of languages was at once genealogical, hierarchical and functional. Aided by organic metaphors like rivers and plants to describe the evolution of languages, he remained convinced about the idea of a fundamental language, the chief candidate of which was the biblical Hebrew of the patriarchs. This fundamental language was the source of secondary languages, which branched off like rivers, or the branches of a tree. The existence of other ancient languages, such as the Syrian, Arabic, Celtic, Scandian and Slavonic, neither falsified nor confirmed Hebrew as the mother of all other languages. In Europe proper, Celtic, the language of 'the German nation', was the oldest and the 'Germanicae Origines' of the Scandinavian, English, Spanish, French and Italian languages (Spegel 1712). All etymological research, he concluded, would have to take into consideration the perpetual flux of meaning inherent in all languages (ibid.: preface).[14] As for lexicographic work, its primary purpose (leaving aside the political or moral aspects) was to ensure *understanding*, a purpose that could be fulfilled only by creating pure linguistic communities.

Interestingly from the perspective of political language, Spegel distinguished between three kinds of meta-languages that were determined by their function: the original language, erudite languages, and vernacular languages (or 'mother tongues'). The first kind was the Hebrew language; the second kind was the languages developed by scholars and kept alive and unified through intellectual reflection; the third kind was the contemporary language of ordinary people. All three were connected and a lack of knowledge of the original language adversely affected the capacity to speak and write in erudite languages. According to Spegel, both Aristotle's and Plato's erudite languages were compromised by their scant knowledge of Hebrew. At the same time, he denied that particular forms of sociability and functions required knowledge of specific languages. Ecclesiastical and secular history writing did not require a working knowledge of either Hebrew, Latin or Greek, nor did persons involved in travel and trade have to speak Spanish, French, or Arabic, just as reading and teaching poetry and oratory did not require knowledge of French, Castilian or Florentine. All of these functions could be carried out in the vernacular if there were enough translations available.

Spegel's main concern was indeed the vernacular in general and Swedish in particular, which he argued had to be standardized to enable communication on the basis of an established common meaning of words. Like Swedberg after him, Spegel held up Germany as a model of state-sponsored standardization, and also England, which excelled in the production of bilingual dictionaries. Similar efforts could be detected in Belgium, Spain, Italy, Denmark, Hungary, China, Egypt and, last but not least, France, which had been blessed with Cardinal Richelieu and the institution of the French Academy in 1635.[15]

In the Swedish case, Spegel considered the year 1537, signifying the first vernacular Swedish translation of the Bible, as both the crowning achievement of standardizing the language and the beginning of its ensuing decline. Between the 1530s and 1540s and the early 1700s, a large number of words had been lost or replaced, or they had changed their meaning but remained in the vocabulary. This was a source of confusion, especially for 'the multitude' or 'the ignorant' who misinterpreted the message of the Bible, with the result that one of the state's tools to ensure homogeneity was disarmed (Spegel 1712, preface).[16] In order for simple folk to understand sermons based on older religious books, ancient but still effective legal codes, sagas and Greek and Roman writings on morals and politics, key terms had to be properly explained or, if necessary, replaced with new or old Swedish words. Indeed, the establishment of a stable and clear meaning of religious, judicial and political terms became a means to create a homogenous political community. As Spegel concluded:

> For it is necessary both in social relations and in government, firstly, that we know the words, with which we speak; secondly, that we understand what these words mean, so that we may properly present, so that others can understand, our meaning.[17] (ibid.: preface)

Spegel and Swedberg wished for Sweden a language and culture founded on the principles and practices of the Greeks and the Romans, the arrival of which would root out foreign influences, in particular Frenchness, and thereby revive the dignity of the Swedish nation. Alongside making this argument, the *Shibboleth* contained a chapter of French words that should be erased from the national spoken and written language. Among them were key political terms like *absolut, administration, auctoritet, conspiration, constitution, discours, justice, libertet, nation, opinion, parti, patriot, politicus, publique, republique, revolution, societet,* and *souverain* (ibid.: 246–198).[18] In addition, the entire language of *civitas* developed by Leonardo Bruni in the civic humanist tradition of the early Italian renaissance (see chapter 2 of this volume) should be replaced, according to Swedberg. Thus, the terms *civil, civilisera* and *civilité* should be replaced with *borgerlig* in the first example, and with a vocabulary centering on the words *höflig* and *höflighet,* the closest English historical and contemporary equivalents of which are 'polite' and 'politeness'.[19] (ibid.: 255). In Levin Möller's French-Swedish dictionary (1745), the equivalent French terms were *courtois, civil* and *honnête* and *civilité,* and *courtoisie, politesse* and *honnêteté.* This choice of translation virtually emptied the terms of the explicit political connotations it had in humanist thought. The connotations instead became *social,* focusing on the quality of manners, or certain social virtues, deriving from court society. In fact, the Swedish term *höflig* does not entail the civilizational pathos of the French term, where to be civilized can be ascribed to an entire people, distinguishing them from the barbarity of the uncivilized. Rather than being applicable to the qualities of peoples or nations, the new Swedish term was only able to point out differences between individuals within the same society, thus providing a vocabulary that was in important ways contrary to the civic vocabulary of the early renaissance. The limited meaning was maintained in Abraham Sahlstedt's *Dictionarum Pseudo-Svecanum* from 1769, where the words *civil* and *civiliserad* were identified as unnecessary foreign words (Sahlstedt 1769: 15).

With results in hand, Swedberg's project for the most part failed miserably: only a fraction of the words he hoped to introduce remained central in the last decades of the century. In 1769, Sahlstedt again listed as useless foreign words *absolut, administration, civil, civiliserad, constitution, justice, nation, opinion, patriot, politique, publique, revolution* and *societet* (Sahlstedt 1769: 5–85). In fact, the vast majority of these words are used to this day, either in the exact form listed above or with minor modifications such as changing the endings from '-que' to '-k'. Interestingly, Swedberg did 'succeed' in replacing two words in ensuing political vocabularies: *civil* and *societet*, which in the combined form of 'civil society' became *borgerligt sellskap*, although Swedberg himself did not put them together. As we shall see it was a term that in a few varieties was used throughout the eighteenth century.

Thus, and in stark contrast to other key social and political concepts in the Swedish language, the Latin *societas civilis* that Bruni coined in his Aristotle translation and on the basis of which numerous vernaculars were issued, was significantly transformed in Sweden into a form very similar to the German *bürgerliche Gesellschaft*. As can be seen in Spegel's explanations following the old Swedish words *borgare* and *borgerskap*, which he hoped to revive in religious and political discourse, the Latin *civitas*-rooted words were available but undesirable. Moreover, his rejection of these words has nothing to do with disdain for French specifically. Indeed, the Swedish word for the Latin *civis* (*borgare*) is mentioned in the context of its equivalents in the German, English and French, that is *burger*, 'burgher' or 'burgess', and *bourgeois*. Likewise, the Swedish word for *civitas* (*borgerskap*), according to Spegel, was the direct equivalent to *burgershaft*, 'burghership', and *bourgeoisie* (Spegel 1712: 62). In Möller's French-Swedish dictionary from 1745, the first of its kind, the same usage is observed, with the addition that the French word for the adjective, status or quality *borgerlig* is both *bourgeois* and *civi'* (Möller 1745). More importantly for our purposes here, this first French-Swedish dictionary also introduces the Swedish word for 'citizen': *medborgare*. Under this entry, the French equivalents are *concitoien, citoien* or *citoyen*. There is, however, little conceptual clarity since this French word for 'citizen' is also treated as a synonym for *sujet* (ibid.).

The equivalent Swedish words given by Spegel and Swedberg suggest that their understanding of the *civitas*-rooted vocabulary was closely related to the life of *the city*, understood primarily as a space for commercial exchange. Spegel's analysis also highlights some of the political or legal aspects of the city that are so marked in classical and humanist writings on the city-state or city-republic, as he speaks about the words *civitas, coetus civium* and *jure sociatus*, and *jus civitatis* as the relevant Latin terms for 'burgership' (Spegel 1712: 62, 606). In a 1773 dictionary, the legal and representative connotations come into sharper focus as notions like *jus civis* (*borgare-rätt*) and *status civilis* (*borgerligt stånd*) are incorporated to a more exhaustive list of words connected to the world of the city and the burger (Sahlstedt 1773: 60). As for the term 'society', or *societas*, a number of terms are used in early eighteenth-century Swedish. Moreover, no stable meaning can be detected, but rather a mixture of two understandings: one that refers to religious community and one that refers to political institutions. Both these understandings conceive of a society as associations for a particular purpose rather than a later concept of society as a preconstituted whole.[20] Both religious and political meanings are listed under Spegel's entry for *samqwem* in his *Glossarium-sveo-gothicum* from 1712. On the one hand, the Latin word *societas* is listed as being synonymous with *consortium, conventus,* and *contubernium,* while the French equivalents suggested are *société, assemblée,* and *congrégation.* As for the English, Spegel suggests that the translation of *societas* is 'legal assembly', which he also detects in the ancient Swedish political meetings. In present usage, he suggests, it denotes all kinds of gatherings involving different forms of sociability, including of course religious and political ones (Spegel 1712: 390).[21] Swedberg's understanding of the term leaned more towards forms of sociability associated with scientific or Masonic societies, emphasizing secular or religious camaraderie (Swedberg 1716: 298).

Translating John Locke: Early usage of 'civil society' (1720)

As this brief discussion indicates, a Swedish rendition of the Latin and French vocabularies of *societas civilis* and *société civile* was in principle available in the first two decades of the eighteenth century. Nevertheless, the Swedish translator of John Locke's *Two Treatises of Government* (1690) argued for the need to explicate the meaning of the philosopher's key terms, and to coin Swedish equivalents. With regard to translations, it was almost exclusively the *Second Treatise* that was of interest. John Dunn's conclusion that it was the *Second Treatise* 'which made Locke into a political thinker of major importance' was recognized by the Swedish translator as well. According to him, the first part, which contained a falsification of Robert Filmer's theological justification of absolutism in his *Patriarcha* (1680), was a simple quarrel not worthy of attention (Locke 1726: 1, translator's preface). Whatever its relative worth to seventeenth- and eighteenth-century readers, it seems fair to say that the higher level of abstraction and less context-sensitive second part must have appealed more to foreign audiences.

To French readers, Locke's arguments first became known through Jean Le Clerc's review in *Bibliothèque universelle et historique de l'année 1690,* which included some translated extracts ('Traitez du gouvernement civil en Anglois', 1690). The *Second Treatise* was published in its entirety, apart from the first chapter, in French in 1691, one year after its original publication in English, and in no less than eight more editions and one abridgement (1790) during the eighteenth century. All of the editions were based on the original translation by David Mazel, which was used in the three other translations that were completed in the eighteenth century: the 1718 German edition, the 1726 Swedish edition and the 1773 Italian edition. All in all, Locke's work on the origins, limits and purpose of government was thus translated into four European languages: French, German, Swedish and Italian, all of which were based on the French edition of 1691. While all of the French editions (except for the abridgment that was printed in the octavo format) were printed in the small pocket book format duodecimo, the Italian and the Swedish edition were printed in the larger octavo.[22] This suggests that reading Locke in the eighteenth century was not a luxury that only the very privileged could afford.

Hans Harmens, who had been appointed state translator in 1722, completed the Swedish translation. The translation was commissioned by a government in search of foundations and a language of legitimation after the rejection of absolutism in 1719. In the debates surrounding the 1719/20 Instrument of Government – the compact that placed political power in the hands of the Estates and the Council of the Realm after the death of Charles XII in 1718 – Sweden's political history and traditions played a central role. The period of absolutism (1680–1718) was described by 'the men of liberty' as a parenthesis in a history permeated by liberty and elected kings that prevailed even before the Succession Pact of 1544, which obliged kings to sign an Accession Charter and swear a coronation oath (Roberts 1986: 2). When Charles XII died in 1718 and left no heir to the throne, discussions among a small group of noblemen and civil servants of a restoration of Gustavus Adolphus's 1634 Constitution, backed up by Pufendorf's and Grotius' works in constitutional law, became real.

The outcome, according to a retrospective 1766 account of the discussions, was an adoption of one basic idea: 'That a Free People enjoy an independent and inalienable right, to create from themselves such Laws as Regulations that, taking into consideration the position of the Country, the character of its People, and domestic and external needs, advantages and reputation that can be determined to be most expedient and sure ' (Fredenstierna 1769: 21–22). In 'free nations' (*frije nationer*) a 1720 pamphlet stated, the rules of succession were dictated by the constitution, not by the prerogatives of a person with absolute power. Contrary to theocratic notions of absolute rulership, the pamphlet's author disputed that the Bible sanctioned uncontrolled monarchy. The book was, in fact open to the three different forms of government outlined by Aristotle and debated ever since – *democratia, aristocratia* or *monarchia* – and the latter could be either absolute or conditional, regulated by laws and contracts (*regnum pactis limitatum*). Moderate or constitutional monarchy meant that, in the name of the common good, certain rights of the King would not be upheld without the direct consent of the people or their representatives (Silvius 1720, §§ 2–4, 21). Of the three possible means to accession of the crown – violence, inheritance or election – the latter was decreed to conform to Swedish traditions. The sister of dead absolutist ruler Charles XII, Ulrika Eleonora, was elected only after she promised to uphold the 'power' of the Council and the 'liberty' of the Estates.

In this context, the problems of civil society – specifically the mechanisms of *societas*, or communion, in a free state – were acute and directly felt. The desacralisation of religion, tradition and authority left a void to be filled, opening the field to varieties of civil morality. In Sweden, where the king since the fall of absolutism in 1719 no longer constituted the sacred centre of politics, the void was deeply felt among the country's political elite. The 'founding fathers' of the 1719/20 constitution had appealed both to ancient Swedish constitutional traditions and the theories of Grotius, Locke, Algernon Sidney and others to override positive laws (that is, existing laws) and institute a government on the basis of what they claimed were universally held norms. The Estates of the Realm were furthermore pronounced to be the carriers of popular sovereignty (Carlsson and Rosén 1961: 96). It is worth pointing out that Locke's second treatise, which contains the ideas about civil society quoted in the previous paragraph, was, on the initiative of the *Estates of the Realm*, translated into Swedish in 1726. Universalistic rhetoric and English political thought notwithstanding, the change in Sweden's system of government in 1719 was above all presented as a return to ancient constitutional praxis. Thus understood, the events of 1719 and 1720 manifested a restoration of historical traditions of liberty and the political practices that they had conceived (Roberts 1986: 59–62; Lagerroth 1915: 254–97, esp. 80–81; Carlsson and Rosén 1980).[23]

The debates surrounding the events of 1719 and 1720 essentially concerned what should be the foundation for a political system without an undisputed centre, or with a centre that was divided among four estates. Our working hypothesis is that in order to make life endurable in the 'unnatural' order that a civil society after all was, the state had to engage not only in the making and enforcement of laws, but also to enlighten the population (or the relevant part of it, however defined) about civil behaviour; to foster, in short, a culture built on the engagement with, and expectations of, others. According to Peter Laslett, the key element in Locke's notion of civil life was what he calls Locke's 'doctrine of natural political virtue'. Whether individuals were organized formally or informally, or even subsisting in isolation from others, this doctrine maintained that it is a constitutive feature of humankind to 'have some tendency to allow for the existence, the desires, actions and needs of other men ...' (Laslett 1969: 110).[24]

The post-1718 government justified the translation of Locke's *Second Treatise* by pointing to the benefits of making it widely known among the people. According to the translator, the effort was significantly marred by the fact that the Swedish vocabulary did not lend itself to serious intellectual work. Fitting foreign terms with Swedish endings provided one possible solution, but the translator concluded that it would more likely confuse than enlighten. 'To translate word-by-word would also make them dark for both learned and unlearned' (Locke 1726, translator's preface).[25] Instead, a compromise would be struck: the translator would avoid foreign words to the greatest extent possible, and invent Swedish equivalents to key political terms. Thus, in the preface, he stated directly that the Swedish term *borgerlig sammanlefnad* was used as an equivalent to *societas civilis*. In the original English text, Locke used three English terms interchangeably to denote *societas civilis*: civil society, political society and commonwealth. In the Swedish title of the work, the adjective 'civil' (as in Locke's 'civil government') was translated as 'worldly' (*werdslig*), denoting a realm for politics that was separate from the spiritual realm. 'Political power' (Latin *Potestas Politica*) was accordingly translated as 'worldly power' (*werdslig makt*) (ibid.: preface).[26]

'Civil Society' in Enlightenment Discourse

In Swedish usage between the 1740s to 1760s, the English term civil society was translated as *borgerlig sammanlefnad*, *borgerligt samqväm* or *borgerligt samhälle* (*Kongl. maj:ts nådigste stadfästelse* 1741: 2; Ehrenpreus 1748: 23; Tessin 1746: 4; Wrede 1743). These terms were used interchangeably to denote what Locke meant when he discussed civil or political society: a form of social organization under a government bound by law; the opposite of a state of nature (Locke 1969 [1690]: 343).[27] At this time, a significant number of Swedish intellectuals were convinced that they indeed lived in a civil society. The patriotic rhetoric surrounding the Academy's goals and activities did not preclude a cosmopolitan outlook among its members. The views of one of its most known members, Olof Dalin, are illustrative in this regard. On the one hand, he spoke with nationalistic fervour when he claimed that the diffusion of enlightenment in Northern Europe enticed foreigners to 'gaze at the Nordic countries with greater curiosity than ever Italy inspired'. On the other hand, he conceived of learned discourse in cosmopolitan terms. 'The entire learned world', he proclaimed, 'now resembles a single Republic in which all People are Compatriots'. The idea of a transnational Republic of Letters was related to the unification of Europe, a process that Dalin claimed had been initiated in the mid-fifteenth century. A new spirit of governance, he noted, had converted the Continent's sovereign nations into 'one Body in which all Powers are members, either to assist or obstruct each other, so that none can reign supreme' (Dalin 1749: 1–4).[28] According to Dalin, the great challenge to citizens in all nations was to advance the tenets of a still young European civilization.

Other academicians praised reason and mused how future generations would marvel at the achievements of 'our enlightened age' or 'this enlightened era' (Elvius 1746: 14; Mennander 1756: 24; Scheffer 1755: 2; see also Tessin 1746: 3–4; Ehrenpreus 1748: 5–9).

Some members explicitly associated the creation and successes of the Academy of Sciences with the country's unique political system after the fall of absolutism in 1718. Relieved of the hardships under absolutism, the 1719/20 Constitution had been described as the work of 'angels' and the Church even changed the wording of prayer so that it read 'To the Honour of Thy Holy Name, and the safeguarding of each and all of us in our blessed Liberty' (Roberts 1986: 59). Thirty years later, Dalin still spoke amiably about 'our Age of Liberty' while a fellow academician referred to 'our blessed government of Liberty' (Dalin 1749: 22; Mennander 1756: 14). [29] The historian Anders af Botin in 1757 wrote that he projected to write a comprehensive work 'which includes the history of the Swedish people after their liberty had been regained' (Botin 1757–64, vol. 1, preface). The Councillor of the Realm, Count Carl Gustaf Tessin, discussed the mutual benefits of 'civil Associations' and the 'deliberations of Men of Letters' (Tessin 1746: 4). In 1771, when the political system of the Age of Liberty was in turmoil, another member identified the year 1720 as a time when 'a new Era for Sweden began to win sway ... The Citizens of the Realm were able, after a tedious and violent storm, to breathe fresher air. Peace and liberty were restored' (Sandels 1771: 11). An important reason why earlier attempts to establish a learned society on Swedish soil had failed, he argued, was the sense of bewilderment or lack of purpose of domestic politics under late absolutism (ibid.).

A Lockean understanding of civil society was put forth in an illustrative speech delivered by Hindric Johan Wrede in 1743. Addressing the means to realize civil society, Wrede maintained that individuals lost their 'innate and natural liberty, or equality' when they became subjected to 'the control and governance of one or many'. The loss of natural liberty was compensated with the acquisition of something even greater, namely 'the security, felicity, and benefits that are contingent on civil Society' (Wrede 1743: 6). Five years later, Carl Ehrenpreus made an analogy that singled out the rule of law as the mark of a civil society: 'The Commonwealth is not unlike a ship', he suggested, 'its rig and canvas are the Law and Justice' (Ehrenpreus 1748: 23).

The concept of civil society was already central in natural law education in Swedish universities in the seventeenth century, which relied heavily on the works of Hugo Grotius and Samuel Pufendorf. Pufendorf, who had served as professor at Lund since 1667 and historiographer of the realm under Charles XI, was especially influential. According to one legal historian, his textbook in natural law, *De officio hominis et civis* (1673) was the key work in instruction in natural law during the Age of Liberty and was translated into Swedish in 1747, accompanied by references to positive Swedish law (Nilsén 2000: 38).[30] As had been the case with the 1726 translation of Locke's *Second Treatise*, the translation of Pufendorf's textbook widened the audience for these discussions, thus also increasing their potential impact on public discourse. According to Per Nilsén, the translation of Locke's work constituted 'a step towards the popularization of debates on the legal and philosophical nature of the state. Only now ... did the Swedish language acquire the first elements of a terminology of its own in this field' (ibid.: 102; Saastamoinen 1999: 16). In the case of Pufendorf's work, however, the addition of Swedish positive law may at the same time have limited the potential reading public to students of constitutional law.

Pufendorf's theory maintained that the condition of fundamental insecurity that reigned in the state of nature, combined with the human disposition of sociability, or *socialitas*, gave rise to the formation of social groups and eventually to states. An initial social contract between individuals renouncing life in a state of nature was followed by a contract between rulers and ruled, whereby the former guaranteed the latter protection and the latter promised the ruler loyalty and obedience. Mutually constrained by a contract, rulers and ruled were thus united in a pursuit of societal perfection. Guided by a collective goal to advance the common good, individuals fulfilled their oath of loyalty by contributing to the best of the whole, while the ruler fulfilled his by protecting the safety and rights of individuals (Nilsén 2000: 40–42).[31]

In the speeches delivered at the Academy of Sciences and disseminated to a wider audience through print, the Swedish words for 'society' – as well as related terms such as 'association', 'community' and 'commonwealth' – were used to describe/prescribe two different social categories. In speeches and writings the word was used in a wide sense to discuss the idea and conditions of civil society, understood in terms of the moral and legal constraints placed upon the actions of governments and individuals. The discourses of civil society encompassed both theoretical and practical approaches to the subject, ranging from theories on humankind's exit from a state of nature to concrete suggestions of how to raise morally upstanding citizens at a particular time and place. The word 'society' was also used in a narrow sense to refer to the Academy of Sciences itself, which was closely related conceptually to the wider sense. At the same time as a supposedly close conceptual affinity between society at large and the learned society of the Academy lent support to the former, this comparative mode of reasoning invited critiques of contradictions in society at large, among them structural inequalities between noblemen and commoners that were absent in learned societies. Thus, while some conceived of the Academy as a replica or microcosm of a larger free society, others presented it as an ideal society in miniature that only partially corresponded to its larger counterpart.

In the 1740s and 1750s, academicians described their small society as founded on the principles of equality and merit, recreating in national context the spirit that permeated the cosmopolitan European Republic of Letters. Conceived of as a particular kind of social organization, the Academy of Sciences was chiefly referred to as a *Samfund* or *Samhälle* – both of which translate into English as 'society' – and used synonymously with a range of related words: 'Societies' (*Sällskaper*), 'learned Societies' (*lärda Sällskaper*), 'Learned Guild' (*Lärda Gillet*), 'this Lettered Society' (*detta Vittra Samhälle*), 'Learned Societies' (*Lärda Societeter*), 'an enlightened Society' (*ett uplyst Sällskap*), 'enlightened Assembly' (*oplyst Samqväm*), 'this little Society' (*detta lilla Samfundet*), and 'Scholarly Societies' (*Vetenskaps Samhällen*) (Ehrenpreus 1748: 2, 28–9; Elvius 1748: 34; Sandels 1771: 1, 8, 9, 15, 25; Mennander 1756: 2; Wrede 1743: 34; Dalin 1749: 22). Regardless of which words were used, they all referred to a particular ideal concept of social organization: an egalitarian and transparent society whose chief characteristics emanated from the ways in which it organized membership and regulated social communication. Learned societies were organized horizontally without recognition of birth or office. Jacob Faggot, an economist, agricultural reformer and the Academy's secretary between 1741 and 1744, did not hesitate to liken the learned society whose daily business he administered to what he called 'the larger society'. He wrote:

> As a small Society this Royal Academy is not unlike the larger Society. There is a head, body and members: There is law and obedience: there is both reward and its deprival: There is agreement, not to sever the links of Association: there is love of virtue and learning: There is a battle against wrongdoing and falsity: There is peace with impartiality in judgment. (Faggot 1743: 38)

Faggot's description of the learned society and society at large must have struck contemporaries as an idealized picture, at least of the latter. In the light of a strict interpretation of the 1719/20 Constitution, the Academy's two major institutional characteristics – meritocracy and rational communication – did however make a conceptual affinity between the smaller and the larger society conceivable. The concentration of power in the Diet made continuous deliberations a central aspect of politics; and according to the constitution, merit was the sole ground for promotion in the civil service. As opposed to the situation in the academies in Prussia and France, the members of the Academy of Sciences did not perform their duties as salaried civil servants, but as scientists and laymen who volunteered their talents (Lindroth 1978–81, vol. 3: 48–52). The Academy shared this feature with its beau idéal, the Royal Society of London, which serviced a nation founded on extensive civil and political liberties.[32] According to the Academy's statutes, it would admit 'no members other than reasonable, honest Citizens who love their Fatherland' to its ranks. 'In a society where Science, reason and industry are the only requisite qualities and advantages', status differences emanating from birth or office had no bearing on becoming a member (*Kongl. maj:ts nådigste stadfästelse* 1741, chap. 1, §10). A contemporary description of the only woman in the Academy, the Countess Eva de la Gardie, illustrates this meritocratic conviction well. As the wife of one of the most powerful men of the realm, Count de la Gardie, one author introduced her as 'the foremost Woman of the Realm,' but added that she was known 'no less for her qualities, than for her eminence.' Her productivity as a writer on economic topics was also noted, suggesting that neither social status nor gender – only merit and patriotism – mattered in the Republic of Letters (Sandels 1771: 25).[33]

The ideal of rational communication was also central to the concept of society that was expressed by academicians. A strict procedure dictated intellectual discourse. After reading submissions out loud, members were invited to peruse a written copy of whatever was reported. The original was dispatched to specialists in the field. In order to separate issues from individuals, criticism had to be presented in written form and submitted anonymously. In the event of controversy during deliberations, the Academy's president, who was elected by rotation every three months, was expected to end the discussion and request written statements (*Kongl. maj:ts nådigste stadfästelse* 1741: chap. 2, §3. See also chap. 4, §3). Forms of conduct and sociability supported the meritocratic or egalitarian credo, which alongside publicity was considered a necessary requirement for learned discourse. Personal qualities such as 'frankness, mutual politeness and friendship,' were stressed in numerous texts and members could refer to the Academy as 'this Beloved Association' and to their fellows as a 'beloved Brother'. (ibid.: chap. 2, §7; Wrede 1743: 1, 35; Faggot 1743: 39; Wargentin 1756: 27). In an age of titles and decorum, the fact that members were addressed as 'Mr.' (*herr*), regardless of what titles they had procured by birth or personal ennoblement, testifies to an egalitarian pathos (Andræ 1980: 34).

The spirit of equality and reason that reigned supreme in the chambers of the Academy of Sciences was, however, clearly absent in society at large, where the culture of privilege was intact and the pursuit of material wealth was believed to rule the desires of men and women. In his persistent struggle against luxury and vanity, Olof Dalin suggested that the Academy was not a reproduction of, but a model *for*, society at large. Contrary to Jacob Faggot, who favourably likened the learned society to Swedish society, Dalin cautiously revealed a gap between society as an ideal and as a reality. He also made one of the earliest references to the term 'middle estate' (*medelstånd*) to denote the large group of 'non-noble persons of standing' that lacked representation in the Diet but possessed significant economic or cultural capital, including lawyers, physicians, engineers, journalists, and others. Speaking about his own social group and a large segment of his readers, he wrote:

> This Royal Academy provides abundant evidence of how superfluous such glitter is in the presence of virtue and worth: four times a year we see the same honorable positions exchanged, sometimes between noteworthies of the Realm and citizens of middle estate without regard to their office. And this is verily one of the most distinguished adornments of this learned Society. (Dalin 1749: 21–22)

Regardless of the rationale behind many commoners' intellectual work, their successes in this field significantly strengthened their relative position in society. The fact that Dalin's 'middle estate' – whose members undoubtedly played an instrumental role in the nation's passage from destitute military state to a prosperous and 'enlightened' state – lacked political representation must have become glaringly apparent with every new discovery and every sign of international recognition. Sten Carlsson's remark below sums up the sentiments that would erupt in the early 1770s: 'In the long run such a state of affairs could not escape serious criticism. The ground was prepared for the rise of a new middle-class opinion opposed to a constitution based on estates' (Carlsson 1962: 60). The reasons why commoner academicians so admired the Academy of Sciences was arguably not that it replicated society at large, as Jacob Faggot had maintained, but that it offered members an egalitarian sanctuary in a hierarchically ordered society beset with legal and social distinctions that issued from unequal corporate privileges.[34]

There was also a much more practically oriented discourse on civil society that discussed the means to achieve a civil society here and now. This discourse did not come about as a reaction to theoretical accounts, but as a more or less pronounced corollary to them. In the circle around the Academy of Science, the prospects and problems of civil society were not discussed in the kind of theoretical terms that were pursued in constitutional law education, but on a very practical level. Although economic growth was the Academy's primary concern, growth was not merely a question of invention and rationalization, or even of its spread among peasants, but also and perhaps most fundamentally a question of nourishing patriotic dispositions. In this way, civic education – processes of learning that addressed society at large rather than being confined to a particular institution like the school or university – became an important topic for reflection.

Although the concept of 'citizen' experienced a breakthrough in Swedish public discourse in the 1790s, questions pertaining to patriotism and civic virtues date back to the 1730s, when they were debated in the nascent periodical press (Christensson 1996: 105–69; Nordin 2000: 328–37). In Olof Dalin's magazine *Then swänska Argus* (1732–34) – the appearance of which one historian characterizes as 'the birth of the Swedish public sphere' – a more personal style of writing was applied as a means to 'nurture, guide and edify the public' (Vegesack 2001: 44).[35] The paper's didactic task was attuned to the brand of enlightenment espoused by the Academy of Sciences in the 1740s and 1750s. Stressing qualities like virtue, industry and frugality, Dalin maintained:

> [W]hen a Realm is virtuous and Wise, then it is strong, but when it is vicious and Foolish it is weak. What is the noblest element of which a Realm consists? Of its inhabitants. Indeed. And therefore I conclude that no Realm may be strong and secure that does not have virtuous and wise Inhabitants. (Dalin 1732–34, no. 2: 17)

The focus on morality and wisdom does not mean that the early journals did not perform a critical task as well. On the contrary, the relationship between the individual and society was at the centre of their concerns, and the normative approach was studiously dichotomous, pitting Stoic qualities like authenticity, simplicity and honesty against artificiality, vanity and foreign impulses. Dalin's satires tended to ridicule the vainglory of the nobility, the most obvious opposite of his eighteenth-century Stoic ideals (Oscarsson 2000: 101–4).[36]

A treatise on civil society: Armfeldt (1765)

In order to better understand eighteenth-century conceptions of the relationship between virtue and civil society we may consider Carl Henric Armfeldt's 1765 dissertation on the means to prevent the degeneration of civil customs. This particular work combines theoretical reflection with practical advice on how to ensure the preservation of order and liberty and offers a detailed account of a view that appears in a more fragmented form in many other contributions treated in this chapter.[37]

Armfeldt's starting point was the challenges posed by the birth of civil society. In a narrative familiar to readers of Grotius and Pufendorf, individuals at some point in history concluded that living in an organized society was more conducive to their wellbeing than remaining in a state of anarchy, even if it entailed a loss of freedom. Ever since human beings shed their God-given liberties in order to obtain 'individual comfort and public welfare', Armfeldt argued, they had incessantly sought the 'means of securing their felicity and laying the cornerstones of the welfare and continuance of Realms and Societies' (Armfeldt 1765: 1). The first step consisted of forming a 'civil commonwealth' (*borgerlig sammanlefnad*), a form of life and social organization regulated by more or less formalized rules of conduct. To transform these loosely configured commonwealths into organized polities, the means to preserve and boost a spirit of civility must be identified. A number of possible means were ruled out: the exercise of brute force, protection by other states, and the accumulation of wealth, all of which would in the end prove counterproductive. As testified by what was known about the great empires of Western civilization, handed down to contemporaries by classical authors such as Sallust, Livy and Polybius, the flourishing of order and liberty depended on the intensity and diffusion of civic virtues. In Armfeldt's words:

> The inhabitants' love of virtue and unsullied customs form the bedrock on which all former dominions have constructed their true felicity, strength and growth. When a noble spirit enlivens a State, when a love of mankind and obedience to the Laws of Nature are revealed in the acts and deportment of its inhabitants; when a zeal for the common weal unites all hearts to love their country, Laws are always revered and cogent; there will exist an enduring serenity and welfare in its Society and a general unconstrained respect beyond its borders. (ibid.: 2, 4)

Armfeldt avoided subscribing to either an idealistic or a fatalistic view of human nature. Human beings were never either good or evil. Virtues and vices were rather in constant conflict, within individuals and within societies. According to Armfeldt, humanity's lowest instincts had always existed among the lower segments of the population. A closer look at the history of humankind, however, showed that the level of civilization has always shifted with a government's relative ability to 'prevent and counter the general dissolution of customs in this country' (ibid.: 5).[38] Morality was clearly understood by Armfeldt as a matter of state policy.

Armfeldt defined morality or virtue (*seder* or *dygd*) as a 'desire and ability to fulfill one's obligations in full compliance with the Law'. The corruption of morals was logically defined as 'the indifference, apathy and failure to fulfil the obligations prescribed by law' (ibid.: 8–9).[39] He further distinguished between three kinds of morality/virtue: Christian, philosophical/natural and civic, each corresponding to their basic source, that is, the Bible, natural law and civic law respectively. The author's emphasis on the responsibilities of individuals towards society should not lead us to disregard the fact that his ideas at the same time placed a significant burden on the state. For although even the best of governments had to realize that complete perfection could never be produced from such materials as the human mind and spirit, the state was ultimately responsible for the prevention of moral corruption. Armfeldt was certainly clear on this, insisting that nothing was more important for 'Civil Societies' (*Borgerliga Samhällen*) than the maintenance of civic morality. Virtues had to be encouraged, vices discouraged, the cardinal question being how it should be done (ibid.: 6–7). Not only the national wealth but liberty itself depended on finding an answer to it.

Because humans are prone to habit and prejudice, and since it is easier to prevent vices from developing at all than to expel existing ones,

Armfeldt argued, governments should prioritize moral education at the early stages of individual development:

> Young people are the greenhouse of the state and he who desires to prevent the country from the impairment of vices and dissolute habits should consider this with ardor ... In the hearts of children many images may be imprinted; they provide a fertile soil in which the seeds of love of their Country, God and Neighbor may flourish and bear abundant fruit. (ibid.: 12–3)[40]

Since the ability of parents to finance and oversee their children's education in most cases was limited, Armfeldt argued that state funds had to be channelled to support a number of public institutions: schools and universities, libraries, laboratories, observatories and botanical gardens. He furthermore maintained that teachers had to be paid better, their status boosted and pedagogical methods modernized. Relying heavily on the French pedagogue François de Salinas de la Mothe-Fénelon, Armfeldt moreover discussed the necessity of educating women, since they reared children, thus performing within the private sphere an essential task that also belonged to the public sphere. To this end, the government should also create schools for impoverished women in the cities. As Armfeldt argued, governments of 'enlightened nations' that hoped to 'maintain their good civil customs' would also realize that they ought to institute charity schools to educate impoverished children in order to make use of a dormant human capital (ibid.: 14–24, 32–33). The government's key role in the realm of civic morality had been phrased by an academician in 1743, who in a speech on the strengths of civil society argued for the government's duty to 'aptly exercise its tutelage over an irresolute Society, to foster virtue and extirpate vices' (Wrede 1743: 17, see also 3, 26–30).

Concluding remark

It is tempting to see in these views from the 1740s, 1750s and 1760s the conceptual beginnings of a welfare state. They were, however, couched in a language of civic humanism that is not usually associated with the language of the welfare state or its intellectual origins. In a dictionary, from 1773, the latter language becomes clearly elucidated as the entries for 'society' (*samhälle*) and 'state' overlap and discuss the individual's responsibilities to the whole in phrases such as the virtue of being 'a useful man in Society' and about the detection of 'evil in the state'. The word *samhälle* is further used synonymously with the social and political terms that Leonardo Bruni helped popularize in European political discourse, *civitas* and *respublica*.(Sahlstedt 1773: 468, 544).[41] Indeed, the 1773 dictionary's entry for 'republic' exemplifies usage by noting the importance of being 'an honorable citizen in the republic' (ibid.: 442).

Notes

* This article was written with the support of the Swedish Foundation for International Cooperation in Research and Higher Education. Comments by Bo Lindberg and Vasileios Syros are gratefully acknowledged.

1. This particular country has been selected neither because it is typical nor because it is more interesting than any other polity in eighteenth-century Europe. It is simply the first country to be investigated in projected further comparative research on the concept of 'citizen' and related terms, including 'civil society'. For a more detailed study of political debate and the emergence of a public sphere, see Hallberg 2003.
2. Among key questions to be addressed are: did the concept of civil society – including concepts in the same semantic field – develop in similar or different ways in European polities? How are key texts transmitted (and translated), diffused and received in different linguistic, political and cultural contexts? What is the relationship between different discourses, such as the legal versus the literary, in respective polities?
3. The language question had been discussed in the country's first academy, Vetenskapssocieteten at Uppsala, which worked under different names and was instituted in 1710. There, prominent members had debated which should be the language of its published proceedings. Since the lingua franca of the scientific community was Latin, and the Academy claimed that it serviced not only Sweden, but the world, it decided to publish in that language. Its Latin language review was, however, supplemented in 1742 by a Swedish review, which was eventually replaced three years later by a combined review and news journal that would survive until 1773 (Segerstedt 1971, 14; *Tidningar om The Lärdas Arbeten* 1742; *Lärda Tidningar* 1745–73).
4. The latter published a weekly economic journal for a wider audience and suggested that Latin be banished from the universities, replacing it with Swedish (Lars Salvius, *Tanckar öfwer den swenska oeconomien* [1738] cited in Sylwan 1896: 151).
5. 'Then said they unto him, Say now Shibboleth: and he said Sibboleth: for he could not frame to pronounce it right. Then they took him, and slew him at the passages of Jordan: and there fell at that time of the Ephraimites forty and two thousand.' (Book of Judges, 12:6).
6. [*förtroligit almenna Samhälle*].
7. The relevant passages are noted by Swedberg.
8. [lära thet Latinska språket, fram för alt annat språk i werldenne].
9. [modersmål].
10. [Hiertat och sinnet är nu mera med fremmande språk och seder helt och hollit intagit].
11. [egen mechtig, enwold Swensk konung].
12. Gustavus Vasa (1523–60) and Gustavus Adolphus (1611–32).
13. Remarks printed in Hernlund 1892: 30–31 n. 1. According to Delblanc 1965: 86–87), Plutarch's biography of Pericles was for the same reason an influential collection of moral examples in Western discourse, from the Renaissance to the Romantic era.
14. [ingen ting så lätt ombytes som Språken, och at therföre hwart och it är genom Tidens Långwarighet, samt långwäga Folcks umgänge och handel, åtskillige Flychtningar från it Land til it annat &c. så förändrat, at om man nu hörde them, som för 1000 år sedan lefde, skulle man them ingalunda förstå].
15. The general sentiment about the elevation of vernacular languages expressed in the Letters Patent that established the Academy was certainly shared by Spegel and his supporters, who of course applied it to Sweden and the Swedish language: 'The French language, which has suffered much hitherto from neglect on the part of those who might have rendered it the most perfect of modern tongues, is now more capable than ever of taking its high place, owing to the great number of persons who possess a

The Concept of 'Civil Society' in Swedish • 81

special knowledge of the advantages which it enjoys and who can augment these advantages' (Robinson 1904: 180–83).

16. [*thet gemena folket ... the enfaldige*].

17. [*Ty thet är ju mycket nödwändigt både uti wårt umgänge och i wåra bestälningar, först, at wj wete orden, med hwilka wj tale om; sedan at wj förstå hwad the samme ord egentliga betyda, som wj måge rätt framföra och andre fatta wår mening*].

18. With regard to the word *souverain*, Spegel paranthetically added that the English tended to add the word 'dread' when using it, as in 'dreaded sovereignty' (ibid.: 601).

19. 'Uncivil' is accordingly translated into Swedish as *ohöflig*, but also *omanerlig* (Swedberg 1716, 276), meaning roughly unmanly, a translation that points in the direction of a language of virtue and honour in the republican tradition. On the changing meaning of the concept *civilité* in early modern France, see Chartier 1987.

20. For a discussion of these two concepts of society see Heilbron 1995; Wagner 2001b. See also Keith Michael Baker's conceptual history of society in the French context, where he notes that the philosophers of the enlightenment claimed that the term 'society' was invented by them, an erroneous claim that nonetheless emphasizes the centrality of the term in Enlightenment discourse, where it becomes the supreme ontological category for understanding human life. To the philosopher, whose task it was to reflect on human thought and action, the *Encyclopédie* maintained, 'la société civile est, pour ainsi dire, une divinité pour lui sur la terre'. Baker 2001: 84.

21. Thus, Spegel listed as Swedish synonyms *samwist*, *omgänge* and added, in addition to the Latin *societas*, the word *conversatio*.

22. I have not been able to identify the size of the 1718 German translation.

23. The precise sources of the 1719/20 Instrument of Government has been a hotly debated question in twentieth-century historical research. See the summary in Carlsson and Rosén 1980: 106–7.

24. On this matter, Locke had referred to Richard Hooker's *Ecclesiastic Polity*, whose formulation is illuminating and worth quoting at length: 'Two Foundations there are which bear up publick Societies, the one a natural inclination, whereby all Men desire sociable Life and Fellowship; the other an Order, expressly or secretly agreed upon, touching the manner of their union in living together; the latter is that which we call the Law of a Common-weal, the very Soul of a Politick Body, the parts whereof are by Law animated, held together, and set on work in such actions as the common good requireth. Laws politick, ordain'd for external order and regiment amongst Men, are never framed as they should be, unless presuming the will of Man to be inwardly obstinate, rebellious, and averse from all Obedience to the sacred Laws of his Nature; in a word, unless presuming Man to be in regard of his depraved Mind, little better than a wild Beast, they do accordingly provide notwithstanding, so to frame his outward Actions, that they be no hindrance unto the common good, for which Societies are instituted. Unless they do this they are not perfect.' Hooker quoted after the Laslett edition: Locke, *Two Treatises of Government*, p. 357.

25. [*At sätta dem öfwer efter bokstafwen, torde åter giöra dem mörke både för lärde och olärde*].

26. The original English title of the *Second Treatise* was *An Essay Concerning the True Original, Extent, and End of Civil Government*. On the details of the English editions of Locke's Treatise, see Peter Laslett's seminal introduction in Locke 1969 [1690]. The Swedish translation was a highly official affair. In addition to being commissioned by the Chancery College, it carried the stamp of royal privilege, was published in the royal printing house and was translated by the royal translator.

27. Locke 1969 [1690]: 343: 'Where-ever therefore any number of Men are so united into one Society, as to quit every one his Executive Power of the Law of Nature, and to resign it to the public, there and there only is a *Political*, or *Civil Society*. And this is done wherever any number of Men, in the state of Nature, enter into Society to make

one People, one Body Politick under one Supreme Government, or else when any one joyns himself to, and incorporates with any Government already Made.'

28. For a discussion of cosmopolitanism and eighteenth-century historiography in Europe, see O'Brien 1997.

29. The standard Swedish dictionary, *Svenska akademiens ordbok*, does not list 1749, the year of Dalin's speech, but 1751 and 1755 as the first instances of this usage of the term 'Age of Liberty'.

30. Pufendorf's social theories are studied in detail in Sellberg 1998. The Swedish edition (Pufendorf 1747) was translated by Anders Wilde and entitled *Friherren Samuel Pufendorffs Twenne böcker om menniskians lefnads och samlefnads plicht, förswenskade och jemförde med Sweriges lag, beslut och förordningar, b. Pufendorffs Jure naturae & gentium samt några lärda mäns skrifter.*

31. As Frängsmyr has shown, these ideas on the origins and constitution of states and societies reached a wide European readership through the works of Christian Wolff, published between 1740 and 1750. Wolffianism became influential in constitutional law education in Sweden as well, especially at Uppsala. Wolff's major works in natural law were *Jus Naturæ methodo scientifica pertractatum* (1740–48) and *Institutiones Juris Naturæ & Gentium* (1750) (Frängsmyr 1972).

32. To some extent, the relatively open structure of the Royal Society of London was the effect of a lack of economic support from the state. Forced to rely on donations and membership fees, it could not afford to be too selective in its recruitment (McClellan 1985: 49). The Royal Swedish Academy of Sciences enjoyed royal protection, was consulted by the government on question within its competence and counted high-level officeholders among its members. There were, in other words, informal ties to the state. (Lindroth 1978–81, vol. 3: 51–59).

33. For a study of learned discourse in France from a gender perspective, see Goodman 1994.

34. For a detailed study of this phenomenon, esp. in German history, see Koselleck 1988.

35. Dalin's magazine had around 500 subscribers and was also sold as single copies. It was also distributed in the provinces (Oscarsson 2000: 98–104). After 1734, when *Then swänska Argus* was discontinued, 30 journals that more or less reproduced its content and form were started, including *Den Philosophiske Mercurius* and *Den Swenske Patrioten* (1734–35); *Skuggan af den döda Argus* (1735); *Thet Swenska Nitet* (1738); and *Then Swenska Sanningen* (1739–40) (Oscarsson 2000: 108). According to a notice in *Stockholms historiska bibliotek* 1755, vol. 2: 150–51, the magazine was still talked about and in high demand in 1755. According to the same source, it was also translated into Danish. Popular demand reportedly resulted in a second revised edition in 1754.

36. On the whole, Dalin did not rebuke noble status, but his critique of status attributes was appropriated in the more systematic campaigns against the first estate that would erupt after his death in 1763 (Carlsson 1962: 56; Hessler 1943).

37. Professor Pehr Adrian Gadd, an influential eighteenth-century academic inquiring into the relationship between patriotism and prosperity, chaired the defence of this dissertation. It is not unlikely that the dissertation was written by the senior academic, which was not unusual in seventeenth- and eighteenth-century academia (Lindberg 1976: 2). For the sake of convenience, Armfeldt is treated as the author of the dissertation.

38. The author in this context uses corporeal metaphors, speaking of the decline of morals as a 'wound ... in the body politic' and 'harmful fluids [...] in the body of the State' (ibid.: 5–6).

39. He also made a vague distinction between virtues that emanated from the intellect, the will and religion (ibid.: 9–11).

40. On the relationship between age and moral education, see also Wrede 1743: 26; Polhem 1745: 9.

41. [*en nyttig man i Samhället*]; [*et ondt i staten*].

Chapter 4

DECLINING DELIBERATION: CIVIL SOCIETY, COMMUNITY, ORGANIZED MODERNITY

Jean Terrier and Peter Wagner

Varieties of Liberty

As a mere provisional generalisation, and speaking at this moment only of the Western context, we can argue that republicanism and classical liberalism are the political philosophies which give an important place to concepts related to 'civicness' and 'civility', including to the concept of 'civil society' itself. These concepts are related to a reflection on the conditions of possibility of collective self-determination (see chapter 1).

Before the democratic revolutions, republicanism, political liberalism and also economic liberalism were united in their support of the idea of self-determination or, more precisely, in their rejection of constraints on human action, be those derived from theological reasoning or from assumptions about a natural hierarchy in the social world. These positions were all advocating political modernity – as we would say in the terminology adopted here – under conditions in which such modernity was not yet generally accepted. The differences between those positions were thus often underemphasized. After the moment of the democratic revolutions, as we have seen, the republican concept of liberty and deliberation was often seen as too demanding, and as a result republican thinking tended to decrease in political significance. Political and economic liberalism then existed side by side, but were often seen as addressing different and separate aspects of the modern problématique (see Wagner 2001c; 2003c; for more detail on this argument).

From the late eighteenth century onwards, economic liberalism – under the label of political economy – seemed to provide a powerful reasoning in favour of the liberation of economic action with a view to better satisfying human needs, to enhance 'the wealth of nations', to use a famous formula. The use of the adjective 'political' before 'economy' shows that this approach was seen as a political theory; however, it tended to predetermine the objectives of a polity in a rather restricted way, namely in terms of domestic peace and material wellbeing. For the reaching of such objectives, it argued, nothing more than an individualist conception of liberty is needed, any stronger conception indeed being seen as potentially harmful because of possible interference with the working of the 'invisible hand'.

Classical political liberalism remained aware of, as well as appreciative of, the diversity of strivings of individual human beings. Unlike republicanism, however, it expected to solve the thus defined political problématique of modernity by procedural rules alone (some of which were intended to restrict participation in deliberation to those human beings who could be expected to be capable of thinking and acting responsibly: in practice, this often meant property-owning male heads of households).

By the end of the nineteenth century, both economic and political liberalism had lost much of their earlier persuasiveness. The belief in self-regulation of the economy had declined in the course both of the 'long depression' and the rise of the workers' movement in its fight against social inequality and declining working and living conditions. The latter also had an impact on the faith in political liberalism. With workers as well as – though less often noted – women claiming full political inclusion, the restricted concept of political participation that classical liberalism sustained became increasingly untenable, at least without strong means of control. At the same time, the political elite could not envisage how a fully inclusive liberal democracy could be established and maintained given their doubts about the capability of 'the masses' for responsible action. Against this background, the late nineteenth–century transformation of liberalism and its consequences for the idea of civil society will be discussed. We shall argue that the terms of the debate shifted, and that an increasingly dominant intellectual concern, on the ruins of classical liberalism, moved from focusing on the question of the best conditions for liberty (a debate in which, as we have seen, the notion of civil society played an important role) to addressing primarily that of the stabilization of a given social order.

The Transformation of Democracy and the Declining Importance of the Concept of Civil Society

This tension between participation and representation, as conceptualized here, is at the core of the problématique of civil society. Without institutionalized representation, no fixation of the deliberative flux of civil society in concretely existing institutions or concretely taken measures can occur. Without permanent participation, representative bodies lose their representativity, thus undermining the legitimacy of social institutions and threatening political cohesion. For Tocqueville, significantly, this question remains open and cannot be solved by conceptual means. He refused both the individualist–liberal assumption that the procedures established in the social contract provided a sufficient answer and the Hegelian assumption that a state that remained external to participation and deliberation was required to reconcile the diverse strivings of the lesser components of ethical life (see chapter 1). Some other authors during the first two thirds of the nineteenth century, among whom we will briefly discuss Germaine de Staël and John Stuart Mill, took broadly similar positions, even though they were much less able than Tocqueville to underpin them by detailed observations of an existing democracy – which may be one of the reasons why the 'transformation of democracy' (to quote Vilfredo Pareto 1966) that occurred in the later nineteenth century was prefigured in their writings.

In the aftermath of the French Revolution, a long discussion started which revolved around the question of the forms of political representation and, more specifically, on the role of the legislative assembly in a representative system. While discussions on representation before that date do not put much emphasis, or no emphasis at all, on the workings of the assembly – particularly telling is Locke's silence in this respect – a great deal of effort was put by nineteenth-century thinkers into the understanding of this crucial representative institution. Hegel, for instance, offered a very elaborate discussion of the role of legislative bodies within the general framework of ethical life – thus inaugurating a long debate on parliamentarianism in German thought which extends, as we shall see, to the contributions of authors such as Max Weber and Carl Schmitt. Similarly, as we have seen, Tocqueville devoted much attention to the question of the relations between 'civil society' and representative institutions. At approximately the same time, we can observe that classical liberals increasingly tended to rethink the question of the relation of the legislative to civil society.

Mme de Staël spoke of the legislative in the following terms: 'To have representative government, to remain faithful to the principle of such government ... one needs to turn it into, so to say, a version of reduced size in the proportions of the larger whole of public opinion' (Staël-Holstein 1980: 172). For de Staël, in a way which anticipates statistical reasoning, the parliament by the very laws of proportion contained all the opinions which one could possibly find in civil society. As such, any law passed by the parliament could be per se taken to reflect the actual demands of the public, without any immediate need that these demands be explicitly expressed by the public itself. What de Staël did, thus, was to reintegrate the processes of deliberation characteristic of civil society within the parliamentary institution, which therefore was endowed with a twofold role: that of deliberation and that of concretization, that is, the crystallization of deliberation in existing laws. She thus shifted the debate from a discussion on social relations, typical for the eighteenth century, to a reflection on the institutional dynamic at stake within the political sphere. We witness here an example of the liberal mitigation of the idea of civil society, even though in Staëlian thought civil society still had the role of the model to which parliamentary debates had to measure themselves, and from which they drew their ultimate legitimacy.

De Staël is by no means the only example of such a mitigation. In his speech on liberty (1819), Benjamin Constant sustained that representation should be the characteristic feature of modern political orders; but his understanding of what representation meant was rather strong, insofar as it denied the centrality of political participation and advocated a proper division of political labour between the individual members of a given society, only a tiny minority of whom were to take care of the daily administration of political affairs. In the large societies of the modern world, individuals are lost in the multitude and cannot make their voice heard in public deliberation. Therefore, Constant logically concluded, 'the individual ... is, even in the freest states, sovereign only in appearance ... If ... he exercises his sovereignty, it is always only to renounce it' (ibid.: 312). On top of this emphasis on the crucial importance of representative bodies, Constant insisted that their role was to act as a deliberating public – that is, a society of individuals bound by speech ('we assemble merely to understand one other ... in order to understand one another it is necessary to speak', Constant 1988b: 222) whose goal was to 'negotiate on matters common' to 'partial interests' (Constant 2003: 327).

John Stuart Mill, in his *Considerations on Representative Government* (1861), defended a related position. Like the two French authors, he thought that the parliamentary institution would automatically mirror, or even express in a more articulate and explicit way, the opinions of the individuals composing 'civil society' – thus rendering any permanent connection between the representatives and their constituency unnecessary:

> the Parliament has an office ... to be at once the nation's Committee of Grievances, and its Congress of Opinions; an arena in which not only the

general opinion of the nation, but that of every section of it, and as far as possible of every eminent individual whom it contains, can produce itself in full light and challenge discussion; *where every person in the country may count upon finding somebody who speaks his mind, as well or better than he could speak it himself* ... where every party or opinion in the country can muster its strength, and be cured of any illusion concerning the number or power of its adherents; where the opinion which prevails in the nation makes itself manifest as prevailing, and marshals its hosts in the presence of the government, which is thus enabled and compelled to give way to it on the mere manifestation, without the actual employment, of its strength; where statesmen can assure themselves, far more certainly than by any other signs, what elements of opinion and power are growing, and what declining, and are enabled to shape their measures with some regard not solely to present exigencies, but to tendencies in progress. (Mill 1995: 257–58; emphasis is ours)

These authors identify the problem of representation as the question of the translation from the diversity of opinions in society to decision-making on behalf of the common, and they identify the parliament as the site where this translation should occur. While they insist on the direction of this process, namely from society towards the decision, they both also recognize considerable problems in this process, problems that require additional devices to secure the success of the operation, or at least enhance the likelihood for such success.[2] Even though they stay within the classical liberal framework, their thinking prefigures the profound crisis that such political thought would undergo towards the end of the nineteenth century. With regard to the question of representation, we may speak here of a transformation of a *philosophical* concept of representation, based on the political philosophy of the Enlightenment, into a *sociological* one, based on the gradually emerging sociology of industrial and mass society at the end of the nineteenth century (d'Arcy and Saez 1985: 9; see also Wagner 1994: 91–96).

This conceptual transformation was mirrored in the decreasing use of the concept 'civil society'. If one accepts the observation that the emerging discourse of sociology can be read as a reinterpretation of the problématiques addressed before by political philosophy (see, for instance, Wagner 1998), then it is easy to recognize that 'civil society' was replaced by the concept of 'society' *tout court*. With this transformation, though, precisely in the light of the 'crisis of representation', the debate was shifted from the processes of deliberation between a multitude of diverse human beings towards the idea that some pre-existing structures of society, now seen as a bounded, coherent whole, would guarantee unanimity or, at least, manageable difference between the members of that society (Wagner 2001b; Terrier 2004).

'Civil Society' and 'Society': the Rise of the Social Sciences and the Crisis of Classical Liberalism

For the founding fathers of liberalism, it was sufficient to define the polity as a collection of autonomous individuals linked by mere interest (Hirschman 1977). This is what Locke suggested when he wrote that 'by agreeing with other men to join and unite into a community' individuals seek to ensure their 'comfortable, safe, and peaceable living one amongst another, in a secure enjoyment of their properties' (Locke 1990: §94).

However, from the mid-nineteenth century onwards, liberalism started to think of the polity as an entity held together by something more than interest. In his *Considerations on Representative Government*, John Stuart Mill argued that the sense of togetherness which characterized the 'feeling of nationality' could have 'various causes', such as 'the effect of race and descent', 'community of religion' or even 'geographical limits'. Mill thought, however, that the strongest bond between individuals was at the same time political and historical: it was collective remembrance, or to put it like Mill himself, a 'consequent community of recollections' of what the polity has gone through in the past (all quotes are taken from Mill 1995, chap. 16: 'Of Nationality, as connected with representative government'). Similarly, Ernest Renan, who described himself as a 'conservative liberal', thought that it was not the community of interest that made a polity, but the existence of a national sentiment which had to do with the awareness of sharing political values, of having a common destiny: 'A historical past, great men, glory (I mean authentic glory), that is the social capital on which one can found an idea of the nation' (Renan 1996: 240).

Such evolution of liberal thought needs to be placed within the broader framework of the late nineteenth-century crisis of European liberalism (Seidman 1983). The liberal understanding of social life, organized around the notion of the autonomous individual, started to be heavily challenged from the mid-nineteenth century onwards, not least under the influence of socialism. Industrialisation indeed meant the birth of the class of industrial workers, who increasingly enrolled in political groups denying legitimacy to the bourgeois state. Conceptually, from the point of view of political integration, one might put the issue in the following terms: for the classical liberals, a polity was taken to be viable even with a high level of differentiation (strong diversity of life orientations) and a low level of equality (as long as the various members of the polity were better off than they would be in a hypothetical state of nature).

The working class movement precisely challenged these liberal assumptions, arguing that no polity could exist with a level of equality as low as the liberals wanted to keep it. The liberal idea of a grounding of the polity in interest could not lead, under the conditions of capitalism, to any stable order. Karl Kautsky, for instance, recognized that interest could hold societies together, but suggested also that in capitalism there were too many diverging interests for a stable polity to emerge. This was because the outrageous material inequalities brought about by capitalist accumulation clearly led to a situation in which some members of the polity had an interest not in the conservation, but in the overthrow of the order in question: 'The goal of the proletariat is the abolition of all class differences. The attainment of this goal would confer to the unity of nations a solidity that has never existed so far. As strong as the common interests of all members of a nation can be under certain circumstances, their action is weakened by the antagonisms between classes' (Kautsky, 'Die moderne Nationalität', in *Die Neue Zeit*, 1887, cited in Haupt et al. 1997: 126).

In order to preserve the social order of which they were the ruling element, the middle classes started addressing the question of what, if not interest, could hold societies together. This reflection took the form an exploration, mainly conducted under the name of sociology, of the regularities and continuities present in social life. The political balance tipped toward a strengthening of collectivist orientations, in which the autonomy of the individual was de-emphasized in favour of a voluntarism of the collectivity. Both socialism and nationalism provided versions of such collectivist political philosophy; but even former liberals resigned themselves to social changes that had displaced individual responsibility from the centre of politics (see Wagner 2001b, chaps. 1 and 2).[3]

At the end of the nineteenth and the beginning of the twentieth century the middle classes indeed recognized that no polity could exist under conditions of both extreme differentiation and extreme inequality. But what needed to be changed was less the level of inequality than the level of differentiation: the members of the polity had to be rendered similar, if not identical, by the diffusion of a unitary culture, a 'common consciousness'. This common consciousness was to develop among the members of a collectivity of interdependent individuals. It ensured that the polity became an inclusive community of identically-minded individuals.

A similar reflection on the shortcomings of classical liberalism can be found in a fairly clear form in the work of the early Max Weber. In his inaugural lecture at the University of Freiburg (1895), Weber addressed the problem of the relationship between the science of economics and the national question. His position at the time was deeply structured by a vision of social life as a struggle for existence. Not only did he believe that human beings were fighting against each other to defend their privileged access to material resources. He was also convinced that, collectively, groups of human beings, including the nation, were involved in such a struggle. In this context, any political measure must be evaluated in function of its correspondence to national interest – understood as that which ensures in the long run the conditions of collective survival. Collective survival is a value not so much because it enables the physical subsistence of individuals, but rather because it allows for the persistence of 'those characteristics which we think of as constituting the human greatness and nobility of our nature' (Weber 1994a: 15).

The young Weber was concerned with the future of the German nation. He believed that its existence was threatened by the weakness of national sentiment in the rising classes – by which he meant both the bourgeoisie and the working class. In the nineteenth century, the aristocracy of Prussian *Junkers* had managed to create a German nation-state, which was the primary condition to safeguard the place of Germany in Europe. Weber called this a process of 'external' unification (ibid.: 22). The *inner* unity of the nation, however, was yet insufficiently advanced. The lack of 'nationalist passion' (p. 26) in Germany gave birth to a situation in which nothing counterbalanced the centrifugal effects of diverging economic interests: the nation was 'split apart by modern economic development' (ibid.). This threatened the capacity of Germany to face the military and economic competition between nations at the international level.

The solution to this plight lay in the '*social unification*' (ibid.: original emphasis) of Germany. An intense '*political education*' (ibid.: 27, original emphasis) was needed to spread 'the earnest grandeur of national sentiment' (p. 28) across all classes of the nation. This was the only way to avoid a situation in which 'the feelings of political community would be stretched beyond breaking point by temporary divergences of economic interests' (p. 21).

The same year as Weber's inaugural lecture at Freiburg, Gustave Le Bon published the results of his reflections on modern society as a 'crowd society' (*La psychologie des foules*). From the viewpoint of the history of the notion of civil society, Le Bon's texts are interesting insofar as the epistemology and social ontology it contains are exactly the opposite of those typically needed for deliberation (and therefore, civil society) to be available as a resource.

First of all, Le Bon argued that there was a way to fight indeterminacy in social life. The social sciences, according to him, could indicate which institutions were most adequate for each social setting, in view of its general characteristics. In *The Psychology of Peoples* [*Lois psychologiques de l'évolution des peuples*], Le Bon asserted that each people possesses a 'mental constitution as stable as its anatomic characteristics; from it its feelings, its thoughts, its institutions, its beliefs and its arts derive' (Le Bon 1906: 5). In such a context, it became possible to argue that some institutions were preferable to others, on the basis of their correspondence with the 'mental constitution' of the people considered.

Establishing institutions that were alien to the traditional *façons de faire* of a given people was either useless or harmful, insofar as they would be rejected as incompatible with the 'soul of the race' (ibid.: 9; Le Bon 1958: 28).[4] In our own vocabulary, we can say that Le Bon proposes a positivistic epistemology for which the truth in social and political matters is attainable by way of scientific reasoning, as it appears clearly in the following quote:

> Institutions and governments are the product of the race. They are not the creators of an epoch, but are created by it. Peoples are not governed in accordance with their caprices of the moment, but as their character determines that they shall be governed. Centuries are required to form a political system and centuries needed to change it. Institutions have no intrinsic virtue: in themselves they are neither good nor bad. Those which are good at a given moment for a given people may be harmful in the extreme for another nation. (Le Bon 1958: 96)

Le Bon's scientism relied on a deterministic conception of social individuals, who are taken to be incapable of any autonomous action: they are unconsciously and necessarily shaped by powerful forces (those of race).

> The conscious life of the mind is of small importance in comparison with its unconscious life. ... Our conscious acts are the outcome of an unconscious substratum created in the mind in the main by hereditary influences. This substratum consists of the innumerable common characteristics handed down from generation to generation, which constitute the genius of a race. (ibid.: 28)

Le Bon's epistemological and ontological premises contradict frontally the conditions of possibility of a deliberating public, including in its less immediate, parliamentary form:

> the parliamentary system represents the ideal of all modern civilized peoples. The system is the expression of the idea, psychologically erroneous, but generally admitted, that a large gathering of men is much more capable than a small number of coming to a wise and independent decision on a given subject. The general characteristics of crowds are to be met with in parliamentary assemblies: Intellectual simplicity, irritability, suggestibility, the exaggeration of the sentiments and the preponderating influence of a few leaders. (ibid.: 187)

Gustave Le Bon's work, in other words, is a particularly clear example of the diffusion of a new understanding of the social as an homogeneous whole of similarly – if not identically – minded individuals. The rise of these new conceptions undermined the traditional enlightened world-view of society as a collection of autonomous individuals, which represented the only fertile ground for a development of the idea of civil society. We find ourselves here at the core of the demise of civil society.

Complete evidence of the diffusion of these new conceptions cannot be given here (see Terrier 2004). It is useful to suggest, however, that they actually managed to make their way in the social common sense of the time. Le Bon's writings are revealing in this respect. They were fundamentally works of scientific vulgarisation and targeted a public of non-scientists. The success of the undertaking was immense. The *Psychology of peoples*, for instance, quickly became a European best-seller (translated into sixteen languages) and in France alone underwent seventeen editions (Nye 2000: 52).

The diffusion of Le Bon's work alone, however, is not sufficient to demonstrate the influence of the new conception of the social. Moreover, it is important to emphasize that Le Bon represented an especially extreme variant of the idea of social homogeneity. It is therefore not our point that the entire late nineteenth century turned Lebonian: this assertion would not do justice to the complexity of the debates that accompanied the birth of the social sciences. If the space at our disposal was not limited we could propose a detailed account of these debates, emphasising the variety of answers proposed by early sociologists to the question of social cohesion. We do wish to argue, however, that it is possible to identify a broad paradigmatic shift around the middle of the nineteenth century which brings to the centre of attention the question of social homogeneity to which notions such as 'race' (Gobineau, Le Bon), 'national character' (Taine, Bagehot), 'organic integration' (Spencer, Worms) 'collective consciousness' or 'collective representations' (Durkheim), and 'solidarity' (Bourgeois) represented a variety of answers. Most, if not all, of these reflections abandoned the idea of autonomy and moved away from the reflection on civil society in its eighteenth-century form, which depended crucially upon a notion of society as a fluid ensemble of autonomous individuals.

Carl Schmitt and the Anti–sociological Critique of Liberalism

As we have seen, early nineteenth-century liberals started to propose a concept of representation which downplayed participation – that is also, the link between the parliamentary institution and 'civil society' – as unnecessary for the thriving of a free polity. They still thought, however, that parliament was a *substitute*, imposed by modern times, for a comprehensive debate that used to take place within civil society itself, as was the case among the ancients. This is the reason why they conceptualized parliament as a 'public opinion *en miniature*'. Many thinkers of the late nineteenth century, influenced by the new conception of society as a homogeneous whole, typically tended to deny that there could be such as thing as 'public opinion': on the one hand, the social homogeneity rendered individuals virtually unanimous, thus making any debate on values and goals almost useless; on the other hand, the cognitive capacities of individuals – as Le Bon forcefully argued – are too limited to allow for general political participation.

With regard to political organization, and more specifically to the parliamentary institution, two solutions were possible in such a transformed intellectual context: either one could sever the link which traditionally connected civil society and parliament, in order to retain the parliamentary institution (this is the choice made by an author such as Max Weber[5]) or one could judge that the link between civil society and parliament was indissoluble. This meant, as a direct consequence, that the parliament had to be rejected as a central institution of modern politics, since its very condition of existence – namely, public opinion and more generally 'civil society' in the sense delineated above – did not exist any more. This is precisely the core of Carl Schmitt's argument, as we shall see, which he presented in a text published in 1923 and entitled *Die geistesgeschichtliche Lage des heutigen Parlamentarismus* (1985), an extremely interesting and revealing critique of classical liberalism, targeting its central institution (the parliament) and its prerequisite (the idea of individual autonomy).

Schmitt started by identifying the ontological assumptions which underlie the liberal faith in discursive processes: as we have already noted above, individuals must be conceived as capable of autonomous reasoning if they are to engage in collective decision-making processes. As Schmitt wrote,

> Discussion means an exchange of opinion that is governed by the purpose of persuading one's opponent through argument of the truth of justice of something, or allowing oneself to be persuaded of something as true and just. … To discussion belong shared convictions as premises, the willingness to be persuaded, independence of party ties, freedom from selfish interests. (ibid.: 5)

According to Schmitt, precisely these reasoning abilities were put at risk by the development of early twentieth-century polities. Liberal societies were increasingly replaced by a new political arrangement which Schmitt called 'mass democracy'. Mass democracy was characterized by the development of parties as groups striving to gain political power ('power-groups', ibid.: 6). In order to reach this goal, parties started to develop a whole series of techniques aiming at winning the support of electoral masses. The appeal to affects and passions, at the cost of cold-blooded reflection, played an important role in this process: 'The masses are won over through a propaganda apparatus whose maximum effect relies on an appeal to immediate interests and passions' (ibid.: 6).

The development of party politics and the deployment of its consequences undermined the very basis of liberal parliamentarianism, namely the public sphere, thus precipitating the parliamentary institution in a crisis. The public sphere, as we have seen above, was taken to play an important role in the conceptual system of liberal polities: it was a mediating institution which tied together the rulers and the ruled. Schmitt was aware of this crucial fact, and implicitly acknowledged that no polity could thrive if some connection between those who exercise power and those upon which this power is exerted was not guaranteed. Thus, he argued that a new conception of political connectivity had to be established.

Societies could not be understood as heterogeneous collectivities of different individuals any longer, merely bound together by a series of discursive links. Instead, they needed to be conceived (and, to a certain extent, actively established) as coherently integrated wholes of identical individuals: 'Democracy requires, therefore, first homogeneity and second – if the need arises – elimination or eradication of heterogeneity.... A democracy demonstrates its political power by knowing how to refuse or keep at bay something foreign and unequal that threatens its homogeneity' (ibid.: 9). Schmitt's position, thus, was that a restoration of the link between the rulers and the ruled was possible if the ruled could recognize themselves in their rulers; if they could count upon the fact, in other words, that the decisions of their rulers were inspired by what constituted the very identity of the collectivity considered. Schmitt's proposal was to ground political cohesion upon primordial qualities, which he called 'substance' (*Substanz*, ibid.: 17); among these qualities he mentions religious conviction (as in the political arrangements of seventeenth-century democratic puritanism) but also, more importantly for us, national survival.

In the political arrangement advocated by Carl Schmitt, the identity of the rulers and the ruled was thus guaranteed without any deliberative mediation. The legitimation of power occurred, at best, through direct acclamation – which was the way in which, by mere deployment of its 'obvious and unchallenged presence' (*selbstverständliches, unwidersprochenes Dasein*, ibid.: 16), the people made their unitary will known. Even acclamation, however, was not necessary to the legitimation of power, insofar as a primordial unity existed a priori between the rulers and the ruled.

For us, Carl Schmitt is interesting insofar as his thought represents one of the possible results of the rejection of the public sphere as a location in which the agreement between individuals bearing different opinions is sought: namely, the justification of authoritarian rule, grounded on assumptions of social homogeneity. Schmitt is unequivocal in this respect:

Compared to a democracy that is direct [*unmittelbar*], not only in the technical sense but also in a vital sense, parliament appears an artificial machinery, produced by liberal reasoning, while dictatorial and Caesaristic methods not only can produce the acclamation of the people but can also be a direct expression of democratic substance and power. (ibid.: 16–17 – the parenthesis is ours)

Schmitt's work helps us to understand the political conceptions behind the dictatorships born during the interwar period; his critique of liberal parliamentarianism mirrored indeed the one proposed by Vladimir I. Lenin in the first two decades of the twentieth century (see Bolsinger 2001). These two political thinkers mainly differed in their view on the nature of the 'substance and force' that could bring about the 'immediate democracy' that they were advocating. This concept of immediacy marked basically a denial of the need for mediation that arises from any diversity within a polity. In as far as the concept of civil society was developed to provide for such mediation through deliberation, Schmitt as well as Lenin can be seen as direct heirs of the long tradition of critique of civil society (as will, in an indirect way, be shown in the analysis of Wilhelminian Germany and the German Democratic Republic in chapter 5).

Despite the similarity of their diagnoses, the sociology and political theory of mass society provided highly different perspectives on the crisis of liberalism and the decline of civil society. The former developed stronger and more rigid notions of the social bonds between members of a polity than any concept of civil society ever had – bonds that thus made political deliberation superfluous or, at least, less significant. The latter insisted on the need for some political voluntarism that would overcome precisely the socio-economic cleavages that otherwise would endanger the polity. Even though this thinking, too, relied on some assumption about a social 'substance' that needed to be homogeneous, it was political will and not the development of society as such that would bring such substance to its full effect.

Excursus: a Discussion of Habermas's Structural Transformation of the Public Sphere

In spite of the fact that Habermas's famous study *The Structural Transformation of the Public Sphere* does not present itself as a work on civil society, it appears evident from our perspective that his reflection on *Öffentlichkeit* and our own enquiry on civil society deal with the same set of historical phenomena.[6] Also, we find ourselves in agreement with Habermas when he identifies in the idea of a deliberating public one of the possible answers to what he calls the 'post-metaphysical' condition – a condition marked by the diffusion of the idea that it is indeed impossible to arrive at any kind of certainty about the natural and the social world by way of mere individual speculation or heteronomous imposition. Lastly, the 'chronology' of the development of civil society we have just proposed is very similar to the one offered by Habermas: the eighteenth century as a moment of diffusion of the public sphere, the later nineteenth century as a moment of crisis of the notion, the early twentieth century as the period of its decline.

In spite of these similarities, there are important differences between Habermas's reflection and ours when it comes to accounting for the decline of the public sphere, or civil society. He identifies two main reasons for the crisis of the public sphere: first, the stratification of society, which undermines the social basis of the public sphere; and second, the rise of the corporate press.

In Habermas's understanding, the emergence of the public sphere was rendered possible by the preliminary development of a consolidated private realm in the form of the bourgeois household. Bourgeois individuals could count on the existence of a sphere in which to retreat, where they could enjoy the tranquillity which is necessary for any individual reflection on public affairs. Furthermore, the bourgeois household was also characterized by a certain wealth, which further enhanced autonomy. The birth of this specific kind of private realm made a new figure possible, that of the *honnête homme* (here the masculine is *de rigueur*, as we shall see), versed in understanding the natural and social world, and thus capable of *having* an opinion – that is, of holding a position backed by communicable arguments. The public sphere, in this context, is understood as the virtual space in which individuals disclose and confront their private opinions, by way of what is aptly described as *publication*, of which books and newspapers are the material support; public opinion, in turn, is the result of the provisional agreement resulting from this confrontation. Habermas argues that this social configuration underwent substantial changes at the end of the nineteenth century.

First of all, according to Habermas, the bourgeois family disappeared. With the diffusion of the division of labour, especially in the form of a generalisation of wage-paid jobs, the bourgeois family was deprived of one of the pillars upon which it built its coherence, namely the common effort to preserve familial property which was seen as an insurance against hardship. This latter role was increasingly taken over by state institutions, with the effect of dissolving traditional family solidarity. With the disappearance of the bourgeois family, the existence of a separate realm of autonomy to which individuals could retreat in order to forge their opinion vanished. As a consequence, the public sphere lost one of its foundations: the existence of a collection of individuals who confront and exchange opinions.

Second, this very exchange of opinions could take place only if the circulation of ideas was supported by an autonomous Press, whose main goals were the diffusion of information, the reproduction and confrontation of various possible interpretations of this information, and the presentation of articulate positions. The Press considered as a whole, in this incarnation, was equivalent to public opinion. With the development of capitalism, however, the Press became a commercial product which progressively lost its connections with the public. When newspapers started to be conceived mainly as products of a privately-owned firm,

> [t]he sphere of the public was altered by the influx of private interests that received privileged exposure in it – although they were by no means eo ipso representative of the interests of the private people as the public ... in the measure that the public sphere became a field for business advertising, private people as owners of private property had a direct effect on private people as the public. (Habermas 1989: 192)

In such a context, individuals were not exposed to the variety of the opinions held by other individuals; they were merely confronted to the endless repetition of dominant positions:

> Publicity is generated from above, so to speak, in order to create an aura of good will for certain positions. Originally publicity guaranteed the connection between rational-critical public debate and the legislative foundation of domination, including the critical supervision of its exercise. Now it makes possible the peculiar ambivalence of a domination exercised trough the domination of nonpublic opinion: it serves the manipulation of the public as much as legitimation before it. Critical publicity is supplanted by manipulative publicity. (ibid.: 177–78)

We are unsatisfied with Habermas's account for mainly two reasons. First, we do not see social changes in family structure as the primary reason for the rise of the public sphere. In our understanding, individual opinion as firm conviction, or the capacity for having one, is not necessarily constituted in the intimacy of the private realm; it appears first as an unstable position, and is turned into conviction in the very process of its confrontation with other positions. *Private opinion as conviction is constructed via the mediation of the public sphere itself.* Changes in the family structure have no immediate or direct effect upon the possibility of the constitution of firm opinions.[7] Moreover, this conviction avoids the patriarchal connotations present in Habermas's text: the reflexive bourgeois is implicitly presented as a *pater familias* whose independence is guaranteed, among other things, by his benefiting from the work done by the other members of the family, most importantly women.

Secondly, Habermas's account entails quite an important amount of (economic) determinism. In his view, the passage to industrial capitalism is the major cause of the development of the welfare state, which in turn causes the destruction of the private realm and of the public sphere which was built upon it.[8] Similarly, industrial capitalism is responsible for the transformation of the Press into a series of commercial products. Our conception tries to avoid insisting on economic transformations as causing the demise of the public sphere. We suggest instead that this demise must be understood against the background of the social and political dynamic of nineteenth-century society, which was characterized by important changes in the prevalent conceptions of togetherness; the decline of the public sphere should be described as the consequence of imaginary shifts induced by the rise of new social challenges.

Notes

1. A prominent mid-nineteenth-century political thinker with republican leanings was Karl Marx – as was noted, but not further discussed by Quentin Skinner in *Liberty before liberalism* (1998). In Marx' view it was mainly the adoption of a bourgeois–liberal conception of economy and politics that stood in the way of 'human emancipation', or the realization of a free political association based on deliberation, no genuinely political problématique related to self-determination. Notably, his political writings operate through a critique of what he saw as a bourgeois concept of civil society, exploiting the double connotation of the German word *bürgerlich* as referring to both bourgeois and citoyen (or to justifications in terms of the *cité marchande* and the *cité civique*, to use Boltanski and Thévenot's terms [1991]). See Abensour (1997) for an argument to read the early Marx as a republican. In this context, it may be important to note that the current German debate retranslates *societas civilis* as *Zivilgesellschaft* rather than *bürgerliche Gesellschaft*.

2. There is some consistency in de Staël's proposal of the proportional argument, insofar as she advocated an electoral system enforcing the principle of one man, one vote. One might wonder, instead, how it can be successfully applied within the framework of John Stuart Mill's political thought: he was indeed in favour of a system of weighing of the votes according to levels of education; in such a context, it becomes difficult to understand how parliament could be taken to be a proper reflection of society.

3. A similar view was also advanced for a political analysis of the emergence of sociology. Robert Nye, for instance argued that 'men like de Maistre, de Bonald, Saint Simon, and Comte, deplored the liberal social and economic ethic that was leading to a dangerous atomization of society. In an effort to contribute to a restructuring of social order, these men drew heavily on theories of organic society that were hierarchical and rich in tradition and purposiveness. These partisan efforts contributed, ironically, to the founding of the modern science of sociology' (Nye 2000: 63). Early in the nineteenth century, however, authors who held such a position were mostly 'conservative' in the sense that they had never fully accepted the modern political condition. By the late nineteenth century, even 'modernists' became inclined to reflect about social bonds that could hold societies and polities together under conditions of – or despite – equal liberty.

4. Le Bon's '*âme de la race*' is translated as 'genius of a race' in the English edition.
5. Weber noted in *Parliament and Government in Germany under a New Political Order. Towards a Critique of Officialdom and the Party System* (1917) that the existence of parliament was 'a condition of the duration' of political rule, insofar as 'any rule, even the best organised ... should enjoy a certain measure of inner assent from at least those sections of the ruled who carry weight in society' (Weber 1994b: 165). However, the tendencies to bureaucratisation in society in general, and in the organisation of parties in particular, had progressively undermined the mechanisms by which the parliament maintained contact with civil society. Bureaucratised parties could not be understood any more as crystallisation of the political position of a given section of society, since '[e]ven in a mass party with a very democratic form of organisation ... the mass of voters at least, and to a considerable extent the ordinary "membership" too, is *not* (or only formally) involved in deciding on programmes and candidates'. Weber chose to defend the parliamentary institution even in such a transformed context, because it had an important effect upon upon political life: it rendered *Führerauslese* (the selection of leaders) more efficient: '[o]nly a *working*, as opposed to a merely talking parliament can be the soil in which not merely demagogic, but genuinely *political* qualities of leadership can grow and work their way up through a process of selection'; the selection of talented leaders 'is *only* possible within a party if its leaders have the prospect of *power* and *responsibility* in the state as the reward of success' (176–77).
6. *Strukturwandel der Öffentlichkeit* appeared in 1962, four years after Hannah Arendt's *Human condition*, and is very likely to have been inspired by the latter. As will be shown (see chapter 9), however, the diagnoses of these two authors should diverge considerably in later works, unveiling differences between these two early works that were originally somewhat hidden behind apparent similarities.
7. From Adorno's work on the 'authoritarian personality' via Habermas to Axel Honneth's plurality of modes of recognition, one of which resides in love, to Hans Joas's elaboration of the idea of 'primary sociality', social theory that broadly is connected to the Frankfurt School tradition has always tried to find one of the keys to understanding 'pathologies' (Honneth) of contemporary societies in the structure of the realm of family and intimate life, conceived as the realm in which conditions for human autnomy are created. This is not the place for an extended discussion of this issue: suffice it to say that in our view the step from family life to the diagnosis of society is larger – in terms of both empirical generalization and conceptual connection – than these authors generally recognize.
8. Consider for instance this quote, p. 143: 'the increase in functions of the state machinery demanded by capitalism in this phase', etc.

Chapter 5

THE WITHERING AWAY OF 'CIVIL SOCIETY' AND THE ORGANIZATION OF SOCIAL LIFE: THE CASE OF GERMANY FROM THE WILHELMINIAN ERA TO THE G.D.R.

Jay Rowell and Bénédicte Zimmermann

In order to understand the rebirth of 'civil society' as a concept to describe the nature of social and political relations over the past two decades, we begin with what may at first glance appear to be a counterintuitive tack by examining the historical process which led to the disuse of civil society semantics from the end of the nineteenth century to the 1970s. During this period, the concept of civil society was eclipsed by the concept of 'society' and 'social organisation': 'liberal modernity' gave way to 'organized modernity' (Wagner 1994). Between 1890 and 1970, the history of 'organized modernity' is the story of an organisational framework of society whose boundaries increasingly corresponded to the borders of the nation-state. This history is that of the restructuring of individual identities, as well as political and economic practices around the central ordering principles of class and nation. Finally, this history is also characterized by a vast movement towards increased standardization and codification, largely through the extension of bureaucratic logics, seeking to reduce uncertainty during a period of intense political and economic transformation (Polanyi 1980 [1944]).

This detour through history will seek to fulfil two objectives. Studying a historical context which resulted in the transformation not only of descriptive languages but also in the reshaping of collective identities and the articulation between the social, the political and the economic could provide some tools to get a better grip on the current re-emergence of civil society semantics and its subsequent effects on the social and political order. Secondly, studying the context from which the civil society discourse emerged in the 1970s and 1980s will help us to understand how the principles of 'organized modernity', its collective identities, organisations, conventions and institutional arrangements, began to erode and what role the critical and normative dimensions of civil society semantics played in this process.

The historicisation of a concept does not simply involve a philological study of a word or its cognitive implications, uses and migrations. While this is a necessary first step to deconstruct categories that are only too evident, we would like to expand the horizon of investigation beyond the historical changes of the semantics of civil society, towards the study of situations where the articulation between the private, public and economic spheres was also problematic, but which did not result in the use of grammars, strategies and procedures based on the category of the 'civil'. It is from this standpoint that we can raise the question of the possibility of using civil society as a tool for historical investigation in a context where actors did not think in these categories, before returning to the contemporary uses of the term, to question the relationship between the 'civil', the 'civic' and the 'social'.

In short, our objective is to develop a form of reflexivity which is not limited to a history of the concept, but which also extends to the categories and forms of action and interaction which have been – or can be – associated with it. By linking together the linguistic registers of interpretation and the 'indigenous' uses of language and action, one can hope to combine conceptual reflexivity with empirical reflexivity, an operation which is inextricably linked to any attempt at achieving critical distance through historical contextualization. For this reason we will anchor our reflection on specific spheres of action: work and housing as two important elements of social organisation in the *Kaiserreich* (1871–1918) and the G.D.R. (1949–1989), each period having, in a particular way, produced a specific form of articulation of the individual with the collective, the political with the economic, without recourse to the themes of civil society.

The *Kaiserreich* was marked by a particular vitality of associations and organisations corresponding to what we would today define as a civil society. At the same time these organisations did not use the semantics of civil society and inscribed their activities in the framework of the nation-state, more specifically around a social topography structured by the 'social question'. The G.D.R. seems at face value to be a strange place to discuss civil society, as it was one of the regimes that proved to be most successful in controlling the space between the individual and the state.

However, it may be interesting on two counts. First, it pushed the structuring of the social through vertical integration to its most extreme authoritarian and bureaucratic conclusion. Second, it belonged to the geopolitical space of communist central Europe where the renewed civil society discourse first emerged in the 1970s. But in the G.D.R., discourse critical of the social and political order did not adopt the grammar of civil society, but rather took the path of what one could term a 'civic society'.

It seems difficult to question the definition of 'civil society', with its underlying postulate of an autonomous space, without asking: autonomous with regard to what? For this reason we examine in the first two sections the challenges of constituting the collective out of the infinite diversity of the individual. In other words, the challenges of creating principals of equivalence essential to the construction of collective identities and interests which are prerequisites of collective action, deliberation, and the production of legitimate binding decisions in a polity.[1] The first section addresses this question from a theoretical standpoint by positioning the 'civil' ideal type with regard to two other categories of the collective: the 'civic' and the 'social'. The second section adopts a more empirical line of reasoning through the examination of the construction and the consolidation of an 'organized society' in the *Kaiserreich* and the G.D.R. The third section seeks to understand the dialectic of autonomy and dependence with regard to the state. In much of the civil society literature, the relationship between the state and society is presented as a zero-sum game, with its many variants, that is, an increase in state power results in a proportional decline in the autonomy of civil society and vice versa, even if there is a general consensus on the necessity of some form of institution external to civil society to guarantee the basic rules of the interaction (Keane 1998c). Despite this, the state is nonetheless generally represented as a unified actor, while it is in fact composed of partially autonomous subsystems constantly interacting with social organisations. The boundaries between state and society, between the public and the private, are therefore variable (depending on the sector examined), ever moving and often porous. Finally, in a last part, we attempt to integrate what can be learned through our excursion into German history into a reflection on the current uses of civil society. This allows us to raise some questions around the two basic elements of the term: 'civil' and 'society', and the evolutions of signification and relationship between these two terms over time. Are 'social' and 'civil' synonyms, complementary or antagonistic? Has there been a shift from the 'social' as a way of thinking about society to the 'civil'? Does 'civil' encompass the 'social' by merely adding a new dimension, or is the 'civil' eclipsing the 'social' in much the same way as the 'social' caused the 'civil' to wither away in the second half of the nineteenth century?

The Semantics of the Individual and the Collective

If the 'social' emerged in the nineteenth century to refer to the connectedness between human beings, the concept 'society' conveys a central tension between the 'oneness' of a group of human beings, therefore implying some sort of boundedness, and the constituent parts, or smaller sub-units (associations, groups, institutions) of which it is constituted (Wagner 2001b: 128–45). The search for unifying principals in the rapidly transforming European countries of the nineteenth century lead to the opening of an 'interpretative market' to make sense of a series of radical and interconnected transformations: the emergence of representative democracy and the extension of suffrage rights to the masses, the increasing division of labour, the rise of salaried employment and the radical transformations of the economy, demography and patterns of urbanization; the revolutions in commerce, transportation and communication, and so on. A variety of competing conceptions based on a reading of the tripartition of the individual, the political and what was increasingly thought of as a partially autonomous intermediate space, or society, dominated political thought in the latter half of the nineteenth century (Heilbron 1995; Colliot-Thélène and Kervégan 2002).

Civil society semantics functioned as a bridging principle between the individual, the political and the economic, but it is not the only means by which these three units were historically linked. One can deductively define three competing ideal-types or regimes of linkage between the individual and the collective that were in place by the end of the nineteenth century and could be mobilized by contemporary observers and players: civil society, civic society and, if one pardons the pleonasm, 'social society' (these ideal types are derived from a reading of Boltanski and Thévenot 1991). The objective of this section is to specify these three competing and partially overlapping paradigms which structured social enquiry and underpinned the social and political orders of modern nation-states over the past two centuries (see, for example, Marshall 1950).

'Civic society' is a system in which the individual is linked to the collective by belonging to a polity, the distribution of status groups being indexed on rights to political participation, itself determined, until universal suffrage, on gender and on property as a definition of stakeholdership and as a guarantee of social, and therefore political independence and responsibility. 'Civic society' is consequently closely linked to the ideal of citizenship, with 'numbers' as its legitimizing principal (Desrosières 1993) and with the postulate of an egalitarian norm 'one man, one vote' (as each citizen is a bearer of a parcel of sovereignty). This ideal did not, however, preclude profound differences in individual rights ('active' or 'inactive' citizens, *Dreiklassenwahlrecht*, and so on) creating a strong hierarchy of capacity within an imaginary holist political society. Unlike 'civil society', the 'civic society' is therefore territorially bounded to correspond with a given polity, and places the emphasis on the individual, who must be ideally extracted from his social context to become a rational and independent actor. This form of organisation creates the legitimizing framework for representative institutions. It is largely procedural in orientation and does not necessitate intermediate forms of social organisation in order to function, even if political parties, governing coalitions and other such organisations can be seen as functional by-products of 'civic society'.

'Civil society', was, as shown in the previous chapters of this book, indexed during the phase of its emergence on the autonomy of the private sphere and the superposition of the private sphere with the economic sphere, before becoming more recently autonomous of its economic roots (Kocka 2004). It designates an intermediate space in which individuals are linked together without recourse to material or economic interests and without direct reference to political identities or objectives. This state of affairs has led Jürgen Habermas to exclude labour unions, employee associations, as well as political parties or clubs from his understanding of this intermediate space (Habermas 1997: 394). The emphasis is placed on self-organisation and autonomy, and procedural inclusiveness (to which we will return), and the legitimizing principle is the respect of pluralism rather than the indexation of legitimacy on numbers or, in other words, numerical representativity.

'Social society' seeks to specify the generic term of 'society' which was dominant for over a century. It can be used as a heuristic tool to get a grip on the specificity of 'civil society', by trying to reconstruct the system of social ordering which civil society is today challenging. In many ways, this term is synonymous to the concept of 'organized modernity' coined by Peter Wagner, although we would like to argue that it does not necessarily imply a state-led organisation of society. However, for the sake of simplicity we will use Wagner's term of organized modernity here. Contrary to civic society, organized modernity puts emphasis more on the collective in the space between the individual and the political, but contrary to the ideal type of 'civil society' developed over the past two decades, organized society is strongly linked to economic structures, the division of labour, and to the question of property. Rather than being based on the idea of autonomy vis-à-vis economic or state structures, the concept designates a vertical linkage superimposing political and economic identities thereby creating powerful mechanisms to constitute classes of equivalence between individuals based not on their civic statute but rather on their position in the productive process, constitutive of common interests and values. The development of this grammar corresponds to the emergence of the 'social question'. In other words, it results from a discrepancy between the normative underpinnings of the civic and the civil semantics and practices in the mid nineteenth century and the perception of a new and menacing reality.[2] Organized society was characterized by the invention of collective property, or the welfare state, which transformed those without property into stakeholders (Castel 1995), and integrated them, through highly structured social organisations, into the political sphere, implying a high degree of territorial boundedness similar to civic society. From this paradigm, it also 'borrows' the legitimizing force of 'numbers', although here numbers are not based on abstract aggregated collectives derived from the rational deliberation of individualized actors, but on the capacity of bureaucratically structured organisations to create local monopolies based on group identities, and to be recognized as the legitimate voice articulating their member's private interests on the public scene.

How can we use these three distinct forms which compete and overlap to understand the ordering of social relationships? Of course the first pitfall to avoid is thinking of these ways of ordering the social in a linear-evolutionist, or, for that matter in a cyclical manner, with the return of civil society semantics after a 150–year hiatus. This raises a series of epistemological problems, such as the possibility of describing a social entity before it exists or when its existence is in doubt (retrodiction), or for that matter, the relationship between a reality in which actors use one set of categories and where historians and social scientists use another set of concepts to make a model of reality (see Bourdieu 1980: 67). This having been said, there is nonetheless a heuristic advantage to see how the three semantic alternatives described above combine, and whether they are mutually reinforcing or mutually exclusive. The appeal to history can also shed some light on the configurations and contexts in which social actors and observers share the same categories, producing a mutually reinforcing spillover, or 'looping effect', to borrow Ian Hacking's (1999) expression, or the contexts in which observers and protagonists promote opposing or overlapping readings of the normative, analytical or practical ordering of the space between the private and the public, between the individual and the political or economic spheres.

The Shaping of Social Relations in the Wilhemian era and the G.D.R.: the Emergence, Consolidation and Hypertrophy of an Organized Society

Having set out the competing discourses which crystallized during the nineteenth century as ideal types, we now come to empirical observations to demonstrate how social theories spilled over into practice, and how pragmatic solutions to perceived political and economic problems led to the emergence and the consolidation of organized society. It was during the *Kaiserreich* that social classes became the organizing principle of social relations, a principle that would be pushed to its bureaucratic extreme in the G.D.R.

The *Kaiserreich* can be characterized by the simultaneous process of national unification and industrial capitalistic economic development. The era was marked by the challenges of inventing new ways to structure space and public action in the context of rapidly evolving territorial and economic realities. Some of the central questions were: the problem of rebuilding links between the individual and the collective at a time when established relationships, and in particular the social topography based on trade corporations, was crumbling through the sheer speed of economic and demographic transformations; the problem of integrating the working class and the risks of revolutionary upheaval; the problem of access to the political sphere blocked by a system which, although democratic in theory, was above all authoritarian.

The associative movement and social forms of self-organisation were extremely intense (Nipperdey 1986), but as most of these institutions were incapable of gaining significant access to political instances, the question of associations was essentially conceived as a problem of its articulation with state structures. If the concept of civil society was not used as such during the *Kaiserreich*, a lively debate nevertheless opposed those who hoped for state intervention to solve the social question and those who preferred the self-organisation of society at different levels of intervention. The terms of the debate therefore opposed *Staatshilfe* espoused by the conservatives and *Selbsthilfe* promoted by liberals and certain segments of the workers movement.

This debate was itself framed by another overriding issue: the definition of the boundaries between the state, the economy and society, categories that were unstable and emerging at that juncture. The issues surrounding the drawing of boundaries between these spheres were themselves structured around the question of the degree of autonomy of politics as either an overarching structure 'external' to society, or as a sphere of action organically linked to society, 'armed' with levers capable of resolving problems, constructed as social questions. Depending until then on the realm of the private sphere, problems such as housing, being ill, old, out of work and so on were translated into public problems giving rise to a social sphere in which the legitimacy of the new polity could be anchored. In this respect, the challenges of integrating the urban industrial working class (Schmoller 1865; 1918) and parleying the perceived risks these 'dangerous classes' posed to the political order were decisive in promoting the emergence of class as a structuring collective actor in society. New social institutions were put into place in which *Homo laborans* was central to the process of identification of the individual to the collective (Arendt

1998 [1958]), whether it was based on an identity claim or the assignment of an identity by an outside authority. These institutions functioned within – and were complementary to – nation building, as organized solidarity was most often built along the same lines as politically defined territories. The *Kaiserreich* therefore can be characterized as a double process in which the social world was instituted as a collective space regulated by public action, and as a context where the political sphere was constructed as a possible space to mediate social conflicts. It is precisely this double characteristic which is today contested by the semantics of civil society through a rewriting of social history in which the 'social' is implicitly posited as a construction competing with the 'civil'.

Class was essential to the authoritarian bureaucratic shaping of society implemented in the G.D.R. While the debate between *Selbsthilfe* and *Staatshilfe* remained central to the Weimar Republic, the G.D.R. stamped out the last remnants of the *Selbsthilfe* logic left after the Nazi dictatorship and legitimized a Soviet-style political order and full bureaucratic control of the economy as the only possible path to solve the inherent contradictions of the social question which had so plagued the *Kaiserreich* and the Weimar Republic.

If one uses Jürgen Kocka's qualification of the G.D.R. as a 'modern dictatorship' (Kocka 1999) as a starting point, one can interpret state socialism on German soil as an attempt which pushes the organisation of modernity to its extreme limit. While Nazi social engineering attempted to replace the class-based ordering of the social with a holist conception of society based on racial criteria, state socialism rested on a classist definition of society which sought nonetheless to promote a non-antagonistic reading of class relationships through the expropriation of the means of production, cemented by the fiction that the G.D.R. was the sole inheritor of all progressive and anti-fascist forces and traditions in German history (Meuschel 1992). It was not only in the countries to the east of the Iron Curtain that central economic planning was seen to be a viable alternative to the crisis of liberal capitalism and to more corporatist solutions, such as those which had emerged in Germany after 1918. However, unlike the *Kaiserreich*, the relationship between the individual and the collective or the role of the state was no longer an unfolding story of possibilities. In the G.D.R., the solid grip of Party and state over social organisations froze the terms of the debate, stymied or even criminalized attempts to reassert the capacity of self organisation of society. Inherited institutions such as labour unions, professional organisations, political parties and parliament provided for a formal expression of social pluralism, but were denied any capacity to formulate autonomous demands. In other words, one can speak of a fusion or submission of society to political imperatives, and a complete disappearance of categories of the 'civil' from public discourse, although this is hardly the whole story as we will try to show below.

In both contexts one can speak of the domination of 'organized society' built on the perceived need to integrate the totality of the population into the national community through the prism of class identities. This reconfiguration of the social became increasingly institutionalized through representative organisations and institutionalized arenas of representation, and was underpinned on a micro-sociological level by the creation of collective property (welfare entitlements, but also cooperatives). In theory, this guaranteed the possibility of autonomous social action by providing the material basis of stakeholdership in society, means to identify oneself and the Other through social proximity/distance, and identification of one's own interests and values and those of other social groups. Having sketched out some characteristic features of both contexts, we now use empirical examples taken from the question of work and housing to show more precisely the ebb and flow between descriptive languages and social practice.

Work, the Welfare State and Collective Bargaining

During the *Kaiserreich*, salaried employment became the central node of social organisation, the fulcrum of the articulation of the individual to the collective, of the political to the social and the economic (Zimmermann 2001). A multitude of protagonists used work, albeit in varying and often contradictory ways, as a central category in order to conceive a new political and social order. Promoted to a category of public action, work provided the means to edify new collectives and principles of social action. It authorized the reformulation of the question of working-class integration by getting around the limits of civic integration in an authoritarian polity (*Dreiklassenwahlrecht*, extremely limited prerogatives of the *Reichstag* such as the political irresponsibility of the government, repression of unions and socialist political organisations). The conjunction of Bismarckian welfare reforms and the activity of labour unions contributed, albeit with opposing motives, to the creation of new social identities and categories. The social order engendered by worker insurance was centred on class logics, but it also implied reinforced coordination between state and society on the one hand and employers and salaried workers on the other. This increased coordination revolved around risk management through mechanisms of collective bargaining, co-determination and *Selbstverwaltung*. Risk, as it is constructed by Bismarckian legislation, defines collective identities around territorial and professional criteria (Kott 1995). This 'reterritorialisation of social ties' (Ewald 1986) identified risk communities with varying contours depending on the nature of the problem (sickness, workplace accidents, old age, unemployment) and the specific combination of professional and territorial logics associating individuals. Insurance schemes and institutionalized negotiations between employer representatives and unions such as collective bargaining which developed during this period ensured that work, through its function as a social regulator, became a mediating instance between the economic and the political and a factor of social peace. These emerging institutions of co-determination and *Selbstverwaltung* were guaranteed by the oversight of the state and the solidity of professional or even corporatist identities from which a social (and in a more limited fashion an economic) democracy emerged, thereby completing the decades-long process of gradual substitution of grammars based on civil society by subsuming and completing civic society semantics.

The G.D.R. represents a radical redrawing of social boundaries and the definition of the relationship of the individual to the collective, but remains nonetheless in relative continuity to the social semantics based on class which emerged during the *Kaiserreich*. In the G.D.R., a class-based discourse structured official representations of society and state, but contrary to the *Kaiserreich*, the G.D.R. thematized non-antagonistic relations between the classes, albeit signifying the exclusion/expulsion of the propertied classes and the former political elite from the political community as well as the negation of conflicting bases of social identification such as religious or regional identities. In addition, the state was no longer seen as a mere guarantor of co-determination or *Selbstverwaltung*. On the contrary, the methodical nationalization of industry and central economic planning placed the state in a direct relationship with social organisations, a relationship which became quickly unbalanced through the ability of party and state to monopolize material and symbolic resources and its willingness to use physical coercion. Another important difference was the organisation of social insurance through the workplace (Hübner 1994), thereby creating a deterritorialization of collective identities and paradoxically weakening class based identities, by reinforcing collective identification with the workplace.

The legitimacy of the social and political order therefore rested on the mobilization of 'numbers', founding principle of organized society. Despite also being based on the legitimacy of numbers, key elements of 'civic society', such as free elections, parliamentary representation and legal guarantees on the rights of the citizen, were discounted as 'formal' bourgeois democracy, and maintained only as empty shells. The political colonization of mass organisations negated any expression of plurality. Collective interests as defined by the ruling party were superimposed on individual interests to varying degrees of success (Lindenberger 1999), while social classes remained until 1989. However, as we will see, these all-inclusive categories (the class of workers and employees in use from the 1970s onwards, which included the intelligentsia) were a much too unwieldy instrument for bureaucratic procedures, in work and housing as elsewhere, leading to an indexation of individual identities on other collective identities.

The Housing Question

Housing emerged in the mid-nineteenth century as one of the key components of the broader 'social question' (Huber 1857). The barricades of 1848 had demonstrated the potential dangers created by the steady influx of rural populations into the ever expanding cities to feed the labour needs of the industrial sector. The problem of sedentarizing and 'domesticating' this floating and 'dangerous' urban population was constructed as a first and necessary step to integrating the working classes into the national community. As was the case for the question of work, the mechanisms of civic society did not provide for obvious solutions to this new challenge, as the electoral laws guaranteed that property owners keen to block any attempts of public regulation held an automatic municipal majority. In addition, attempts to solicit the central state were structurally doomed to failure as central decision makers saw housing as a problem to be solved by local authorities according to the principle of subsidiarity.[3]

In the mid-nineteenth century, liberal and conservative reformers who remained within the realm of civil society semantics based their hopes on charity and education of the working classes towards more hygienic and moral lifestyles as the path to better the living conditions of the urban working classes (Huber 1857). Others placed their hopes in private ownership based on the British model of 'cottages' (Zimmermann 1991), but the only concrete applications during the *Kaiserreich* were paternalistic solutions, such as those of Krupp in Essen, where entrepreneurs built homes for their workers in an effort to reinforce loyalty to the workplace and to the enlightened entrepreneur. It was only with the development of the public health movement in Germany and its linkage to an increasingly professional municipal administration in big cities, that the first municipal regulations on housing were introduced, giving rise to a process which would eventually blossom in some cities into a highly inventive and wide ranging municipal public housing policy in the Weimar Republic (Reulecke 1997).

The development of a conception of *Staatshilfe* at the municipal level, however limited in scope during the *Kaiserreich*, was reinforced by the creation of institutions based on *Selbsthilfe*. This process did not give rise to a conception of insufficient housing as a risk similar to old age, sickness, and so on. The problem was rather seen to be a consequence of these risks as well as imperfections in the functioning of the housing economy: an increasing number of associations and housing cooperatives pushed for housing reform along the lines of *Selbsthilfe*.

The idea of housing cooperatives was for a long time stigmatized by the revolutionary wing of the S.P.D. and later by the K.P.D. Friedrich Engels (1872) had in effect criticized housing reform based on cooperatives as a trap for the working classes, as cooperatives tied workers to a particular employment basin and could prevent them from exploiting the only real capital they possessed, their labour force. Housing cooperatives represented a form of collective property, built around the sharing of contributions and of risks. By pooling resources of workers who would not be able individually to finance property ownership, cooperatives allowed them to collectively raise credit. At the same time, housing cooperatives also created new links with local administrations and industry, as entrepreneurs and town councils financially supported cooperatives for specific professions or civil servants by lending money or providing land to build on. The number of housing cooperatives grew from 1,342 in 1913 to 4,390 by 1930, and included members of political parties, salaried workers of a business, professional groups, civil servants and members of religious communities.

In the housing sector in the G.D.R., the state controlled both supply, through central planning, and demand, through the administrative rationing of living space and stringent rent controls. This policy was justified by the critical state of housing following the destruction of 20 percent of the housing stock during the war and the claim that central planning and administrative redistribution of existing living space was the only means to solve the century- old 'housing question'. Cooperative housing was reintroduced in the G.D.R. in 1954, but as in other areas, the *Selbsthilfe* component of cooperatives was quickly reduced and cooperatives came under the control of the *Kombinate* to house their workers (Rowell 2004a).

In the day-to-day administration of the housing 'market', the dominant reading of social topography along non-antagonistic class lines was of little use in deciding who got what, when and how. Administrations devised – and had to reconcile – three principles of distribution, each providing partially contradictory linkages of the individual to the collective. To paraphrase Marx, housing was simultaneously distributed to each according to his means, to each according to his needs, and to each according to his politics. Means refers to a retribution based on the reading of the importance of the worker to economic development. In this framework class had less bearing than professions with particular skills that were in short supply or needed in the sectors of the economy that were given utmost priority. But housing was also distributed to 'each according to his needs', in which needs were either based on housing conditions, or social, medical or demographic identities – large families, families with members with a handicap or a contagious disease such as tuberculosis. Thirdly, to each according to his political engagement, which sought to reward political loyalty or allocate resources to those with relations to people in 'high places'.

In other words, the administrative procedures which identify the different qualities of the individual by assigning identities and priorities in the distribution of scarce goods were indexed on collective identities which only partially overlapped the class-based definitions, and produced other principals of distributive justice. What were the effects of this system on the operations of linking the individual to collectives and the relationship of these collectives to society as a whole?

It is interesting to examine how this variety of distributive principles was reappropriated by individuals when they came into conflict with the housing authorities. With the political control exercised on social institutions, the expression of discontent rarely took the form of collective action, but the individual forms can be studied through the analysis of individual letters of petition, or *Eingaben*, the only institutionalized form of administrative recourse in a system without administrative tribunals. The individual letter-writers identified themselves by attaching their personal identities to collective identities. They reappropriated administrative or political categories of society in a strategic manner, thereby identifying themselves in terms of class, if it was to their advantage, or in terms of political loyalty or as valuable contributors to the national economy if this was advantageous. Many emphasized their connections and political relations by joining letters of recommendation, while others attempted to singularize themselves, by placing themselves outside the bureaucratic categories, their suffering, old age or hard luck in life appealing to the compassion of the decision maker (Rowell 2002).

If one looks at the evolution in the use of these collective identities over time, explicit references to social class identities, professional identities or political engagement tended to become more infrequent, while there was an increasing use of argumentative resources based on 'civic society' norms and categories. In the 1970s and 1980s letter-writers increasingly motivated their claims by mobilizing legal arguments (whether laws or central party resolutions) and more frequently asserted decent housing as a right, affirming that the state, as holder of the monopoly on the building and distribution of housing, had an obligation to decently house each and every citizen of the G.D.R.

In general terms, one can view the general erosion of the legitimacy of state socialist regimes during the 1970s and 1980s as the result of a growing discordance between the orthodox communist ordering of the social, still based on class and the neutralization of institutionalized social organisations articulating social interests and identities on the one hand, and the identities and representations of social topography produced in everyday life and interactions with the administration on the other. If in Poland, Hungary or Czechoslovakia, this gap of signification was filled (at least in part) with the semantics and the beginnings of a self-organizing civil society; in the G.D.R., collective action based on civil society remained very limited. However, one can argue that there was a return, if partial, diffuse, and on an individual level, to the norms of a 'civic society' to order the social in the face of the increasing inoperativeness of class categories (not to speak of national identities in the G.D.R.), to not only make sense of the world, and to attribute one's place with regard to others, but also, and perhaps most importantly, in the daily operations of state institutions themselves, which sorted and classified individuals with categories other than those which dominated public discourse.[4]

To conclude, one can schematically resume the two case studies in the following way: In the *Kaiserreich*, the reconfiguring of social space between the individual and the polity during the period of rapid industrialization and nation building was partly the work of the state, but also partly of a self-organisation of society which sought to recreate links between the individual and the collective on the basis of class structures within the framework of the nation-state. The civic and social principles structured the social and the political, although not without friction and debate. Their pre-eminence ensured that the 'civil society' semantics and themes were pushed to the margins. The hereditary rights of the aristocrat and the bourgeois became less 'natural' and their centrality in the social and political order progressively yielded to the figure of the citizen, bearer of civic and social rights granted and guaranteed by the state. This long process changed the contours of the public sphere, modified the forms of expression and the regulation of conflicting social and political interests in the public domain. The G.D.R., on the other hand, inherited the framework of an organized society but pushed its logic to the extreme, while amputating the *Selbsthilfe* dimension and reinforcing the authoritarian bureaucratic features contained in *Staatshilfe*. However, bureaucratic overload set into motion a process by which the institutions of 'organized society' lost their ability to provide individuals with a cognitive and procedural framework which structured collective identities on a professional or territorial basis.

Contrary to some other state socialist societies, the 'vacuum' was not filled by an attempt to reorganize society along the lines of a civil society, but rather took the shape of a limited re-motivation of the 'civic', based on individual rights of the citizen (to vote, to travel freely, to be decently housed, and so on). From these developments it becomes clear that the relationship of social paradigms to the state is essential in getting a better grip on the specific combinations of these forms of social (self)organisation. We examine this aspect more closely here before returning to more contemporary issues of the relationship between the civil, the civic and the social in a context where class and the nation, the two founding principals that structured organized modernity, are increasingly challenged.

Collective Identities and Configurations of the State

If the previous section centred attention on the issue of collective identities in the context of the 'social question', in this third section we focus our attention on the relationship between collective forms and the configurations of the state. The starting point of our discussion is the widely held idea that civil society is autonomous of the state, or somehow outside its grasp. This claim is of course central to the rebirth of the concept in Eastern Europe during the 1970s, where civil society proved to be a powerful arm to criticize state socialist systems which had more or less neutralized society as an autonomous sphere of action. If this powerful affirmation of a form of legitimacy outside of the sphere of state control proved to be extremely corrosive to communist authority in Eastern Europe, its use in Western Europe and elsewhere has not been without consequence on the legitimacy of state institutions. This reading of civil society seems however to imply that in a system based on 'organized modernity', social relations were entirely orchestrated and subservient to the state. In this light, the *Kaiserreich* and the G.D.R. can be seen as a sort of litmus test in that both states were authoritarian in character and groups were predominantly articulated in relation to the state which sought to limit, or at the least to rationalize and render more predictable, the pluralistic expression of social interests. However, at the same time, it would be too simplistic to assert that social relations were entirely organized *by* the state – at least in the *Kaiserreich*. It may be more exact to think of society as a mediating space *between* the state, the individual and the economy.

Contrary to the idea of a binary opposition between state and society, which is implicitly included in the contemporary conception of civil society, our historical retrospective will place the emphasis on the plurality of possible configurations between social groups and state institutions. In doing this, we will attempt to cast light on the dynamic nature of this interaction, on give and take and collusion between state and societal actors which cannot be reduced to a 'zero sum' game. This pragmatic approach to the state through the prism of specific sectors of public action such as worker insurance, unemployment and housing, builds a picture of the state as a complex reality in constant evolution. This holds even for authoritarian states such as the *Kaiserreich* and the G.D.R. (Zimmermann 2001: 167ff.).

This differentiated approach to the state and public action seems essential to countering methodological pitfalls such as reliance on a priori reasoning or excessive modelization which oversimplifies complex realities. Anchoring theoretical speculation in empirical observation is vital if one is to avoid reified models of the state, sweeping generalizations or a reduction of the state to a mysterious black box where inputs are magically transformed into outputs. This implies that the state is not a given, an intangible and pre-existing structure, but rather a complex and contradictory set of institutions traversed by competing efforts to frame social reality (Goffman 1974). Following Max Weber, the state can be defined as a category that represents determined types of human cooperation (Weber 1964: 1034ff.). Consequently, the fluidity of the boundaries between state and society or even the imbrications between the two terms comes into view, thereby revealing the supposed hermetic analytical separation of state and society as a fiction (Birnbaum 1982).

The impulsion for the lively associative culture of the *Kaiserreich* did not emanate from the national political and administrative institutions. A number of associations pushing for social reforms, such as the *Verein für Socialpolitik*, the *Gesellschaft für Sozialreform*, the *Verband Deutscher Städtestatistiker*, the *Verband Deutscher Arbeitsnachweis*, the *Städtetag* or union organisations created a dense network advocating policy reforms. Vectors of innovation and laboratories of social enquiry and experimentation (Schiera 1992; Nipperdey 1986), these associations did not perceive their action to be part of social self-organisation autonomous from the state or in opposition to it, thereby making the use of 'civil society' as a label to qualify such organisations quite problematic. On the contrary, the activity of these reformist networks was directed towards the state and sought to place the reformist projects on the central state agenda, with the aim of reinforcing state intervention, seen as essential to meeting the challenges of industrialization and rapid social transformation.

As a result, associations were theorized as being complementary to the state rather than in opposition to it. As a space of solidarity and self-organisation of individuals, a tightly woven fabric of associations was, in the liberal conception of Robert von Mohl and Lorenz von Stein, a necessary intermediary between the individual and the state, a space of social self-regulation which could help take the wind out of the emerging class conflicts (Pankoke 1972). Associative life was therefore intellectually constructed as a space to regulate conflicting social interests in society. In this capacity, associations played an essential role in the liberal conception of the German state and the theory of subsidiarity as a space of dialogue and confrontation which structured public debates. But if associations did structure the debates on public policy in many areas, for the most part they were unable to translate their proposals and objectives into policy at the national level (Zimmermann 2001: chap. 7). This shows the extent to which collective actors organized around the semantics of the 'social' are nevertheless confronted with the 'civic' problematic of the accessibility (or inaccessibility) to state structures.

The general problem of accessibility to the state needs to be further specified and thought of in terms of the differentiated political and administrative scenes in which associative actors and political actors interact on different levels in a game fraught with conflict, compromise and mutual instrumentalization. As we have already shown, at the level of national politics and even at the level of the regional states, formal democratic procedures did little to counterbalance authoritarian structures which largely insulated these political scenes from societal input. It was at the municipal level where the boundaries were the most porous between public institutions and private interests. However, even at the national level one can observe intense exchanges between representatives of interest groups and political or administrative personnel which created a 'reformist constellation' (Topalov 1999) via the *Verein für Socialpolitik*, for example.

Differential degrees of accessibility to the political spheres therefore depended on the identities of the actors involved, the policy fields in question and the issues at stake. The conditions of access to political institutions produced effects in return on the strategies and structures of social organisations operating in and around these fields. One can describe this relationship as a kind of homology between the differentiated political fields and organized interests.[5] Even those who were strongly attached to *Selbsthilfe* and opposed *Staatshilfe* did not conceive of their action without reference to public intervention. The latter enabled action, by providing legal guarantees and laws to frame the scope of individual liberties and contractual arrangements. If the logic of *Selbsthilfe* is hostile to bureaucratic reforms imposed from above, state intervention, in the form of neutral arbitration and conciliation, was nonetheless considered to be essential to the ability of non-state actors to resolve the social question. As a result, even for the most hardy tenants of liberalism or social self-organisation in Germany, the state was seen to be essential to guarantee liberties and procedures for peaceful conflict resolution (liberty of association, right to strike, and so on). During the *Kaiserreich*, the state was viewed as a mediator or even an arbiter in the process of collective organisation, even by those who did not enjoy direct access to centres of decision or those who were hostile to direct state intervention.

The G.D.R. shared the authoritarian characteristics of the *Kaiserreich* but the party-state made any autonomous attempts at accessing the central state all but impossible. The tight grip on 'mass' organisations and unions severely limited forms of articulation of social interests and transformed them, at least in theory, into 'conveyor belts' of the will of the Politbüro of the ruling party. The extreme centralization of the state and the bulimic concentration of decision-making at the central level meant that decision-makers were totally reliant on information provided them by disciplined state and party bureaucracies. This extremely hierarchical articulation of state-society relationships tended to rigidify the moving borders and sectoral differences between central state actors and social dynamics which had existed during the *Kaiserreich* and the Weimar Republic.

However, both within these organisations and above all outside them, informal horizontal interactions developed based on instrumental networks of exchange, allowing for a partial compensation of the rigidities of institutionalized interest articulation (Huinink and Mayer 1995). In other words, the increasingly formal and ritualized forms of integration of social logics into the state apparatus stimulated the development of informal modes of interest articulation, centred largely on individual and informal interactions rather than on the expression of pluralistic collective interests which could be construed by the ruling party as a challenge to its authority. For example, faced with the failure of the state to repair or to modernize old housing stock, many inhabitants mobilized family, friends and relations to acquire, sometimes illegally, building materials and skilled workmen to do the job. The same dynamics were at work in the extensive building of 'datchas', some quite elaborate, in what one could call informal forms of *Selbsthilfe*. This process can also be seen in the partial instrumentalization of workers' brigades for private purposes (Kott 2001), but also in the working of housing commissions. These were formed by volunteers, and part of the routine tasks of housing allotment fell on their shoulders. In order to prevent a demobilization of these volunteers, the administration had to allow them limited forms of autonomy in deciding who got what type of housing and when. In other words, what ensued was a widening gap between informal networks based on trust, mutual give and take, and face to face relations, and the organized, highly centralized network of organisations controlled by the party (Rowell 2004b). Why did this not result in the development of a civil society discourse as in other central European countries with the onset of economic stagnation and eroding legitimacy of party leaders in the 1980s?

One can portray the emergence of a civil society discourse in much of Central Europe as the result not only of the erosion of the legitimacy of party dictatorship, but also as a crisis of the languages used to describe society, the state and the relationships between them. After the failure of attempts to reform and to humanize state socialism from within (in 1956,

1968, and so on), dissatisfaction with the existing order in Central Europe brought critical intellectuals to try to transform society from 'without', from another locus of social legitimacy seeking to modify the perception of society and its relationship to the state. In Poland, or to a lesser degree in Czechoslovakia, critical intellectuals were able to disassociate the connection between class and nation which was central to the claims of legitimacy of the dominant communist parties, and to mobilize (and redefine) a society on the basis of a civil society discourse by using the nation and/or religious identities (as in Poland) as unifying principles. This option was not available in the G.D.R. where other 'outsider strategies' such as 'exit' (Hirschmann 1970, 1993) in the form of emigration was a possibility (both for the protagonists and for the state, in the case of Wolf Biermann). Organized opposition of the 1980s rallied around 'moral causes', pacifism, ecology, individual rights such as the freedom to travel, to voice dissent, denunciation of electoral fraud and other issues simultaneously based on universal human values and rights centred on the individual. This individualized expression of rights based on citizenship and activating the semantics of 'civic society' was also at work in the correspondence of frustrated candidates for housing. Critical discourse insisting on 'civic' norms rather than 'civil' ones were more pronounced in the G.D.R. than in other Central European contexts due to the weakness of religious or national based forms of collective identity and the prevalence of individual and informal modes of access to state structures.

The renewed interest in civil society in Western Europe since the 1980s via Central Europe has coloured the term with a distinct connotation placing it in opposition to the state. While civil society could be used in the context of the *Kaiserreich* to qualify the vivacity and the relative autonomy of the associative movements in the sectors we have discussed, the retroprojection of current conceptions of civil society could be misleading. Social organisations were not pursuing an agenda opposed to the state, but rather were seeking access to it. In addition, while current conceptions of civil society place the emphasis on pluralistic deliberation, on fluidity and inclusion which deconstruct established social categories, representative institutions and decision making procedures, the associations in the *Kaiserreich* sought to work together with state actors (where this was possible) in a common effort of stabilizing, reshaping and making intelligible the social. This process contributed to the reduction of the plurality and uncertainty at a time when social and political changes were taking place at breathtaking speed.

This is where a historical comparison between current changes in the relationship between governments and the governed and past models of state-society articulation can be helpful. Current uses of civil society discourse and norms convey, in the context of established democratic welfare states, a critical dimension not unlike that which was successfully turned against state socialism. In its many variants, civil society discourse seeks to reinvent democracy, to further political pluralism and inclusiveness, to remedy the perceived sclerosis of the welfare state and of corporatist arrangements, to modernize bureaucratic structures, and so on. In its critique of organized modernity, civil society discourse stigmatizes the inherited institutions and patterns of engagement between society, the state and the economy as obsolete and 'old fashioned', a normative charge which is equally shared by neo-Tocquevilleian liberals, representatives of the 'new left', heralds of the 'third way' (Giddens 1998) and by political representatives (particularly in such supranational institutions as the European Union). If the existing institutions, collective identities and procedures have undoubtedly been increasingly contested over the past decades, does civil society provide a credible alternative or even a mechanism to complete and reinvigorate existing democratic institutions without further undermining them?

Power, Procedures and the Reordering of the Social

One could claim, from a Kuhnian perspective, that the development of a new grammar of civil society in the last decades is linked to the diagnosis that the existing languages, social and political institutions and arrangements have lost their ability to accurately describe social phenomena, and that beliefs in the capacity of 'old' social institutions to articulate the individual to the collective are waning.

This diagnosis is well known and can be resumed by several key words: crisis of the welfare state, which is not only budgetary, but also philosophical; crisis and decline of 'old' forms of social representation and institutions such as unions, employer organisations, churches, parliamentary democracy, the family, which are seen to be too unresponsive, too unrepresentative, too corporatist, or too 'out of touch' with rapidly changing realities; crisis of the nation-state and the emergence of multi-level governance; crisis of the political elite, too cut off from the preoccupations of ordinary citizens, and a decline of traditional forms of participation in the political process.

Independent of their political or even ideological dimensions, the current debates on 'globalization' imply a radical rethinking of the roles played by the state, the nation and established institutions in the structuring of interactions between the individual (and families) and the collective, in much the same way that the crisis of 'liberal modernity' provoked a proliferation of social enquiry in the middle of the nineteenth century. The modern nation-state, constituted between 1850 and 1970 as a constructor of relations of equivalence between heterogeneous and often contradictory political, social and economic logics, has been confronted with growing difficulties in playing such a role over the past thirty years. These difficulties have given rise to the production of a plethora of signifiers built around the notions of plurality, flexibility and mobility which have become the new political and economic imperatives. There was accordingly a movement seeking to unfetter a series of institutional and cognitive constraints, an opening of the horizon of possibilities which stands in stark contrast to the period 1850 to 1970, characterized by the quest for a reduction of plurality centred on the definition of generic principals of equivalence making possible (if imperfectly) the organisation of society around the central logic of numbers (Desrosières 1993). And this is precisely where the concept of civil society seems essential: simultaneously an *indicator* of the recent shifts in social organisation, and an *operator* of this shift by transforming social practice and collective identities.

One of the defining characteristics of civil society, and for that matter, the core of its claim as a legitimate form of collective organisation (and as an analytical tool), rests precisely on the principal of pluralism; in other words the openness and fluidity of social organisation and its indetermination, central to claims of greater individual liberties and autonomy at the heart of the innovative potential of a reinforced civil society. The re-emergence of the semantics of civil society as an analytical tool to describe the space between the private, the economic and political sphere was not only made possible by the erosion of the capacity of other words to describe current changes but also by the linkage between the analytical and the normative dimensions of the concept based on the systematic opposition between the 'new' and the 'old'. This opposition has taken several forms, such as innovation and reactivity versus resistance to change, horizontal relations as opposed to vertical relations, creativity as opposed to rigidity, participation versus delegation, autonomy and self-realization versus dependency and hierarchy, self-organisation versus co-optation, and the list can go on.[6] In other words, these different semantic registers have opened an interpretative space for a concept meaning many things to many people (Gosewinkel and Reichardt 2004). Civil society is used by social and political actors in competition with one another as well as by scholars or intellectuals who see their role as making shifts in society and in polity intelligible. Without going so far as to lend these uses a performative function, the replacement of 'old' semantics by the 'new' is not a neutral operation,[7] but has accompanied and perhaps accelerated the reshaping of the way we think about the mediation between private and public.

Two important questions arise: (1) How far does civil society, as an *analytical concept*, allow us to understand and describe current socio-political transformations? What does the concept allow us to see, and what might its use mask from sight? (2) Does the *normative* dimension of the concept give a framework for these transformations – in other words, does it provide a viable alternative to inherited institutional arrangements and institutions? While it is impossible to provide definitive answers to such questions, we will at least try to raise five points an link these broad contemporary questions to the historical cases presented above.

(1) The uses of civil society in Eastern Europe and Western Europe since the 1970s differ in the degree to which they contest state-centred arrangements: in the east by setting up a 'counter society' outside all state-directed social organisations and decision-making structures; and in the west as a tool to renew, complete and reinvigorate a model of state-society arrangements centred on the welfare state. The 'rediscovery' of civil society in the west, via the critical intellectuals in the east, nonetheless resulted in a relatively radical separation of civil society organisations and practices from the state (and from the economy) which has proved to be extremely corrosive to the arrangements, social institutions and collective identities structured around the compromises which emerged a century ago during the constitution of the welfare state.

This raises two questions. The first is the problem of using civil society to describe situations and contexts in which the actors and commentators do not use the term. In the *Kaiserreich*, one can speak of civil society in the sense of a dynamic and relatively free emergence of self-organizing groups and associations. However, if we were to transpose the idea of free deliberation, of openness and fluidity which marks the current conceptions of the functioning and the objectives of civil society organisations and procedures, we would miss the fact that most societal organisations in the *Kaiserreich* sought to increase the predictability of social interactions by institutionalizing procedures and groups, by linking the individual to the collective and the collective to the state.

The second question is the relationship between the three paradigms of social order which we outlined in the first section. As we saw, the ordering of the social which occurred during the *Kaiserreich* sought to complete and to structure the 'civic order' by providing institutional and cognitive links between individuals and collectives. What is the relationship between civil society, civic and organized society today? Does the recourse to the civil compensate for deficits or shortcomings of organized modernity, as some definitions would have it, or does the critical potential undermine both the civic order and the inherited social order? As we have argued, civil society is built upon the norms of self-organisation, on plurality, indetermination and the fluidity of social organisation. In this respect it is simultaneously complementary to the two other organisations of the intermediate space between the individual and the state, but it also opposes the two, in the sense that the legitimizing principle of plurality can be seen as being opposed to 'numbers'-based legitimacy in its civic variant (votes, referendums, parliament) or its social variant (representative interest groups, neocorporatist arrangements, social insurance, and so on). If this last interpretation is correct, does civil society provide a viable alternative? In other words, can procedural legitimacy built on plurality and inclusiveness replace numbers-based legitimacy at the heart of representative institutions as a workable form of organisation of a multi-level polity?

(2) Trying to answer this question brings us to a second broad point. It displaces the centre of gravity of the definition of civil society away from its organisational aspects, which, as we have seen, raise a number of problems, towards the procedural aspects of the notion which is espoused, at least formally, by all the players of the civil society game. In this light, civil society is essentially a procedural question, an arrangement with minimally predefined rules of engagement between participants in deliberative decision-making. All the players agree to abide by a series of guiding principals imposed by an 'external', mediating entity taking the form of the state (in a wide sense, that is not limited to the nation-state): (a) discussion and communication as the overarching norm of engagement, fluid arenas or forums of discussion (Callon, Lascoumes and Barthes 2001) where there is no pre-established dominant player and where there is a principle of equality between all participants; (b) discussion and deliberation as a rational means to obtaining agreements; (c) agreements which may be contractualized and codified, but which are never definitive, and therefore open to rediscussion and constant adjustment.

These norms are not only prevalent in the space of social self-organisation, but also have become increasingly important as a form of interaction between civil society organisations and economic or political actors. They have even become a dominant mode of functioning, at least on paper, in such international organisations as the European Union with its 'open method of coordination' (De La Porte and Pochet 2002). If one is to adopt for a moment a cybernetic metaphor, one can say that civil society in its effects on public action signifies a rearrangement or reordering of inputs, by marginalizing institutional gatekeepers, by fluidifying pre-existing social and political categories, and by opening up the public sphere to new issues and to marginalized social groups. However, if one turns to the 'outputs', the problem becomes more delicate. One can argue that the diffusion of the procedures characteristic of civil society has simultaneously weakened the social basis and the procedures of civic and social society (increasing voter apathy, decreasing 'classical' forms of political participation and engagement, contesting of the representativity of unions, political parties, employer groups, religious communities, and so on), and at the same time failed to produce new categories of public action (legal definitions, populations identified and targeted for public action, and so on) with enough stability and solidity to make decisions 'stick' and to become binding for all members of a polity. In the world of organized society (at least in societies with democratic procedures), the arenas of decision were structured by the respective 'weight' of the participants based on the number of citizens they were credited with representing. In the procedures of civil society, where no participant can be legitimately excluded, where inclusiveness and not numbers structure deliberations, it is difficult to see how binding decisions engaging the entire population of a polity can emerge.

This dilemma carries with it two apparently contradictory risks: On the one hand, the fact that many international organisations appear to build their democratic credentials on a 'dialogue' with civil society without making a concerted effort to build 'numbers' based legitimacy (either through elections or through neo-corporatist arrangements) opens the problem of the instrumentalisation of NGOs, and a reduction of civil society to a series of 'selected' NGOs commonly denounced in the civil society literature. It points to the risks of an autonomisation of the political sphere, particularly acute with the increasing delegation of policy decisions to regulatory agencies placed outside the control of representative institutions. On the other hand, one can identify the opposite risk, more perceptible in the context of the nation-state, in which civil society procedures and discourse have undermined beliefs in collective social actors (and their representatives) and thereby eroded functioning categories and instruments of public action without having contributed to the emergence of minimally stabilized alternatives. The problem, in other words, is that the open-endedness, the fluidity and undetermined nature of civil society procedures undermine any attempts to define and stabilize a definition of the 'public good', or even the interests or the identities of collective groups, thereby failing to act as an effective counterbalance to the powerful individualizing forces of 'turbo capitalism' which raises the spectre of an increasingly atomized society.

(3) Civil society discourse and procedures pervade political and bureaucratic structures keen to draw upon the legitimizing force of this new imperative. Ideas and procedures such as 'governance', contractualizing, public/private partnerships, open coordination, new public management, the increasing recourse of political parties to candidates from 'civil society', are expressions of this rising awareness that 'top-down' decision-making and implementation no longer seems

adequate in an increasingly plural and fluid social reality. In a nutshell, these procedures seek to reinforce linkages to the governed which have become distended through the crisis of traditional forms of representation.

But where does this leave the concept and ideals of civil society, first invented in the eighteeth century in the context of absolutism and later rediscovered as a tool to contest bureaucratic socialism and the rigidities of the welfare state? The dilution of the boundaries between state and non-state actors and institutions raises the problem of performance evaluation and, more fundamentally, the question of responsibility and accountability through the essential operations of assigning blame and credit where it is due. This interweaving of public and private, of the social and the political, could paradoxically lead to a weakening of the capacity of individuals to organize and mobilize, as one of the key repertoires to the constitution of collective actors and action is founded on the triptych 'naming, blaming, claiming'. Not only does this raise the question of mobilization and participation, but perhaps more fundamentally, these new modes of public action sap many of the foundations of popular democratic sovereignty. Contrary to representative institutions, whether they be parliamentary or corporative in nature, many of the public institutions legitimized through procedural inclusion of organized civil society are not bound by social input as would be the case (if imperfectly) by an electoral mandate. As a result, many institutions, such as the growing number of independent regulatory agencies seeking to reinforce popular legitimacy through 'open' coordination with organized groups from civil society, have a more or less free hand, as they are not responsible to voters and as the input from civil society organisations is consultative.[8]

(4) This brings us to the fourth point, related to the procedural dimensions of the civil society concept: the question of power relations within civil society organisations which are usually only mentioned when discussing the instrumentalisation of civil society by the state or other political bodies (the infamous GONGOs, for example). By placing the emphasis on equal and open access to deliberation, on plurality and inclusion, the question of asymmetric resources and power relationships is largely absent from the debate, perhaps due to the slippage between the normative and the analytic aspects of the concept. The master word of procedural civil society discourse is the figure of consensus-building, a notion which is not far from consent of the governed in more classical terminology. In other words, the prevalence of civil society discourse and practice has operated a shift away from overt conflict and opposition in decision-making and public action (crystallized, for example, in the oppositions between capital and labour, or political parties polarized

around left and right or government and opposition, or the majority and the minority) to a more consensual, depoliticized political culture (Jobert 2003). However, a vast body of scientific literature has emerged since the 1950s which has discussed the sociological limits to the pluralist school of political science, criticisms ranging from the unequal ability of groups and individuals to mobilize and get their interests heard, to the ability of dominant groups in society to restrict access to the arenas of decision. In other words, while the civil society concept provides in theory for an increased potential for citizen involvement and say in who gets what, when and how, the sociological reality of the capacity to participate, not to speak of the capacity or the competence necessary to weigh on the outcome of discussions and deliberation, remains one of unequal access to these forums of discussion. This inequality becomes perhaps even greater in the context of forums on the supranational or international level, where NGOs are increasingly professionalized and armed with expertise. A group's claims are therefore most likely to be heard because of the ability of its representatives to produce an immediately recognizable and 'useful' discourse for political and administrative decision-makers, and not because of the number of citizens it purports to represent.

(5) This brings us to a final point: the problem of participation seen in a historical perspective. A number of recent contributions to the debate on 'social capital' have advanced the argument that the development of the welfare state actually reinforced the vitality of non-state and non-market associations, thereby putting a dent in the commonly held idea that a lively and dynamic civil society requires a relatively weak and self-limiting state (see the contributions of Skocpol, Perez-Diaz, Worms in Putnam 2002). Of course, as the Eastern European example shows, an overly strong state does not guarantee the unfolding of civil society, although it does seem in some instances to have furthered informal networks and trust, working both within and outside official institutions while opposing them. However, as we – and others – have argued, autonomous social organisations emerged historically in close relation (and not just in opposition) to the specific forms and structures of state and nation building. In particular they were related to the welfare state (Skocpol 1992; Tarrow 1996), which appeared to have provided a solution to the problems of 'bridging' between social capital and trust on an interpersonal level and trust in broader overarching institutions.

One of the principal challenges of the later half of the nineteenth century consisted in the task of 'bridging' between the individual/ interpersonal and the collective through the organisation of society around class and the nation, and in particular (but not only) the institutions of the welfare state which assigned identities, created classes of equivalence, mechanisms of solidarity and sharing of risk between members of the same national polity. While these measures tended to rigidify identities and social institutions by tying them into highly codified and bureaucratized institutional arrangements, they also reduced uncertainty and provided clear categories on which public action could be articulated and debated. However, at the same time, the integrative (if rigid and totalising) logic of organized society can also be seen as a precondition to the unfolding of the 'civic society', as it solved the problem of the relationship of property ownership to citizenship, by providing the emerging social groups who had no property but their own labour with 'collective' or 'social property' (Castel and Haroche 2001), thereby transforming the – *de jure* or *de facto* – disenfranchised into stakeholders in the polity and bearers of a legitimacy and a 'dignity' sufficiently stable to authorize their participation in public affairs. With the decline of the 'social state' and the fluidification of the social, the question remains open whether the identity resources linking individuals to the collective are consistent enough to ensure the sociological conditions for an effective participation of the majority, or whether pluralism will supplant 'numbers' as the ultimate form of social and political legitimacy, at the risk of being confiscated by a minority of 'super citizens', with the time and the identity and cognitive resources necessary to realize the normative ideals of civil society.

Conclusion

This last point is a essential to the question of the emergence of a European civil society which is developing (or being developed) without solid pre-existing substrata of 'civic society' based on citizenship rights corresponding to the European polity (on the development of a European civil society, see Kaelble 2003). European citizenship rights remain embryonic and the results of elections for the European parliament do not significantly alter political outcomes in EU policy or the composition of the governing elites of the EU. In addition, the institutions associated with organized modernity which were forged on a purely national level are practically non-existent at the European level and increasingly challenged at the national level. Can civil society develop and realize its normative potential for emancipation without a solid basis of civic society, or the integrative aspects of organized modernity at a supranational level? Can the structuring of social relations on the sole basis of civil society norms, where organized society institutions are relegated to the ever weakened level of the nation-state and where civic society is blurred by the multiplication of territories of sovereignty and citizenship, remain democratic, if one accepts the egalitarian dimension of sovereignty in a democracy as 'one man (or woman), one vote'? The answer to this question depends in part on the vision of the future of the European Union: that of a Europe limited in social policy to regulating procedures leaving responsibility for the conception and maintaining of social equity and justice to the member states, or that of a European Union which takes the risk of constructing a collective normative and ethical framework capable of resynchronizing the civic, the civil and the social in the multiple overlapping polities of contemporary Europe.

Notes

1. As opposed to atomized individuals theorized by the totalitarian model or atomized or radical individualism in market economies.
2. The current debate on civil society is posed in similar terms. For example, Lars Jorgensen envisions civil society as a 'meeting place for debate and common endeavor', implying 'the right of each individual to participate in the workings of society, and the recognition that periodical elections and referendums are not sufficient' (Jorgensen 1996: 36).
3. It was only the outbreak of First World War which incited the *Reichstag* to vote the first of a series of nationwide laws protecting the dependants of soldiers mobilized for the war effort from eviction.
4. Helmut Steiner showed that in the mid-1960s each political party, administration or mass organisation had its own way of categorizing its members. As a result, more than 20 different ways of classifying social identity and origin coexisted in a political system perceived to be perfectly centralized (Steiner 1997: 246).
5. It is precisely the lack of congruence between the structuring of policy fields at the level of the European Union and the organisation of interest groups at the European polity that is one of the key challenges to the European project.
6. The inextricable link between the analytical and the positively connoted normative dimensions of the concept and the fact that most attempts to define civil society do not proceed by designating what civil society is, but rather what it is not (i.e. non-state and non-economic actors) poses the problem of the inclusion or exclusion of groups corresponding to this definition but which are constructed on values which do not correspond to the positively connoted analytical/normative inferences of civil society (religious fundamentalists, tribal organisations, communitarian groups, the mafia or GONGOS, etc.). Attempts to refine the definition by placing the emphasis on self-reflexivity or procedural criteria such as 'open' decision-making or participation could be a solution to this problem, but entail the problem of ad hoc theorizing, and risk drawing arbitrary boundaries. What seems essential is not the typology or the a priori definition of what is or is not a civil society, but the process by which new social semantics emerge, which leaves room for historical contingency, and allows one to understand how many of the 'old' social institutions and organisations have themselves embraced the semantics of civil society, to counter the erosion of their existing bases of legitimacy.
7. As the central European uses of the concept of civil society in the 1970s and 1980s show (see chapter 6), this signifier does contain a powerful normative and practical potential to subvert other languages of society and to produce real effects on the signified.

8. For example, during the recent convention to draft a European constitutional treaty, representatives of organized civil society were given three minutes to voice their claims. This exemplifies the norms of inclusion, but also demonstrates the limits of the exercise, as groups of different sizes and importance were given the same amount of time to make their case, and this consultation of civil society occurred during the exploratory phase of the drafting of the constitution before the delegates got down to the 'serious' business.

Part III

Widening

Chapter 6

THE SECOND RENAISSANCE OF CIVIL SOCIETY IN EAST CENTRAL EUROPE – AND IN THE EUROPEAN UNION

Jody Jensen and Ferenc Miszlivetz

It has become quite common to talk about a revival of the concept of civil society from the 1980s onwards and to identify East Central Europe as one major site of that revival. This chapter provides a critical review of these occurrences, but, beyond taking stock of the civil society debate in East Central Europe, it aims at elaborating a broader European perspective. Our analysis emphasizes the historically specific forms of interaction between East Central European countries and the West during the post-Second World War years that witnessed a series of major political and economic transformations and the gradual dismantling of the welfare state in the respective parts of the European continent. It is argued that, although genuine dialogue between the two parts of Europe was impeded before 1989, these transformations shaped significantly the nature of the emerging NGOs and, as a consequence, had a large impact on the developing forms of democracy and civil society in Europe. New practices have arguably become available to individual and collective actors of civil society since 1989 and the concurrent creation of a radically new language on the issue suggests a renaissance of the civil society debate and the opening up of new avenues for the conceptualisation of the polity and for political *praxis* both in Europe and globally. Furthermore, though, it is argued that we are witnessing a passage from traditional modes of dialogical negotiations between governmental organisations and civil society actors to the processes of *co-*

optation of civil society. By using the term co-optation, we attempt to conceptually grasp – and critically discuss – the potential dissolution of sharp antagonisms and contradictions in the globally emerging contexts of interaction between states and new forms of civil society. The rebirth of the concept and the formulation of a new vocabulary and language can be traced to such important social movements as *Solidarnosc* in East Central Europe.

The Message of *Solidarnosc* and the Language of Civil Society before 1989

Entrapped in the ambiguities of the Yalta system's *Realpolitik*, East Central European societies proceeded on a long path of learning in order to find the right language and modes of self-organization and articulation required to defend their values and identities vis-à-vis dictatorship and authoritarian rule. Revolts and revolutions of workers and intellectuals during the 1950s, and the more peaceful but radical reforms 'from above' that culminated in the Prague Spring in 1968, were heroic, but ineffective experiments.[1] At the same time, these bitter lessons contributed a great deal to the emergence of a new political philosophy and 'strategy' and to the social practice of civil society. The emancipatory powers of East Central Europe needed new ways and forms for self-expression. Adam Michnik's reconceptualization of civil society heralded a new language which arose from strong needs that could not find proper channels for expression.

> The essence of spontaneously growing Independent and Self-governing Labour Union solidarity lay in the restoration of social ties, self-organization aimed at guaranteeing the defense of labor, civil, and national rights. For the first time in the history of communist Poland 'civil society' was being restored, and it was reaching a compromise with the state. (Michnik 1985: 124)

This development would not have been possible without a gradual but nonetheless fundamental change in political thinking and strategy expressed in the renaissance of civil society that was necessarily coupled with the birth of a new language. Curiously enough, at another periphery, Latin America, discussions around the same kinds of ideas were taking place simultaneously. According to Fernando Cardoso, 'In Brazilian political language, everything which was an organized fragment was being designated civil society. Not rigorously, but effectively, the whole opposition ... was being described as if it were the movement of Civil Society' (cited in Kaldor 2003: 75; see chapter 7 for a broader discussion).

Although no direct link can be found between intellectuals in the two peripheries, Mary Kaldor admits the term reflected an emerging reality in

Latin America that echoed the way it was used in East Central Europe. She quotes the Brazilian Francisco Weffort whose words parallel those of Jacek Kuron, arguing the need for the rebirth of civil society:

> The discovery that there was something more to politics than the state began with the simplest facts of life of the persecuted. In the most difficult moments, they had to make use of what they found around them. There were no parties to go to, no courts in which they could have confidence. At a difficult time, the primary resource was the family, friends and in some cases a fellow worker. What are we talking about if not civil society, though still at the molecular level of interpersonal relations? In a situation of enormous ideological complexity, the discovery of civil society was much less a question of theory than of necessity. (Kaldor 2003: 75)

Driven by a curious missionary spirit, the Communist parties in East Central Europe considered it their duty to either cut the horizontal fibres of civil society, or to hinder their development. Society, they believed, kneaded into an atomized mass, would indeed deliver reliable and obedient subjects. The state, intertwined with the Communist party, helped to demobilize society in many different ways: by the dismantling of democratic and social actors, and by monopolizing interest intermediation through the 'etatization' of trade unions, and so on. By far the most effective means of demobilization was the atomization of society through the destruction of social networks and the undermining of social identities and value systems (see chapter 5 above for an analysis of the case of the G.D.R.).

Fortunately, the complete liquidation of civil society failed. Undercurrents of civil existence were never totally eradicated from the collective consciousness. Social networks survived in semi-latent and semi-legitimate forms, and in the mid-1960s their slow regeneration began. After the trauma of the 1956 Revolution, the nature of the dictatorship started to change throughout Soviet bloc countries. A 'paternalism' or 'enlightened socialist absolutism' emerged in Poland and Hungary that was in harmony with the precariousness and transitory character of East Central European history. The early attempts at liberation taught independent-minded East Europeans to look for alternative methods to democratize their regimes and increase autonomy and political, social and cultural freedom within the seemingly stable framework of the bipolar world order.

In Hungary, the first alternative was the introduction of economic reforms and a cautious, state-controlled opening towards the world economy without political change in the 1960s. The internal contradictions of this reform experiment reached a climax in the early 1980s and led to the end of the unwritten compromise between the state and society. The artificially maintained image of the country as an economic success story became untenable. This was the historic turning point for Hungarian society that then started to rid itself of political paralysis and social muteness. Self-mobilization from below, in different grassroots activities, gradually emerged. With the evolving political and economic crises, the culture of silence was gradually replaced with more open dialogue among formerly isolated circles of independent-minded citizens. Cautiously, the media became involved in the new critical discourse and the long list of taboo themes began to shrink. In other words, a new public arena emerged to openly and critically discuss social, environmental, cultural and, in a restricted way, political issues. In the 1980s, a modern critical discourse promoting dialogue was born in Hungary.

In Poland, *Solidarnosc*, quickly became a nationwide, self-supporting political, cultural, social and economic network and a metaphor for an emerging civil society. The political philosophers behind the movement deliberately built their strategy on non-violence, involving the party-state and local authorities in a dialogue with representatives of the officially unrecognized movement. The enforcement of dialogue, in the form of radical demands and systematic negotiations, was tempered with the readiness to compromise. Non-violence and strong solidarity characterized this unique East Central European social movement. As part of the new logic and discourse, the adjective 'civil' was reborn and began to spread since it proved to be the single common denominator for different social and political actors searching for alternatives. A common denominator, or a 'probing concept' was much needed at a time of high uncertainty, fragmentation and also broadening horizons. 'Civil' in everyday parlance, meant autonomous, independent, non-military, non-violent and non-official. The very existence and pervasive success of *Solidarnosc* proved throughout the region of the Eastern bloc that there was a chance to peacefully challenge from below the authoritarian and dictatorial Soviet-type regimes and their apparatus.

The organization of civil movements differed from country to country according to historical traditions, the nature of the dictatorship, political culture and social structure. A wide variety of civil initiatives, movements and associations emerged at the beginning of the 1980s in Hungary in the absence of a large and strong independent moral authority like the Polish Catholic Church which functioned as an umbrella. At an early stage, there was a strong tendency for cooperation and solidarity among these civil groups called 'alternative social movements' or 'civil initiatives'. There was a unifying and consciously shared concept of civil society that had its origin in the political thought of István Bibó, a prominent and independent political writer and historian.[2] Bibó introduced the metaphor of 'small circles of freedom', which was subsequently used and developed further by the emerging student movement, environmental and peace groups, and other initiatives during the 1980s. The common vision of the alternative movements and new civil organizations was a natural outgrowth of these 'small circles of freedom' that developed into interdependent networks and alliances. Their gradual emergence created a mutually reinforcing network during the second half of the 1980s.[3] Rivalry among these groups remained secondary to the unifying force of challenging the authorities of the party-state until the democratic elections after the fall of communism in 1990. Significantly, when they surfaced, all these actors employed the new vocabulary of a wholly new language.

There is widespread agreement in the literature on the East Central European Velvet Revolutions that civil society was pivotal to the overthrow of communist regimes in 1989 (Bernhard 1996).[4] More recent evaluations of the 'alternative movements' and their civil society discourse during the 1980s provide different interpretations. In his recent book, John K. Glenn talks about the 'monocausal logic and conceptual imprecision' of many of these interpretations.[5] Glenn's conclusion is that we need to reconceptualize civil society 'as a master frame with which civic movements across Eastern Europe sought to mobilize public support in light of changing political opportunities' (Glenn 2001: 26–27).

The literature on civil society first concentrated on the democratic opposition movements during the Cold War, usually taking *Solidarnosc* as an outstanding model of social self-reliance and political resistance. But soon the concept was used for the analysis of fundamentally different societies from the United States via the former Soviet Union to Africa and the Far East. Civil society became the agent of cross-border, transnational cooperation and organization and has been gaining in global dimensions ever since (see Budiman 1990; Arato and Cohen 1992; Bozóki and Sükösd 1993; Elander and Gustafsson 1995; Dragovich, Liebich, and Warner 1995; Tismaneanu 1995; Yamamoto 1995; Hall 1995; Rueschemeyer et al. 1998).

Parallel to its increasingly widespread usage, the complexity and comprehensiveness of the concept of civil society can be discovered in the most recent literature. Michael Muetzelfeldt and Gary Smith's analysis reveals the one-sidedness of most of the earlier, biased civil society approaches that either over-emphasize the importance of the state or of civil society. They consequently suggest a more balanced view and emphasize that what they call the 'mutually emergent approach' offers a more complex understanding of the relationship between the state and civil society:

> In contrast to those who give primacy to either civil society or institutions of governance, we emphasize their mutually emergent features, and recognize the importance of the two-way interaction between civil society and

governance. This mutually emergent approach emphasizes the reciprocal constitution of a strong facilitating state and a strong civil society ... (Muetzelfeldt and Smith 2002: 58) [6]

More importantly, as the following paragraph indicates, this perspective has the advantage of acknowledging the intricate relationship between state and civil society and the difficulties inherent in any attempt to arrive at a systematic theorisation of the modes of their relation.

States are not homogenous, and have contradictory features because of their contradictory position in relationship to capital and civil society ...This approach provides an analytical framework that allows for reciprocal socio-political reproduction between state and civil society. This in turn opens the possibility for developing models for action that build civil society and good governance through virtuous cycles of effective active citizenship. (Muetzelfeldt and Smith 2002: 59)

This more sophisticated, complex and balanced approach was elaborated in the civil society literature by Martin Krygier.

Poland has a special and far-reaching significance for many themes. For it was there, more than anywhere else, remarkably resilient, and was ultimately successful beyond anyone's imaginings ... Much can be learned about civil society from the manifestos, struggles, ambitions, and fate of *Solidarnosc*, from what it understood civil society to be, and from what it failed or was uninterested to understand about the concept ... (Krygier 1997: 59)

Krygier detects the important difference between civil society *in statu nascendi* and a well-established and functioning civil society.

Civil societies depend upon distinctive configurations of economic life, civility among acquaintances and strangers, and tolerant pluralism. These in turn depend upon particular configurations of state and law, and gain support from particular sorts of politics. In each of these domains, civil society has ... elements that *Solidarnosc* did not have ... Moreover, the elements interrelate. A truly civil society has a strong – though not despotically strong – political and legal infrastructure and liberal democratic politics. (ibid.: 64)

The problem is that a 'truly' civil society does not exist. Real civil societies, however, might have and should have ideals and therefore the foundation of an ideal type can be useful (Alexander 1998). Real civil societies may even be measured against such an ideal type. Jadwiga Staniszkis pulls us back to the soil of Central and Eastern European realities:

The creation of a civil society is a much more complex process than mere political liberalization: it demands both property rights reform and deep cultural change. It is painful, just as is the creation of new politics occurring now in the Eastern bloc. Not only the old, facade institutions are activated (thus is usually the first step, before new institutions are created and oppositions recognized) but both the old and the new elites have to resist the temptations of unlimited power. The evolution from the situation when only society (not the ruling elite) is bound by rules to the legal structure limiting all actors is not completed yet in the Eastern bloc; oppositional reformers as well as 'revolutionaries from above' of the old establishment demonstrate temptation to use techniques (and philosophy) of the prerogative state in the name of reform. (Staniszkis 1991: 26)[7]

These temptations are real and have not been successfully resisted by either the old or new power elites. Real civil societies in the new member states, future accession and non-accession countries are weak and dependent on weak states which often try to over-compensate for their incapacity by over-regulation, bureaucratic authoritarianism and fake social dialogue. The 'mutually emergent approach' can be applied to post-communist societies, but the circles connecting power, institutions and civil society are far from being virtuous.

For some Western authors, the main characteristic of 1989 was its complete lack of innovation. Mary Kaldor agrees that the Velvet Revolutions of that year did not produce new policies or strategies for governments, but she argues that the period of the 1980s, preceding the revolutions, was fomenting with ideas. Precisely thanks to the emerging movements, 'small circles of freedom', a new understanding of citizenship and civil society accompanied with cross-border networking, 'transnationalism' was born. Kaldor claims that 'the notion of European or global civil society, which could be said to have emerged during this period, in some sense encompassed or encapsulated this strand of thinking' (Kaldor 2003: 50).

From the outbreak of the 1956 Revolution onwards, there was tension between the non-acceptance of Soviet domination and the logic of the bipolar world system throughout the region. Original and effective ways were found to democratize and support the building of a new relationship with the political ruling class. After the failures of 1956 and 1968, *Solidarnosc* proved efficient and victorious. It revitalized and reformulated the concept of civil society. East Central European dissidents and independent intellectuals and activists digested the lessons of 1956 and drew new conclusions by the late 1970s and early 1980s. The new way of thinking and articulation of the basic values of civil society represented by Michnik, Kuron, Konrad, and Havel, among others, regarding the relationship between an oppressive authoritarian state on the one hand, and society on the other, contributed greatly to political and theoretical conceptualization. The change in thinking and acting in civil society was supported by powerful 'external' international trends as well. The 1975 Helsinki Accord's third basket on Human Rights helped Charta '77 in Czechoslovakia, KOR in Poland, and the democratic opposition in Hungary to act more openly not only within their societies, but also with each other.

At the core of these ideas and analyses was a strong belief that events could proceed in new, historically unprecedented ways. Terms and phrases of a new language, such as 'parallel polis' and the 'power of the powerless' surfaced in the new discourse of dissident movements. This new vocabulary expressed a new attitude towards the weakening authoritarian regimes. Vaclav Benda, a Charta '77 spokesperson, emphasized that the 'parallel polis' does not compete with power, and accordingly Charta '77 was seen not as a political movement, but rather as a 'civic initiative'. In short, the new language signalled a new type of politics from below.

The birth of the new language and new thinking was primarily restricted to the national level, but there were also promising cross-border civil initiatives. There was regular cooperation between East Central European opposition groups and alternative movements in order to strengthen each others' cases and support each others' activities (Kaldor 1997: 8). This risky and unprecedented enterprise produced a growing regional – that is, Central European – awareness of a shared and common identity that strengthened solidarity. There was not only cooperation among the main democratic oppositional movements, but also among smaller movements and groups, such as environmentalists, peace activists and professional associations. In order to protect the emerging civil society and its new social movements throughout East Central Europe, Vaclav Havel suggested the need to establish an alternative European Parliament for social movements which became the Helsinki Citizens' Assembly.[8]

Kaldor draws our attention to the fact that the emergence of social movements and citizen groups was global. The 'growth of small circles of freedom' (*Solidarnosc*, Charta '77, the East German Swords into Ploughshares, the Dialogue Groups, the Polish *Wolnosc i Pokuj*, the Hungarian Danube Circle and Fidesz, and so on) did not occur in isolation. The 1980s also saw the re-emergence of strong and dynamic social movements in the West. This was an expression of the need to radicalize democracy and of the emergence of a new public sphere. Together with the birth of a new language, East-West dialogue began in Europe and reflected a hitherto unprecedented global consciousness and responsibility. This dialogue certainly expanded the space for a new European and global public for East and Central European movements, which successfully filled up the new public space. The artificial military bureaucratic and ideological division of Europe became unacceptable to younger generations that had not witnessed the terror of the 1950s. For them, the new language and thinking was a natural given. Suddenly a new *Zeitgeist*, a new 'feeling' began to radiate from the civil discourse of the 1980s. The attitude: 'I have the right to make my voice heard' gained momentum within the alternative movements. It was this common feeling that bound them together and created a common language and milieu for civil society.

Despite widely different political and cultural contexts, there was a fundamental consensus among the participants of East-West dialogue that one could no longer remain silent on fundamental political, social and ecological issues. The new language became the common denominator for all of these public concerns and provided the loose, rather psychological connections of belonging to a new community of independent civil movements and initiatives. Kaldor argues that the Western peace movement contributed 'transnationalism in practice' to the new discourse of the emerging Central European civil world. END (the European Nuclear Disarmament movement) and the European Network of East-West Dialogue that grew out of it demonstrated that networks can be effective and that cross-border networking is not only possible but fruitful in terms of protest, defence of human rights and the elaboration of new concepts and ideas. It is also remarkable that concepts such as *empowerment, participation, deliberation, transnational and European public sphere*, even *global civil society*, were born in the mid-1980s. All these concepts, ideas and phrases later became objects of academic research and a new language of power in the 1990s. Curiously enough, there is very little investigation of and interest in their recent origin.[9]

After 1989: Institutionalized Democracy and the Linguistic Turn in Civil Society Discourse

The rapid establishment of new institutions of representative democracy radically changed the dynamics of civil society. An overwhelming majority of former civil society activists became members of the new political elite and occupied leadership positions in the new institutions and political parties. Accordingly, their perception of civil society versus state relations changed dramatically. The leaders and the ideologues of the new political elite claimed that the time for social movements was over. They stated that grassroots mobilization was unnecessary, if not downright dangerous for new democracies. Political parties, they said, provided sufficient arena for the competition of ideas, ideologies and socio-political alternatives. According to this neo-liberal and at the same time etatist credo, the everyday political participation of citizens is unnecessary. Their role should be restricted to maintaining the new institutions and to legitimizing the political regime by voting every four years in 'fair and unharrassed elections'.

Following Fowler (1996), among others, we can identify civil society as the social environment where interest groups turn themselves into political parties, competing to become the ruling regime. In the case of East Central European countries, one has to alter this general truth according to the special socio-economic and historic context. A gap developed historically between the rulers and the ruled due to the lack of a strong middle class who, after the period of successful capital accumulation and saturation of wealth, would support the social and cultural sphere. In the absence of a strong democratic culture, the values of solidarity, social responsibility and citizenship could not develop. Citizens view themselves and were indoctrinated to view themselves as helpless, exposed subjects at the mercy of the state and its authorities. For good historical reasons, citizens (who are still called 'state-burghers' after the German *Staatsbürger*) and official authorities were – and in many transition countries still are – mutually suspicious of each other. It is important to recognize this special relationship between the rulers and the ruled in order to form a realistic picture of the present state of civil society in East Central Europe.

Although this attitude towards power started to change during the transition, the survival of paternalistic and authoritarian elements remained significant determinants in the relationship between civil society and the political elite. The attitude that 'it was always like this and will always be this way – so what can I do?' which characterized post-Second World War East Central European societies was challenged by the new social movements of the 1980s. This period, which we can call the 'golden age of the renaissance of civil society', proved rather short-lived in terms of erecting strong roots for a new political culture based on the rights and duties of engaged citizens. After the first democratic elections in 1990, continuity remained strong in public institutional life. The restoration of authoritarian patterns of behaviour, between citizens and their institutions, remained tenacious.

If we accept Jeffrey Alexander's conceptualisation, that civil society can be viewed as the universal expression of social solidarity, we might also say that without trust there is no civil society. In East Central Europe, illusions rapidly vanished at the beginning of the 1990s. The central values of civil society were quickly marginalized. Alexander observed the following:

> Just when intellectuals in Poland and Hungary were celebrating the return of civil society as an idea ... [they] are not at all sure they want it ... The practical task of social reconstruction makes these social ideals difficult for the intellectuals to sustain. (Alexander 1998: 1–2)

Amidst the joy of bringing down the communist state, numerous institutions and movements took up the adjective 'civil'. Borislaw Geremek said in August of 1989: 'we don't need to define [civil society], we see it and feel it' (cited in Smolar 1996: 24). Jiri Dienstbier's famous formulation, that 'civil society is in power' quickly became ironic, although the former spokesman for Charta '77 was certainly correct in observing the great stream of former 'dissidents' towards positions of power. With the formation of political parties, however, civil society lost its moral constituting power for the public good. The new political elite believed that moral civil society, along with its movements, had fulfilled its destiny, and should now stop stirring up the waters – some even stepped forward openly against the idea of civil society. Vaclav Klaus, for example, went so far as calling it a perverted idea, seeing in it the ideology of collectivism and an ambiguous third way.

After the Velvet Revolutions, civil society went through a real metamorphosis – some of it disappeared completely, some of it was transformed. Several movements turned themselves into political parties; local initiatives either faded away or were co-opted by local politics, and many civil organisations were forced to sell themselves in a financial or political sense to survive. A desperate struggle awaited those who managed to preserve their identity: they needed time, willpower, money and expertise to continue to operate. In the meantime, a process of disintegration and atomization rather than civilization swept the region of East Central Europe.[10]

During the last decade, sociological literature – especially in Poland and Hungary – has repeatedly called attention to the continuity in institutional and social mentality. Aleksander Smolar speaks directly of a new 'socialist civil society'. 'Shadow society' is the term he uses to describe the collection of informal social relations that were created by people in the 1970s and 1980s to defend themselves from the existing forms of authoritarianism (Smolar 1996: 35–38). These genuine, grassroots networks of social cooperation contributed greatly to the acceptance of shock therapy and the initial hardships of the transition. In time, however, as enthusiasm for 'a return to Europe' receded and the pain caused by the reforms intensified, the emphasis shifted to the defence of material-existential interests. The re-strengthening of the anti-liberal, etatist hierarchy of values came together with nostalgia for the socialist state that had offered a certain kind of protection and security. In societies that have uncertain futures, democratic politics with half-established and not entirely accepted rules and practices frequently deter or alienate rather than attract the majority. The trust invested in informal family relationships and close ties of friendship then gains weight.

Smolar calls it the irony of history that real socialism found refuge precisely in the very world of civil society that it had previously sought to strangle. Even though this phenomenon is not characteristic of the ever-changing sphere of civil societies in East Central Europe as a whole, it reveals a number of deep contradictions that determine social values and personal life strategies. The presence of trust at the social level provides the basis for order and dependability. After a short-lived rise in social trust, cooperation and solidarity, the societies of democratising East Central Europe are once again characterized by distrust and a strong tendency towards atomization. In the post-Cold War period the challenge for civil societies in East Central European countries is twofold: globalization and European integration. In order to address these challenges, local non-governmental organizations (NGOs) and civil society organizations (CSOs) have to link their domestic activities to the global – or at least regional – context. Networking is already very much present, but its full potential has not been realized. Escaping from their narrow and parochial framework and political climate, they need to find donors who are able to cooperate as partners and equals with commonly shared values and goals.

The breakdown of the communist party-states in East Central Europe, coupled with the retreat of the welfare states in the West, naturally gave birth to NGOs both in theory and practice. The negative definition of NGOs refers to the lack of something, to the uncertainty and unpredictability of the transitory epoch. This situation is naturally comprised of positive tendencies as well, like the further articulation of the need for social democratization and participation of citizens in decision-making. Potentially, NGOs could play a vital role in buttressing and facilitating social democratization and citizen participation. This is, however, not self-evident. In many cases, NGOs are not genuine agents of authentic civil society. In weak democracies, loaded with an unelaborated and anti-democratic past, they are often creatures of governments, parties or individuals who employ them to enhance their power, prestige or material interests.

One of the main problems with the new NGOs in political cultures dominated by the lack of trust, independent resources and traditions in citizens' initiatives, is their limited legitimacy in the local societies. NGOs either turn to the state, automatically losing their independence, or look for external resources. In both cases accountability and transparency become questionable. It is also very often the case that western (mostly American) donors, sometimes with the best intentions, are ignorant of local, social, political and cultural conditions and are therefore unable to select the appropriate partners from civil society. In many cases those who receive internal financial support are those who are already in the external circle of a global NGO elite. They possess not only the necessary language, Internet and application-writing skills, but are able to 'talk civil society' fluently using the most trendy and fashionable buzzwords.

On the other hand, the East Central European development of NGOs and CSOs reveals a consciousness of their role in strengthening democratic values, mobilizing society for participation, and contributing to a new civil culture of decision-making and dialogue. This is required to strengthen their bargaining capacity with authorities on local, national and international levels, but this is also not a given. According to Lars Jorgensen:

> There are some risks in taking on civil society. It is of course perfectly legitimate for NGOs not to be openly political or to take sides in whatever constellation of parties or factions which is forming at a given moment, but they must recognize that their work has political aspects and relate to the authority of the state and to the political development of their society. (Jorgensen 1996: 36)

An unbalanced and undemocratic relationship, based on a new dependency between Western donors and Eastern NGOs can seriously undermine and bias this potential. Therefore, a critical assessment of their relationship and its development during the transition period is of crucial importance. Sometimes well-intentioned donors impose their values or policies on recipients who then act rather as dependent agents instead of as genuine local actors in the civil sphere. The scarcity of domestic resources, a growing dependency on state support and an unequal, dependent relationship with Western donors, combined with a growing rivalry rather than solidarity among NGOs, has seriously undermined the spirit of an independent civil society in transition countries. This tendency is reinforced by the emergence of a global and local NGO elite with high technical skills and 'networking capital' that contributes to the fake image of a civil society constructed from above (Jensen and Miszlivetz 1998a: 83–98).

Civil society, with its proliferating interfaces, is a remarkable asset for the global, regional and domestic representatives and configurations of the emerging bureaucratic, political and market players to demonstrate their allegedly 'good intentions'. In this context, by 'talking civil society' and nominating and signifying 'civil society', these social actors become themselves part of civil society. The slippery language and the new praxis of 'dialogue with civil society organizations' initiated by non-CSOs (from above or from the outside) have the potential to dissolve sharp contradictions and antagonisms. 'Civil society speak' can smoothly annihilate diametrically opposing interests and provide mutually satisfying results. This process we can call the 'co-optation of civil society'.

'Talking civil society' provides the common denominator for Western donors, the new NGO-elite, and national governments who want to 'co-opt' them. It can be lucrative to display the 'right' liberal democratic values and at the same time avoid the uncomfortable consequences of strong and genuine civil societies. 'Co-opting' and taking over means surpassing and weakening. A new network of dependent NGOs undermines rather than serves the interests of genuine civil society. However important and inevitable the institutionalization of civil society is, we can only move beyond the practical and theoretical deadend if we assume that civil society is not equivalent to the sum total of NGOs. The permanent slipping between the terms 'civil society' and 'NGO' is a source of theoretical inconsistency, practical misunderstanding and political or ideological manipulation.

In the second half of the 1980s, it did not seem illusory that East-West dialogue would lead to a sustained cooperation of civil society which would strengthen autonomous, democratic social space in the East and revitalize democracy in the West. After the 1989 transformations, however, the situation changed fundamentally. With the disappearance of the bipolar logic, the common foundation for wide social mobilisation also disappeared. Opinions on the unity of Europe were too divided. Once the main political and ideological barriers fell, economic, welfare and security concerns came to the forefront. In contrast to unconvincing rhetoric, the reality showed that the western half of Europe was turning its attention inwards. It cautiously closed itself off, while in the eastern half fragmentation, disintegration and uncertainty became the main features. The concept and language of civil society did not altogether disappear, but it underwent a metamorphosis in comparison to the practice and visions of the 1980s (Jensen and Miszlivetz 1998b: 141–70).

Increasingly professionalized civil organizations and NGOs replaced or outnumbered bottom-up initiatives and movements. In places where the *ethos* and mentality of civil society was preserved from the 1980s, it was either incapacitated against nationalist tyranny (as in several republics of the former Yugoslavia), or it was pushed into the background, as in Hungary, Poland and former Czechoslovakia. A new world was created by the mid-1990s, the world of professional NGOs, civil organisations and foundations. Most of these NGOs took over some of the responsibilities of the state, and they did not have particularly warm feelings about the civil *ethos* or new forms of cooperation. Those civil organisations, however, which carried out their work in the fields of human rights, minority questions, education, culture and the protection of the environment, had every right to regard themselves as institutions of civil society. Most of these have integrated into international – predominantly Eastern or Western European – networks, as a result of which their weight and ability to survive has increased considerably. In the second half of the 1990s, the symptoms of fragmentation and introspection also seemed to have diminished and the idea of Central European cooperation once again gained modest influence in the civil sphere.

Civil Society and European Citizenship in the New European Space

If we consider civil society to be a sphere of solidarity, we need to be able to answer the question: what causes and maintains this solidarity? This is especially important in the post-1989 period within the framework of the European Union and European integration. There have been many criticisms of the EU's unification policy and the concept of a European social and political community. These critiques, a typical example of which can be found in the work of Timothy Garton Ash (1998), usually agree that in a social sense it is impossible to talk about a unified Europe; there is little reward in having a European *telos* if there is no European *demos*.

It is true that EU member states have voluntarily given up a considerable part of their national sovereignty and, in general, European nation states have indeed become weaker after the Second World War. They are no longer capable of exercising control over a great number of economic, political and ecological processes. Thus, the framework in which democracy had previously operated has weakened, and in certain cases it has fragmented. This would not present a problem in itself had a new political form replaced the old. This has become a focus of the present debate: can we accept the European Union as the new framework, or are we to accept the re-strengthening of European nation states? At the moment, there is one point on which the advocates of both the strengthening and the weakening of nation states agree, namely that Europe as a political and social framework still lacks coherence. It is therefore unclear what the basis and framework of a Europe-wide civil society could be. Victor Pérez-Diaz argues that neither international markets nor transnational voluntary associations and bureaucracies have the capacity to create the solidarity and trust that could form the basis of a democratic European political community (Pérez-Diaz 1998). Without a vivid European public sphere, there will not be European citizenship.

During the decade after the collapse of the Berlin Wall, European societies have been predominantly made up of national societies whose citizens are mostly concerned with problems at the national or domestic level. The discourse of agitation for Europe was inconsistent with the actual policies of main political protagonists and as a result it was not easy to formulate narratives that contributed to strengthening the feeling of belonging to a European community. Apart from the feeling of belonging to a community, the other dominant values of civil social associations are trust, a readiness to cooperate, and inclusion. According to Dahrendorf,

> A civil society is a society of citizens who have rights and accept obligations, and who behave in a civil and civilized manner towards each other. It is a society which tries to make sure that no one is excluded, and which offers its

members a sense of belonging as well as a constitution of liberty. (Dahrendorf 1997: 78)

How strong are these values in the societies of the EU member states? What are the chances that they might be extended to the societies of Central and Eastern Europe once they become integrated into the enlarged European social space? The answer to the first question is rather ambiguous. Recent empirical studies have shown that nationalism has decreased significantly within the EU Fifteen, and the willingness to cooperate between former adversaries has increased decisively. In contrast, certain social groups and countries who have suffered material losses as a result of the ongoing process of expansion have employed tactics that are far from civilized. What values the EU Twenty-five along with potential new members will represent, especially in terms of national identification in the coming years, is hard to predict. Nationalism, it seems, has not been eradicated in the new European border regions.

However much the most important constituting values and elements of a civil society might be present Europe-wide, the common public sphere that would facilitate the evolution of a transnational civil society has not yet developed. The creation of a European public sphere, which is of utmost importance for the development of a European civil society is, according to Pérez-Diaz, hindered for a number of reasons:

(1) Due to economic and political uncertainties public interest is focused predominantly on questions inside the framework of the nation state (such as levels of unemployment, the question of the welfare state, and so on).
(2) the conduct of the European transnational political establishment contradicts its own rhetoric; on the level of day-to-day management it still follows the vested interests of nation states.
(3) the criterion of accountability is missing.
(4) the logic of the Founding Fathers is still in effect, according to which any step forward in the realm of economics or finance will induce a chain reaction on a European level and will facilitate social and political interaction.
(5) the fragmentation arising from the diversity of languages and cultures is further accentuated by the lack of common myths and a common historical narrative.

Pérez-Diaz is certainly correct to point out that the expansion of a European public sphere will first of all be the result of active citizenship, and not exclusively the work of a transnational political class, and 'secondly, this citizenry could develop a certain critical awareness towards performative contradictions in European policies' (Pérez-Diaz 1998: 236). At this point we enter a vicious circle: the commitment and attachment of Europeans will only strengthen once their institutions guarantee them a greater number of substantive civil rights than any other political medium. Without this it is indeed hard to imagine an efficient European civil society. But who in fact will convince institutions of this necessity? Who else but the sporadically dispersed elements of transnational civil and social networks and institutions, together with the citizens who make them function? This act of creation and emergence would be a magic trick worthy of Baron Münchhausen.

The EU's soft spot is that its institutions are not thoroughly transparent and lack democratic social legitimacy. The democratic deficit during the 1990s continued to grow. The consensus that was symptomatic of the integration-orientated elite drained away after the Cold War. This consensus played a key role in the regular and effective cooperation between Western European governments and societies. This is no longer clear in the case of Eastern enlargement. The Director of the European Policy Centre, John Palmer, mentions a growing turmoil and doubt in connection with the fundamental aims of European integration (Gillespie and Palmer 2001). Palmer comes to the conclusion that the 'Future of Europe' debate – owing to the uncertainties surrounding fundamental aims – cannot mobilize a critical social mass. This standpoint is also underpinned by public opinion polls from the *Eurobarometer*, the lack of social resonance after the Convention debates, and the aloofness of the Western European political arena. One should not be surprised by the failure of Maastricht where the creation of a polity was attempted from above. The Amsterdam and Nice Treaties attempted to implement long-term reforms in order to reach a civic engagement with the broader political community or the creation of a normative order that is maintained by the independent source of the input-orientated legitimacy (Gillespie and Palmer 2001).

These forced attempts from above to create a common identity or the public comprehension of public good have regularly flopped. Dimitris Chryssochoou indicts 'Amsterdam as having failed to incorporate any substantive civic rights in a formal 'constitutional' document addressed to the citizen directly, thus reflecting the insistence of sovereignty-conscious states on codifying existing trends in both jurisprudence and legislation' (Chryssochoou 2001: 5). In other words, national interests overshadow the broader vision. Amsterdam and Nice – adjusted to fit the EC's and the EU's developmental history – were under the necessity of creating and/or addressing the political community, in spite of which policies were produced and developed. Chryssochoou argues that without the normative frames of transnational civil society, institutionalization at the European level will not occur.[11] We can agree that the 'Europeanization' of civil society could significantly influence future reforms and aid in the creation of a civil identity from 'the present fragmented *demos*'. Agreements based on costs and benefits are inadequate and unable to generate civil engagement. Therefore, it is difficult to say what fundamental reforms should look like.

When we contemplate civil society we encompass more than just society with the notion; the phrase contains added value. When we discuss the notion of European civil society it connotes a further qualification. If we study present European societies with their democratic forms of government and, on the other hand, the lack of democracy at the transnational level of the EU, it reveals why the notion became so relevant to decision-makers, bureaucrats, politicians, regional planners and also for civil society activists. These actors, one way or another, are the architects of the new Europe. The future of Europe depends on the extent to which they will be able to cooperate, compromise and mobilize their social environments on the questions that will determine the European constitution, political community and society.

Today, European civil society is more a promise than a *fait accompli* and there are no guarantees, despite the fact that there are visible signs of emerging representations of a European civil society. Caution is necessary when employing the notion, otherwise we fall into the traps of ideology, wishful thinking and illusion. For the time being, we have to deal with open and unanswerable normative questions. Can the formulation of European civil society become instrumental in the handling of social exclusion and open new channels of social affiliation? Will this result in the implementation of new policies, thereby activating participation in the processes of integration and Europeanization? Or, on the contrary, will there be only protest? In other words, is there any substantive change in attitude on the part of civil society organizations towards more effective cross-border cooperation and networking?

From the early 1970s to the end of the 1980s, the notion of civil society primarily functioned as an umbrella concept and encompassed social movements and initiatives, as well as trade unions and the critical discourse of the independent white-collar workers. After that the notion moved through from the world of NGOs in the 1990s to reach its widest usage at the beginning of the new millennium. It appears in the reports and projects of the European Commission, the UN and the World Bank as well as in the programs of political parties, governments and multinational firms. Although the meaning of the notion varies with the cultural, political and institutional context, the practice proves what Jeffrey Alexander argued that all of these actors would create their own civil societies in order to qualify themselves and their activities. Civil society relates in this way to the public sphere – to a defined manner and mentality as well as to the community of NGOs. This expanded usage preserves the ambiguity of the notion. It can serve to fight political battles, to mantle social and political problems, but can also turn into the language of power.

The need for new players and movements ensures prominent status to the concept of European civil society. It is often the only tool to link the contradictory processes of integration, Eastern enlargement and Europeanization. It suggests that there is a European way to restructure and unite disintegrating elements of society, political community and culture. All this can happen under the conditions of equal access to opportunities, democratic participation, individual freedom, peace, social welfare and civility. For centuries the development of civil society was exceedingly inequitable in Europe as it was confined to certain segments of societies in Western Europe. From its rebirth through the 1980s it has gained newer and newer connotations and conquered wider social spheres; in the process, the notion itself has been democratized. Today Europe is a broadening, multi-level social space. Individuals, NGOs, and coalitions provide its colours. Social innovators, independent media, and trade unions act out the European drama. At the end of the twentieth century, the lack of bipolarity, the acceleration of globalization and widening European integration led to the beginning of an era different from the last 250–300 years, when civil society was principally evoked inside the borders of the nation state. Today civil networks increasingly cross national borders and there are signs that its leaders perceive the complexities of this new period. Many civil society groups in Europe lobby governmental and intergovernmental organisations, form coalitions with international associations and experiment with new forms of cross-border cooperation. These new cross-border networks can potentially create new identities or resuscitate old ones in new forms and in this way contribute to the social Europeanization of Europe. When attempting to understand the transnational mobilization of interest groups, sub-national agencies and citizens, we need new notions and a new central concept.

The 'Great Signifier' in the White Paper on European Governance

The gap between rhetoric and reality is uncontested. It seems that civil society serves as an umbrella and shelter, the redeemer of the European project. European elites need their own civil society as well as national governments and political parties. Under these conditions, European civil society discourse could easily become the new language of dominance and power if genuine civil society is unable to articulate itself at the transnational and European levels. The crucial question is whether the frames and structures needed for the development of a transnational,

European civil society will come into existence in the near future. This would be the moment for simultaneous democratization both from below and above. Then, the alienating and unspeakable techno-bureaucratic language that determines the operation and *ethos* of the EU would loose omnipotence. However distant this may be, it is not impossible that the language of unilateral bureaucratic 'provisions' will be superseded by the language of social dialogue. How can we overcome the present situation? Can the EU escape from its crisis of social legitimacy and perpetual monologue disguised as dialogue? If we want to look for answers, it is worth examining the EU's own self-reflections.

The *White Paper on European Governance* released by the European Commission in July 2001 was produced in response to the demand for strong self-reflection and can be recognized as an attempt to start real dialogue. What counts most from our viewpoint is that civil society and the citizen stand at its core:

> Democratic institutions and the representatives of the people, at both national and European levels, can and must try to connect Europe with its citizens. This is the starting condition for more effective and relevant policies. (*White Paper.* 3)

The *White Paper* emphasizes that immediate reforms are needed. At the same time, the authors make clear that the power of the Commission alone is not enough:

> The Commission cannot make these changes on its own, nor should this White Paper be seen as a magic cure for everything. Introducing change requires effort from all the other Institutions, central government, regions, cities, and civil society in the current and future Member States. The White Paper is primarily addressed to them. (ibid.: 3)

The most important recognition in the *White Paper* is that (similar to many official EU declarations released in the past years) the continued success of integration depends on stronger and more effective interaction between 'regional and local municipalities and the civil society' (ibid.: 9). At the same time, authors of the document hold the nation states responsible for what invariably refers to the survival of state-centred thinking and a hierarchical approach. The Commission disengages itself from responsibility to:

> Establish a more systematic dialogue with representatives of regional and local governments through national and European associations at an early stage in shaping policy. (ibid.: 4)

In spite of its weaknesses and imperfections, the *White Paper* can be regarded as a change in the process of European construction. It is an official recognition that the process is not proceeding on the right track and that the Commission has reached its limits. To develop further it needs to find new and different partners:

> European integration has delivered fifty years of stability, peace and economic prosperity …Yet despite its achievements, many Europeans feel alienated from the Union's work. (ibid.: 7)

At one point the self-criticism goes especially deep and elicits, *expressis verbis*, the possibility of the paralysis of the Union:

> The decreasing turnout in the European Parliament elections and the Irish 'No' vote also serve to show the widening gulf between the European Union and the people it serves…. There is a perceived inability of the Union to act effectively where a clear case exists, for instance, unemployment, food safety scares, crime, the conflicts on the EU's borders and its role in the world. (ibid.: 7)

Then the critique turns against the member states:

> By the same token, Member States do not communicate well about what the Union is doing and what they are doing in the Union. 'Brussels' is too easily blamed by Member States for difficult decisions that they themselves have agreed or even requested. (ibid.: 7)

After the critique and expression of frustration, the *White Paper* examines the role and possibilities of civil society. This is a new development in the history of the EU that reveals the birth of a new rhetoric, that is, the *White Paper* emphasizes civil society's outstanding role in the creation of the future Europe. There is a whole sub-chapter on the topic of civil society entitled 'Involving Civil Society'. This not only enhances the possible role of civil society, but also emphasizes its responsibility in the shaping of good governance. The first recommendation of the closing chapter ('From Governance to the Future of Europe') also looks at civil society. It recommends the restructuring of the EU's relation to civil society in order to promote mutual responsibility and accountability. The EU admits the need for civil society, so it urges dialogue with it. In as much as this experiment continues according to the five fundamental principles laid down in the *White Paper* (promotion of transparency, participation, accountability, efficiency, and coherence), it can create a new context driving the process of integration and Eastern enlargement through new channels. If it remains just rhetoric, it can only worsen the already tarnished credibility of the EU in the circles of institutionalized and non-institutionalized civil society.

Acknowledging the crises and accepting the problems coupled with the recognition that there is a need to create a new relationship with a wider circle of actors is noteworthy. The *White Paper* gives the impression that the community method, amended with the civil society method, could be an efficient mechanism on which to base the future of European integration. It is also remarkable that the notion is not limited to present EU countries, but is extended to the civil societies of the (then) accession countries as well. It is questionable, however, whether the initiative to establish transnational dialogue with civil society will meet the expectations, aims and visions 'from below'. Developments so far are not reassuring. At present, most European societies – both member and candidate countries – are fairly sceptical about influencing European affairs. A refreshing exception is an Internet publication entitled 'Common Europe' (http://www.common.org.pl/), published by independent Polish intellectuals and NGOs in 2001 who identify themselves as 'the voice of Polish non-governmental analytic centres'. They share and support a vision of Europe 'where solidarity is a common standard, which is not divided between better and worse Europeans, and which is not founded on a fear of unification'.

Similar to the *White Paper*, they believe that the involvement of citizens in the process of shaping the new political and social image of a common Europe is the key to the real and democratic legitimation of European integration:

> The voice of European citizens is increasingly heard as a result of the activities of various civic organisations – associations, foundations, churches and informal groups. We are witnessing the birth of a European civil society, which, despite all its deficiencies, is a real expression of the concept of solidarity, the fight against social exclusion, discrimination, and for a clean environment and education. The activities of the organizations of civil society reach into those areas where the state cannot act effectively, and stop integration being limited to elites. (ibid)

Echoing the challenges of the *White Paper*, the authors of the document encourage 'civil dialogue' and the involvement of civil organisations.

Despite these seductive calls from different corners of Europe, our mindset and our language are still determined by an economic and technical efficiency that is controlled from above, by governments and intergovernmental organizations. Larry Siedentop warns that we are still 'sacrificing at the altar of economic growth instead of citizenship' (Siedentop 2000: 217). While analyzing the evolution of European democracies and the historical differences between them, Siedentop purports that Europe, which is principally covered by a French political design, was basically engendered in economic terms (ibid.: 226). Similarly to Chryssochoou, he criticizes first of all the European elites who he believes are the cause of moral and institutional crises in Europe since they fell victim to 'the tyranny of the economy language' (ibid.: 226). The rediscovery of civil society at a European level, combined with the introduction of openness, participation and accountability from above, can be regarded as an attempt at rectifying this imbalance. It is hard to deny that since 1957 European construction arose primarily through economic mechanisms. Consequently, it has its own peculiar reasons for employing the language of market efficiency and bureaucratic control which has blanketed the language of politics and leaves little space for the development of the language of civil society. As a consequence, a common language for the European public is still missing. We are witnessing an interesting experiment, that is the creation of a new European language and public sphere simultaneously from below and from above.

Europe's New Role: the European Project in a Global Context

The protection and enlargement of the values of the European social model is unthinkable without a European Union that takes a leading role in world politics. Politicians, visionaries and social scientists like Delors, Fischer, Jospin, and Habermas emphasize plausibly and consequently that a European constitution would increase the ability of member states to act together by providing the legal framework. In this way, too, something that was lost at the national level could be regained – the ability to have a voice in world politics. On the one hand, there is fundamental agreement on this among leaders, experts and analysts of the EU; on the other hand, there is no consensus on what kinds of changes and reforms are needed to strengthen and make more effective the representation of European interests and values.

As questions about the European construction and Europe's role in the world mount, world system theory can increasingly be found under the surface in analytical essays. José M. Magone, who set out one of the most complex and comprehensive approaches, borrowed the title from Immanuel Wallerstein, *The Modern World System and European Civil Society: A Reconstruction of the Long Durée of the Modernity of the Millenium* (Magone 2000). Magone based his analysis on the postnational constellation and continues by examining the slow but fundamental change in the international system. He argues that this change resulted in a paradigm-shift in the field of international relations, and that essentially the nation state is no longer the only or central player in international society. The EU which itself is a 'result' of this slow and radical metamorphosis, significantly contributed to this much-analysed paradigm-shift.[12]

Magone's approach is new, because he connects world system theory and European integration to the change in the role and function of

European nation states and the transnationalization and Europeanization of civil society. Other notions, however, such as democracy, civil society, sovereignty, regionalization, representation, identity and multi-level governance also need rethinking. Magone considers the EU as a political system *sui generis* that was created by a set of treaties.[13] He first examines what impact the world system and the capitalist world economy has on the realignment of the European space; whether a new political economic structure could be created as a counter-balancing force to globalized financial capitalism (ibid.: 3). These questions are relevant because while the European nation states have matured to the level of intergovernmental cooperation, in other parts of the world, completely different trends are proceeding. Consequently, the sharing of power and hegemony at a global level is greatly asymmetric. The international system, especially as represented by international organisations, has reacted slowly. Magone's important recognition concerning the future of Europe is that 'although a global multilevel governance system is emerging, it is asymmetrical in its integration in different places of the world' (ibid.: 2). This asymmetry and dilatory institutional reaction opens the door to civil society in the new, enlarged European space as well as in the global arena. Logically, we have reached a crucial point: will the European Union as a political system *sui generis* together with civil society mobilize towards the paradigm-shift; in other words, diluting national-orientated capitalism with 'proactive cosmopolitanism' (ibid.: 3).

This does not mean that we should consider the EU or European civil society as a blueprint for the world or a completed project. Rather cautiously we could speak about tendencies and possibilities. One outstanding trend is the transformation of the Westphalian system of European nation states into a post-Westphalian system which replaces conflict with cooperation and networking. In the new world of increasing complexities and interdependencies, the much appreciated institutions of global governance such as the UN, IMF, World Bank or WTO have to be restructured in order to survive. A possible positive outcome of this restructuration is that the American model of twentieth century capitalism would be replaced by a 'global negotiated model' (ibid.: 14), and into this new model the EU could transfer genuine and innovative elements. This is the point where European civil society enters the scene since its role has become indispensable.

Those who are concerned about the possibilities of an emerging European *demos* understand well that a common currency or the single market are not sufficient to establish a political community in the minds of people. Eurosceptics and opponents of a more unified or deeply integrated Europe deny the democratic legitimacy of a supranational institutionalization, claiming that a European *demos* as such does not exist. Consequently, the process of constitutionalization lacks its subject:

there is no European collective singular. Habermas strongly disagrees with this view, arguing that a political community does not necessarily presuppose a community of common origin, common language or common traditions. On the other hand, it is true that in the course of European history, democracy and nation states developed in a circular process, strengthening and consolidating each other. Civil society could be interpreted primarily within the boundaries of the nation state:

> There are two lessons to be learnt from the history of the European nation states. If the emergence of national consciousness involved a painful process of abstraction, leading from local and dynastic identities to national and democratic ones, why, firstly, should this generation of a highly artificial kind of civic solidarity – a 'solidarity among strangers' – be doomed to come to a final halt just at the borders of our classical nation-states? And secondly: the artificial conditions in which national consciousness came into existence recall the empirical circumstances necessary for an extension of that process of identity formation beyond national boundaries. These are: the emergence of a European civil society; the construction of a European-wide public sphere; and the shaping of a political culture that can be shared by all European citizens. (Habermas 2001: 16)

Although the political structure of a democratic European Union still needs to be constructed, Habermas believes that the process of construction has reached a critical point where conscious state-building can take the lead. Therefore, the process of constitutionalization plays a decisive role in further development.

The importance of a new, European public sphere and interrelated publics is salient. Without it, it is impossible to imagine overcoming the democratic deficit and the crystallization of a positive European identity. This new European public sphere will most likely take the shape of a network which 'gives citizens of all member states an equal opportunity to take part in an encompassing process of focused political communication' (ibid.: 17). One of the inevitable consequences of the European transformation process is that the European nation states increasingly lose their all-encompassing ability to control. The demand for collective control over negative externalities transferred a lot of power to Brussels that used to be under national control (such as environment, migration and the fight against illegal trade). The establishment of the single market required a set of measures that would be impossible to control at the national level.

The process of sharing power for the time being favours Brussels over national governments and modifies the relation between central institutions and municipalities. This change is quite advanced in the case of the Western European societies, but still remains a long-term aim for new and future member states from East Central European countries and the Balkans. If new players, such as independent social groups, movements and initiatives, successfully adapt to the possibilities provided by new supranational structures, their survival will not only be assured but will also expand the narrow national public spaces. In the words of Yves Mény, they will contribute to changing national squares into a European circle. These attempts, however successful they may be, will not immediately and automatically lead to the evolving of a homogeneous European public sphere.[14]

This European experiment and the talk of European civil society from both above and below (and, to a certain degree from in-between, by social scientists) certainly contributes to expanding horizons, including linguistic ones, even if the existence of such a civil society (to what extent, in what forms and how efficiently?) still invites inquiry. This attempt at the creation of a more or less unified European public sphere has the character and the precariousness of an experiment, while it is certainly conditioned by the European civil society discourses emanating from both above and below. As with every other social issue, social scientists themselves undoubtedly contribute to the wealth of the experiences and visions concerning the ongoing creation of the languages of civil society. Not only does this proliferation of discursive perspectives open up unprecedented possibilities for the future development and further democratisation of the nascent European polity, but it also invites further reflection, research and actions on the part of social scientists and civil society actors alike. It can only be hoped that the present chapter succeeds in showing the urgency with which this task announces itself and its importance for the future of democracy and pluralism in European civil society, while pointing at the same time towards the conceptual and theoretical developments that are necessary to adequately understand the complex and often indeterminate current state of affairs.

Notes

1. They all assumed a rapid and fundamental political change: the reclaiming of national independence and the immediate withdrawal of Soviet troops from Poland, Hungary and Czechoslovakia.
2. István Bibó was a minister without portfolio in the government of Imre Nagy during the 1956 Revolution.
3. Besides single-issue movements, a whole set of colourful initatives oriented more directly towards actual social and political issues also came into existence. By the mid-1980s, discussion and study circles known as the 'Club Movement' and the 'Movement of University Colleges' emerged around the country. Communication and networking among these new groups occurred naturally and created a special spirit for civil society and dialogue. A strong feeling of solidarity and the new experience of increasing

freedom of expression released creative energies and blurred or hid the political, cultural and ideological differences between them.

4. See also Butterfield and Weigle 1992: 1–2: 'expanding independent activism increasingly contradicted the legitimacy and power base of the single ruling party, leading to the end of Communist rule'; and Arato and Cohen 1992: 64: 'groups, associations, and indeed movements outside the official institutions would have the primary task of pushing the reforms through'.

5. 'They obscure the impact of the Leninist regimes as repressive agents and negotiating partners in the reconstruction of the states. These regimes were not simply overcome by political protest led by independent groups but shaped the patterns of reconstruction independently of the efforts of the movements. They cannot explain the reconstruction of the state because they lack a model to explain the interaction between states and movements that created the political institutions of post-communist states ... They misunderstand the strategic nature of the discourse of civil society and the conditional nature of public support for the civic movements' (Glenn 2001: 24).

6. This aligns with Krishan Kumar and Michael Walzer's analyses; see Kumar (1994: 127–30) and Walzer (1995: 170): 'Only a democratic state can create a democratic civil society: only a democratic civil society can sustain a democratic state.'

7. Staniszkis's evaluation stresses the continuity in East Central European societies after 1989 and sees the self-limiting strategy of social movements as rather defensive, and not suited to fundamental social change. She believes that 'from the perspective of the society the aspect of continuity is more strongly experienced than the sense of change, and this perception itself ... may take on the features of a self-fulfilling prophecy, inducing social apathy and feelings of revolution for the elite only ...' (Staniszkis 1991: 181).

8. The Helsinki Citizens' Assembly (HCA), established in 1990 in Prague, is the only international and institutional offspring of efforts to create civil networks across borders in the 1980s. It reveals a significant continuity in the protection of human rights and support for local grassroots initiatives.

9. The term 'European civil society' was introduced in the public debate in the late 1980s (see Kaldor 1991 and Muetzenfeldt and Smith 2002).

10. Elemér Hankiss observes: 'Millions of people have lost, or fear that they may lose, their traditional roles and positions in the sphere of production and distribution. They have lost their way in the labyrinths of social and industrial relationships, which are in the midst of a chaotic transformation. People no longer know what the rules of the new game are, what their duties and rights are, what they have to do for what, what is the cost and reward of what? There is no authority to tell them; there are no values to refer to' (cited in Smolar 1996: 34).

11. Chryssochoou's critique of European elites – in accordance with the opinions of numerous European social scientists – reaches the gist of the problem: 'The significance of tying the self-image of the elites to the dialectic between citizenship and *demos*-formation is that no common civic identity may come into being unless all major actors engaged in European governance see themselves as part of a polity-building exercise that has to evolve from the lower level upwards. Likewise, a transnational political space must be built up in the everyday networks of civic engagement, instead of being constructed from the top down' (Chrysochoou 2001: 17).

12. See, for example, the works of Jürgen Habermas, Jeremy Rifkin, Iván Vitányi, etc.

13. Magone regards this phenomenon so important that he introduces a new term: 'treatism'.

14. William Outhwaite, too, believes that the European integration process requires 'some sort of civil society dimension'. He tries to answer the question whether we can talk about an emerging European civil society by looking at European identities and

European institutions. 'A European identity might be seen as taking shape in opposition to, on the one hand, national or subnational identities of a traditional kind and, on the other, alternative supranational identities such as an Anglo American Atlantist identity ...' (Outhwaite 2000: 135–36). Outhwaite understands the significance of the European experiment to establish transnational, European identity via postnational citizenship and constitutionalization for global citizenship and global governance. 'Europe is pioneering a mode of governance, this time transnational rather than national, which gives some practical embodiment to the current extension of democratic thinking into conceptions of cosmopolitan democracy' (ibid.: 135–36).

Chapter 7

PLURALIZED GLOBALIZATION: CIVIL SOCIETY DEBATES IN EAST ASIA AND LATIN AMERICA

Shin Jong-Hwa and Peter Wagner

In the preceding chapter, the analysis of the recent retrieval of the concept of civil society was begun with a focus on East Central Europe, where this process started. Motivated not least by disillusionment in this region, the concept was only in a second step gradually transformed and the European Union became more and more the polity that the users of the concept were addressing. During the early period of East Central European retrieval, in turn, the political history of Western Europe had still been marked by the consolidation of the democratic Keynesian welfare state. This was the model of a nationally organized democracy that certainly did not rely on any strong concept of civil society – even though it did not abandon all such thought as radically as *ancien régime* and Soviet-style socialist societies did (an analysis of which is provided in chapter 5). Furthermore, it was not only the case that towards the end of this period cracks in this model became ever more visible – in a multi-faceted attempt at rethinking the political discussed in chapter 9. In addition, developments outside Europe and North America, such as de-colonization, attempts at liberation from Western models of political and economic development, and the gradual emergence of non-European forms of modernity, provoked a critical revival of political thinking also beyond the European experiences. In this chapter, we provide elements of a comparative perspective on extra-European uses of the concept of civil society, focusing on the cases of East Asia and Latin America. In chapter 8 of the book, we will turn to an analysis of those debates that, in a context of so-called globalization, detach the concept of civil society from any existing polity and point to the distant horizon of a cosmopolitan order.

East Asia, Latin America, Europe: Civilizational Patterns or Regional Experiences?

After the end of the so-called Cold War, the rigid political tension between the East and the West in Europe has eased and divided political cultures in Europe have been gradually reintegrated within the institutional process of Europeanization. As discussed in chapter 6, the interest in civil society has considerably increased in the new polities in Central and Eastern Europe. In a sense, the idea of civil society served to project the possibility for reconstructing democracy in the region. East Asia and South America were also parts of the global scale of political change in the last two decades of the twentieth century. While the collapse of Soviet socialism and the enlargement of the European Union are significant for understanding the democratization of Europe, however, different kinds of political influence were at work in East Asia and South America. In particular, the internal dynamic from the rise of the Asian economy and the political tradition of democratic resistance in both regions need to be pointed out.

Just as a state has its national territory, civil society often has its boundary as well – in discourse as well as in practice. A particularity of East Asian discourse of civil society is the fact that each national discourse has been rather rigidly established, at the expense of cross-boundary inspirations. Across the region it is only Japanese civil society that has shown a high international capability, at least if the contents of civil society activities include humanitarian agendas in international politics. In spite of this fact, even Japanese society is very sensitive to critical opinion from abroad concerning Japan's historical legacy in the twentieth century. And while Japanese civil society simultaneously shows openness to international affairs and seclusion in domestic affairs in terms of measuring actual political influence, its Korean and Chinese counterparts have focused on their own political problems and hardly ever taken positions towards international affairs, with the notable exception of issues of Japanese hegemony in the region.

Compared with the regionalization of the debate about civil society in Europe, increasingly referred to as Europeanization (see chapter 6), we witness here a rather different attitude towards regional identity. A strong national identity in China and Korea is not well combined with any regional one. Most of all, the Chinese and Korean discourse for understanding regional identity is shaped by the historical experience in which the Japanese idea of Great Asia caused military conflicts in the region. Due to this legacy, regional politics is being developed very slowly compared with economic cooperation. Besides, in both state and civil society symbolically harmonized national voices often emerge with regard to regional issues, even though there are serious tensions between the two in domestic affairs. In other words, the national idea remains a major underpinning element of civil society in East Asia. This is so today despite the fact that major political problems in each country are unlikely to be solved within the national boundary. Questions such as the unification of Korea, humanitarian issues in China and North Korea, or the influence of right-wing extremists in Japanese politics cannot be successfully dealt with unless political actors in the region work together, since these apparently national issues have regional implications, in terms of their possible effects that spread beyond the border. Thus, debates about civil society need to address ways of dissolving current boundaries.

One way of responding to this exigency is to broaden the spatial extension of the concept from nations to world regions. The preceding chapter has shown that something like a regionalization of civil society debate happens in Europe, a reopening after the nationalization of the concept two centuries ago (as discussed in chapter 3). One can explain this regionalization in Europe by virtue of the fact that European integration also brings something like a European polity about – civil society being in search of the polity towards which its concerns are directed. As plausible as such an explanation is, in recent years another idea has also found new interest – the idea namely that, rather than national societies, regional civilizations may be the appropriate focus of that kind of political sociology that takes an interest in the varieties of civil society and its related discourses (see, for instance, Arnason 2003).

For the East Asian discourse of civil society, indeed, it has been argued by some scholars in East Asian regional studies that origins of civil society – without that name – can be found in the traditional political culture. In such light, the current debate about civil society was analysed in terms of linking those traditions with the newer conceptual importations from the West. This phenomenon reflects the scholarly attempt in regional studies to identify, with the help of categories of European thought, a region's political traditions, and to trace the historical sources of orientations in contemporary political culture. An analysis on the public sphere in Ming and Qing China (Wakeman Jr 1998), for example, partly illustrates how traditional Chinese politics had its own political mechanism for the public. Also, the suggestion to analyse faction politics in Chosun Korea as an early form of civil society has been introduced in this academic trend (Haboush 1994; Cho 1997).

What, though, is to be gained by reconsidering some political cultures and customs in the name of civil society and the public sphere? It goes without saying that re-evaluating the political traditions that have been critically dealt with is an important task for historically oriented scholars. However, there are also two other elements in this movement. First, previous political historiography in the East Asian region did not have a balanced view towards its own past. When the modernist world-view began to attract a majority of intellectuals, it appeared to be very efficient in interpreting social, economic and political problems; and concomitantly the regional and national political traditions were heavily criticized by the emerging new modes of thought. Thus, any new interpretation of previous politics using the terms 'civil society' and 'public sphere' meant at the same time a critique of such modernist historiography and a rebuilding of the long-term political tradition in which the modern idea of civil society is seen as having endogenous roots. Interestingly, the scholars in this trend do not show strong relativist views in cultural studies, because their initial idea was to analyse the Confucian political tradition as comparable to the European one, rather than arguing for any fundamentalist view on Confucian politics. Secondly, the idea of Confucian backgrounds of civil society reflects a certain socio-economic awareness that Confucian culture and its organizational implications contribute to economic development. The debate on Asian values shows the discursive process in which the result of (partial) economic success motivates the reinterpretation of socio-economic culture that has to some extent been inadequately treated in the modernist perspective. Regrettably, the end of the discursive process was the justification of authoritarian political culture without creatively linking the idea of democracy with Confucian backgrounds.

While the legacy of Confucianism serves as a – sometimes doubtful – means to conceptually hold together an East Asian civilization, treating Latin America as one region seems at first sight unproblematic for plain cultural-linguistic reasons. The name Latin America reminds of its cultural background in Southern European colonization and migration, while North American culture is said to have originated through English and 'Germanic' – German and Scandinavian – movements. Furthermore, the differences between North America and Latin America stem not only from their language-based cultural particularities but also from political and economic features related to their initial colonization (Hartz 1964). In the perspective of identity formation, one can recognize that presenting themselves as Latin American despite highly different origins also served as a means for detaching from Europe (Fuentes 1999; Rhee 1999; Larrain 2000). Thus, drawing a distinction between Latin America, on the one hand, and Europe and North America, on the other appears to be a relatively straightforward analytical exercise.

However, finding possible common elements across many countries in Latin America requires nevertheless careful consideration (Skidmore and

Smith 1984; Wiarda and Kline 1985). In this vast subcontinent, the nation-states have highly different scales and geographical locations as well as economic and political orientations. In particular, small states in Central America and huge states in South America have produced different political and cultural identities. Thus, the aggregation of national experiences in the history of civil society is not always inclined to producing the 'Latin American case' as such. Considering this issue of conceptually creating a regional group, we suggest four categories through which national cases in the region should be analysed. First, native American civilizational experiences are seldom introduced as intellectual resources for civil society, even though they constitute political motives in the history of conflicts. Secondly, the independence from Spanish and Portuguese powers did not entirely eliminate colonial legacies. The tensions between major actors in the new political and economic situations after liberation are sometimes related to colonial experiences. Thirdly, and most recently, Latin America as a whole has been the place in which economic and political conflicts over so-called globalization have been most explicitly articulated.

Last but not least, the influential power of Catholicism needs to be mentioned. No one can ignore the importance of religion and its role in the historical shaping of Latin America since the European arrival on this continent (Rhee 1999). Starting with missionaries aiming at 'enlightening' the natives during the colonial period, to the considerable support from many priests for the independence movement, to the contributions to the civil and human rights movement in the contemporary period, the political intervention of religious groups have shaped the history of Latin American politics (Vallier 1970; Kim 2003). Although the history of European politics, including the current process of eastern enlargement of the European Union, also shows the influence of Christianity, unlike the Latin American case, the relationship between state and Church in Europe has been marked by strong tensions during the past two centuries. Even if one could call the decline of religious power in Europe a long-term process of deep cosmological rupture, the Latin American socio-political environment could certainly not be properly described merely as disenchantment. Even though one may argue that native civilizations in the region were mainly swept out and replaced with Christianity, the observation of the existence of religious power might lead to the impression of a cosmological continuation which also affects institutional arrangements.[1]

All these observations notwithstanding, and in contrast to the East Asian case, Latin American discourse of civil society hardly touches upon any civilizational backgrounds. The radical civilisational rupture after the expansion of Spanish and Portuguese power in the region and the full adoption of European institutions, later, leads South American discourse to rather parallel the European one; and the origin of civil society is normally dated to the time of importing European thought (Davis 1972). Modern European political thought already began to take root in the eighteenth century and many intellectuals no doubt identify with this heritage. As Chakrabarty (2000) points out for South Asia, European culture and value-systems are deeply embedded in the regional context and, for this reason, an analysis of politico-cultural constellations would need to partly proceed by reconstructing a European culture that can be described – in an absolutely non-pejorative sense – as 'provincialized' European culture.

Such a view, if adopted in general terms, would however tend to overestimate the difference between East Asian and European debates while similarly exaggerating the similarities between Latin American and European discussions. In a long historical perspective, Latin American and European political developments have diverged as often as they have converged (Larrain 2005), whereas a linkage to Western-style democracy is a rather recent occurrence in East Asia. Although they have different civilizational backgrounds in terms of religion, politics, and intellectual thought, many political scientists in both regions have recently analysed democratization processes on the model – often stylized – of contemporary Europe, in terms of consolidated institutional politics without severe violence and the emergence of democratic civil society. The appropriateness of such an approach is discussed on pp. 172–73. Similarly, the two regions have witnessed highly different economic trajectories. The European economy, long the core of advanced capitalist development, experienced a deep crisis between the twentieth-century world wars while simultaneously the Latin American economy prospered. Currently, in turn, the latter faces severe economic turmoil while Europe is relatively stable. Introducing East Asia into this comparison, we see with the recent Japanese and Korean experiences impressive growth patterns against an earlier historical background of seclusion from the world economy. The relation between economic and political developments are taken up in the concluding section of this chapter.

In this double light, we need to return to the question behind all of this volume, namely that of whether the development of European civil society itself can be seen as a linear process without political ruptures in contrast with which other regions are 'late developers' or need to recast their own traditions. The civilizational approach does not seem to properly answer this question. In fact, if one tries to find the common elements of civil society among different national experiences in a long-term perspective since the eighteenth century, different ideological spectrums of political actors and particular aspects of public spheres in which the mode of actors' interactions are specifically situated become easily visible (as shown in the preceding chapters). In spite of some historians' attempt to identify the core contents of civil society across time with a view to conceptually reconstructing civil society in order to evaluate non-European experiences, their retrojecting attitude in dealing with the concept is not always fruitful. Historically available examples of civil society before 1945 often do not meet normative standards. In particular, early ideas of civil society many of which were based on the newly rising economic and political classes' exclusive interests, are not acceptable in contemporary political discourses. Any historical approach to civil society invariably reconstructs it for a particular historical epoch. That is why, methodologically, any such attempt should be seen as dealing with concrete historical experiences rather than with either timeless concepts or civilizationally determined expressions. To critically assess the specific features of such historical experiences is necessary for re-conceptualizing civil society in order to readopt it for contemporary Europe and other socio-political constellations. Such a rethinking of the relationship between civilizational backgrounds and civil society opens the way for a perspective in which the former never determines the latter. Rather, civilizational backgrounds make political resources available that can be mobilized by political actors to address problematic situations. It is from such an angle that we will now look at the two specific features of the East Asian and Latin American constellations mentioned above – the social embedding of democracy and the political roots of economic development.

(Civil) Society against the (Authoritarian) State? Radical-democratic and Conservative Interpretations in East Asia

Analysing the discourses of civil society in both regions, it is not difficult to see that the argument about the universal principle of democracy is often intertwined with that about its unavoidably cultural, that is particularistic, interpretation. The scholarly attempt to link one's own political tradition to what is called the modern idea of democracy in looking for the origin of civil society can be an example of the latter, while the critique of strong authoritarian states is based on the former. The formation of political actors for civil society is always situated in historical experiences; thus one needs to understand for each context which political issues the actors have used to develop their own visions and practical solutions to problems. At least as far as three states in East Asia – the Chinese, Japanese and Korean – are concerned, the crisis of state sovereignty in the nineteenth century paved the pathways in a long-term direction, even though rather different short-term or medium-term solutions were adopted: the socialist path by the Chinese and North Korean states; the authoritarian developmentalist state by the Japanese, South Korean and Taiwanese ones.

When the end of Soviet socialism increased the doubts about possible radical political change in general, the rise of the discourse of civil society raised not only positive perspectives but also negative ones. The positive viewpoints include an increased feasibility of widening the public sphere and enlarging political agendas and the negative ones concern the possible de-radicalization of social movements. If the Chinese debate could be classified as an example of the former, the South Korean debate is rather mapped on the latter constellation.

In order to understand these different attitudes, it is necessary to identify why, when, and by whom the idea of civil society was presented. Interestingly, in what was called the advanced (industrial) democratic societies, the civil society debate did not flourish during the 1990s. It was rather in what was called developing countries with authoritarian states that the discourse developed considerably. This means that 'civil society' was a sufficient first concept to promote the desire for the further development of political democracy. For instance, while South Korean, Taiwanese and Chinese political discourses have widely introduced the concept of civil society, Japanese politics did not welcome it in any similar way. Besides, the Chinese discourse on civil society includes the question of how to democratize state-centred organized politics, whereas the Korean counterpart to a considerable degree includes the critique of civil society itself. Thus, the introduction of a new political discourse – here, civil society – is always situated and appraised in the political environment where political actors hope to get a grip on new prosperous ideas, on the one hand, or are reluctant to abandon their own political attitudes, on the other.

It is in this light that we can now ask why many social and political scientists displayed negative views of civil society in South Korea until the first half of the 1990s. The particular aspect of the Korean debate comes from the change of Korean politics around 1987 when the authoritarian state based on military dictatorship was successfully challenged by democratic movements. Since 1980, when the state was occupied by the military elite, the counter-state actors also increased their capacity of resistance. In this process, many counter-state actors analysed Korean situations with the help of Marxist doctrine and tried to find political alternatives with a view to radical political change. While their contribution to the democratization process was significant and opened the path on which military power was going to be fully eliminated from politics, the institutional changes were much less significant: parliament was still in the hands of conservative politicians; the state was still quite hostile towards any collective social movements. Within this situation, the introduction of civil society discourse was partly manipulated by conservative political networks and instrumentalized by them to resist the rising power of radical political actors. Even though many advocates of civil society had shared democratic goals with radicals, Marxist actors and scholars heavily criticized the new discourse for fear that it could fragment the democratic forces.

Although conservative elements are found in the idea of the endogenous origin of civil society, the political actors who took initiatives for building democratic society always included critical actors that stood against state structures that were conceived as problematic, thus accepting the classical idea of the dichotomy between the state and society. This in fact means that building civil society has been a political project that aiming to overcome the current political problems caused by the existing state. However, each country in the East Asian region had a specific political situation, most clearly related to the respective role of the state in the modernization process. When the state took the role of main modernizer, especially in East Asia, the members of national societies developed different attitudes to it in relation to the impact of imposed societal changes felt by them. The experiences in an authoritarian state and the relationship between the state and anti-state actors have certainly enhanced the struggle for democracy. However, if undemocratic political experiences have increased the democratic desires of the people, the emerging opposition between the state and anti-state actors has often undermined the actual ways to reach democratic restructuring – and this in various ways.

The Chinese experience shows the existence of rather weak democratic actors outside the state, with the state trying to minimize the possibility of emerging political actors. The Korean experience, in turn, reveals how the state has always been under criticism from strong counter-state actors. Also in the Japanese experience, both the state and other political actors have become dependent on institutional solutions. These rather diverse historical formations of politics in the East Asian region driven by different political practices after the nineteenth century have shaped the major actors' political orientations and the relationship between them.

The use of the concept of civil society in the Korean discourse is the one most comparable to the European debate. In terms of building a democracy that is always at risk of being shrunk by the state, the forces of civil society are in most cases critical of the state, and political actors see the state as the main obstacle to democracy. Thus, the state and (democratic) society are in strong tension. The Chinese case, though, is different in that the state is still the main political force determining the direction of politics. The relatively small scale of social movements in China and the dominance of politics by the state has led the Chinese discourse of civil society in two directions: first, the recognition of the role of the state as the guardian of civil society; secondly, an emphasis on how to minimize political fluctuations in the process of democratization.

Here, there is no need to say that the history of Chinese politics, like the experiences in other countries in the region, shows the state's dominance over other political forces. However, while Japanese and (South) Korean politics, and to some extent even the Taiwanese one, successfully increase socio-political forces outside the state in order to counter-balance its influence, Chinese and North Korean politics have not accomplished this. Arguably, this problem stems from the different path to political modernity under the impact of communist political culture. However, one should remember that the earlier political culture was exclusively dominated by a small political elite. It is important that we carefully identify, above all, the reasons why the state is often treated as the subject of promoting civil society instead of 'societal' forces taking the initiative.

The Chinese state has succeeded in justifying its political legitimacy, even though it has from time to time faced legitimation crises around the Cultural Revolution and the violent oppression in Tiananmen Square. Stronger legitimation crises, though, have marked the Japanese and Korean experiences. The failure of Japanese politics in the Pacific War made the state concentrate on institutional politics and bureaucratic affairs, and the legitimation crisis of the state in Korean politics due to the colonial legacy, the Korean War, and military coups provided a political environment for non-state actors to contest state authority. In other words, the political balance between the state and its counter-forces is asymmetrical, not only in their actual powers but also in their ways of constituting the discursive boundary between 'state' and 'civil society'. The historically shaped discourse of civil society for Chinese politics unveils that the state has the role of the guardian for (civil) society. The ultimate task of the state for political development in China is to achieve the gradual progress of democracy without facing radical political fluctuations. When Korea arrived at economic development by a state-centred modernization programme on the one hand and succeeded in accomplishing democracy by the anti-state actors' political contributions on the other, in Chinese politics, political development, like economic modernization, became part of state policies.

The relationship between the state and non-state actors is changeable. We can point to the Korean case for support of this thesis. Before Korea entered into the democratic transition – historically the period before 1997 – many scholars of Korean studies subscribed to one of the two following ideas: either a strong state encountering a weak (civil) society, or a strong state opposed to a very contentious society. The argument for the latter idea was to prevail around the emergence of civilian government and the disappearance of the military dictatorship, when scholars wished to identify how democratization was achieved (Koo 1993). While the discourse of the relationship between economic development and democracy was influenced by the role of the middle class in political change, some scholars tried to understand how historically the democratic actors were constituted in modern political history.

However, after the democratic actors took state power with the support of socio-political movements around 1997, the discourse came to include the role of non-government organizations for extending the democratic environment in relation to the state. New governments opened the policy-desks to socio-political activists and in many cases welcomed the participation of non-government organizations in the policy-making process. Thanks to this changed attitude of the state, the tension between state and counter-state actors has eased more and more. Around this phenomenon, the thesis of the opposition between a strong state and a contentious society became less attractive for understanding Korean politics.

Interestingly, when the combative relationship between state and society is being transformed into cooperation, the conceptual division between the two also becomes indistinct. As in Chinese politics, in Korean there is acceptance of a functional division of political labour in the promotion of democracy. Of course, this Korean phenomenon is very different from its Chinese counterpart: neither state nor civil society now enjoys powerful influence over the other, while the Chinese state strongly monitors civil society organizations. It is still unclear as to how long this coordinated role-playing in Korea will last. If the conservative networks take state power again, the relationship will return to the confrontational style of the past.

Democracy and Development: Comparing East Asia with Latin America

As mentioned above (p. 163), the relation between the pre-existing native American civilizations and the newly expanding European ones has only rarely inspired a civilizational analysis of South America. However, an emphasis on colonial legacy has in a different sense become the guiding thread for understanding the foundation of Latin American polities in a nation-building process that, although it witnessed early independence from the European powers, remained in a situation of economic dependency.[2] Larrain (2006) interprets this relation between political sovereignty and economic weakness in terms of a type of modernity that shows strong autonomy but weak control. Theoretically, once independent states emerge from colonial power, however, the power relations between protagonists radically change. The hegemonic physical power with potential violence moves out of the hands of the state elite from the colonial power. Any external economic and political powers need to deal with the elites of independent states as the institutional partner in order to efficiently justify their dominance over a nation-state's domestic affairs. For these reasons, the initial development of the independent state should be investigated in terms of how the newly emerged state elites have become a focus of modernization since the nineteenth century.

In a comparison of Latin American and East Asian paths to modernity, the difference in the historical moment of national independence in Latin America – the nineteenth century – and in East Asia – the twentieth century – must be emphasized, particularly in relation to how Latin America had been deeply integrated into the world-economy since the colonial situation. In fact, the development of the colonial economy began here as the supplier of natural resources and a few agricultural items – coffee and cotton, for example – on the one hand, and as the market of European industrial products, on the other. This historical shape of the Latin American economy did not change when the states achieved independence. The agriculture-based capitalism with export-centred economic activities underwent strong fluctuations whenever the European and North American markets faced a crisis. Besides, the persistent devaluation of agricultural products compared to imported machinery from Europe and America prevented the growth of national economies in the region.[3]

Furthermore, in contrast to the process of building new modern states after independence in East Asia, there was no clear disruption of the class structure of colonial Latin America. The exceptional socialist revolution in Cuba and the rise of other socialist movements in the region did not coincide with national independence. Besides, the phenomenon in Latin America corresponding to the post-Second World War rise of developmental states in East Asia – South Korea and Taiwan – during the period of state-led import-substitution policies in the mid-twentieth century was considerably less successful. In other words, the coincidence of a modernist project of economic development – in either socialist or capitalist terms – and a radical turn from the colonial legacy in the economic and the political sphere, which can be identified as the two interdependent axes of East Asian ways to modernization, did not happen in Latin America. Thus, the temporal cleavage between the building of new nation-states and the project of state-centred organized modernization appears as a crucial feature of Latin American political history compared to the East Asian one.

One of the common aspects of East Asian states is that they exercised rather strong ideological control over the members of the national societies. In the colonial period, colonial states not only mobilized socio-economic resources for the Japanese empire in order to support its military expansion, but also utilized collective propaganda emphasizing the need for self-sacrifice in the national interest. This ideological pressure was not exceptional for the entrepreneurs, and the tradition has been continued and even strengthened in the context of the nationalist idea of economic modernization. The role of the capitalist class in the military-style organized modernization was neither hegemonic over the state nor equal to the state. For this reason, the state has been not only the major political actor, but also the primary economic one.

In contrast to East Asian experiences, the major economic actors in Latin America were a capitalist class that did not face the pressure to minimize their political voices. In the period of the struggle against the colonial powers, many landowners, like intellectuals, welcomed a liberal idea of economic activity in order to protect their interests from Spanish intervention, and they advocated the independence of the state. Since then, the strong link between economic interests and political participation has been firmly rooted in Latin American political culture. Even during military dictatorships and populist regimes, the capitalist classes have maintained their political voice in relation to the state. For scholars in East Asian studies this provides a stark contrast to the Asian style of economic restructuring processes led by a strong state that minimizes any counter-response from the economic actors.

Thus, many political economists have argued that one of the main sources for the rapid development of the East Asian economy is the state that efficiently mobilizes other economic actors. This state-centred development strategy has been praised also as a viable institutional alternative for non-East Asian states. However, one needs to keep in mind that the high economic capability of the state has grown from two historical experiences that are particular aspects of East Asian politics. First, in the East Asian context, political actors in general and the state in particular have always taken the initiative over economic actors in dealing with economic issues. In other words, the latter have not had enough political power to control the state, on the one hand, nor have they been successful in transforming their economic interests into political thought, on the other. Although South Korean and Taiwanese states experienced military dictatorship, like many Latin American states, their attitudes to capitalist economic actors have not always been friendly, and in many cases the states tried to subordinate economic actors with a view to achieving high economic performance in order to allocate resources through state planning.

Secondly, the state's embodiment of the motives for modernization has been a litmus test to legitimate the state in relation to other competing ones. The hostile attitude between the two Chinese states –

China and Taiwan – and between the two Korean ones – South Korea and North Korea – as well as the uneasy relationship of these states with Japan – the former colonial power – basically shape nationalist ideas and systems of state-led mobilization. In short, the state as the disciplining agency has devoted itself to industrialization.

Of course, the relatively successful industrialization performance has been concomitant with political dictatorship. Up to the end of the 1980s, indeed, Latin American studies provided some theoretical tools for East Asian studies. The experience of military dictatorship, the overall situation of weakly rooted institutional politics were introduced to indicate the state's overwhelming power in relation to civil society. Besides, finding a possibility to overcome 'authoritarian rule' became an important academic agenda for political scientists (O'Donnell et al. 1986). It is only during the global trend towards democratization since the late 1980s that military dictatorship has lost its attraction and its political power in both regions. However, while East Asian economies survived the financial crises of the 1990s relatively well, many of their Latin American counterparts once again failed to overcome economic turmoil.

One East Asian case in particular, that of South Korea, deserves a comparative analysis with the Latin American situation. The emergence of a democratic state in Korea coincided with the economic crisis due to the collapse of the exchange rate of the Korean currency. This is one of several recent cases that demonstrate the problems emerging from the dependence on international capital of a national economy: the currency crisis in Mexico in 1995 and the Asian crisis in 1997 both reignited economic turmoil in their respective regions. In Korea, specifically, this meant that in 1997 the newly emerged democratic regime had the task of persuading non-state actors to accept the economic policies guided by the International Monetary Fund. Although it unsurprisingly faced severe criticism from its supporters – workers, farmers and other forces of the democratic movements – the new state overall succeeded in the task of economic restructuring. The high increase in the number of unemployed and the introduction of labour flexibility have to some extent been accepted as an inevitable problem in the course of overcoming the national economic crisis. In other words, although the state's neo-liberal economic policies became disputable political issues, they did not directly challenge the legitimacy of state. If the same policies had been pushed by an authoritarian state, one can assume that the anti-state actors would have produced serious anti-state political resistance.

Similarly, it seems, the status quo of the Latin American economy has been shaped by the economic policies suggested by international economic institutions, especially by the International Monetary Fund. In a situation of high debt, many states in the region had to accept the IMF's policy guidance, which strongly demands the privatization of major industries and the liberalization of financial markets. This external pressure influenced the states' policy orientations almost regardless of the considerably wide ideological spectrum of the state elite.[4] While the IMF's policy guidelines were diligently adopted, the Latin American situation has not improved: indeed, one could even argue that it has degenerated.

Such worsening – or at least not improving – economic situation must be taken into account when one observes that in Latin American politics, in contrast to most East Asian countries, violent conflicts among political actors are – shall one say: still? – a possibility. In Mexico, the Chiapas region and the Zapatista movement continue the tradition of military resistance. Venezuela experienced a military coup in 2002. In Argentina, Chile, and Peru, the conservative political network maintains strong ties with the military elite. The institutionalization of non-violent political communication is certainly not accomplished in any consolidated way. In the light of some likelihood of states again failing to deal with economic turmoil, one is inclined to describe the contemporary Latin American economic and political situation as a 'never-ending permanent crisis' (to use the terms of an East Asian observer: Rhee 2002).

In spite of deeply rooted institutional problems, however, Latin American civil society is likely to develop its democratic capacity. The institutionalization of democratization processes in Chile and Brazil would accelerate the development of non-violent relationships among political actors in Latin America. Nevertheless, this straightforward expectation is not easy to accept for scholars of this region who have seen repeatedly emerging violent events, and then one will have to note that external power has been one of the key factors in halting democratization and domestic pacification. During the Cold War period, the U.S. supported many military dictatorships in visible and invisible ways in order to suppress social movements and eliminate the possibility of emerging democratic regimes. Although the degree of intervention is comparatively low, East Asian states witnessed a similar phenomenon. However, since the collapse of the Soviet bloc and the rise of the U.S.A. to hegemonic power in international politics, the focus of both ideological tension and security debate in East Asia has been on North Korea. At the same time, the rise of the Chinese economy has been a primary concern, in terms of its potential impact on the power balance in the region. Thus, these two issues have become the main variables for the future of civil society in East Asia with regard to the impact of external intervention.

If in Latin America, in turn, the weakness of economic development seems to remain the main factor affecting the activities in the political sphere, this does not exclude the possibility that political problems concerned with external powers and violent confrontations among political actors will be as influential as before, for two main reasons.

First, global social movements, as a counter-force of economic globalization, have considerably developed against the institutional endeavour of global governance based on economic interests. A nation-state did not have a proper political voice when it faced policy pressures from international economic institutions. The history of Latin American politics shows how each state has been too fragile to resist global-scale industrial and financial capital. Many social and political conflicts, which were analysed in terms of an underdeveloped democratic culture, were indeed more connected with the state's economic dependency on external economic factors in policy-making processes. The gradual increase of international solidarity in dealing with neo-liberal policies in international economic debate may in a long-term perspective change the global power relations. The global social movements try to exert their influence over domestic politics as much as over the policy-making of international institutions. With the support of international opinion, international actors have directly and indirectly criticized the authoritarian state and thus made any decision to return to violent suppression much more difficult.

The second reason for the continued influence of political players is that democratic forces in the region have become stronger with the accumulation of political experiences of resistance to the authoritarian state. In spite of harsh military dictatorships and rigid conservative networks in formal politics, democratic actors in labour and farmers' movements have increased their political capacities. Not least against the background of several political confrontations with the state, they often have an affinity to socialism, a socialism that has developed its own particular aspects connected to the region's specific, historically shaped problems. The question of land ownership, strong ethnic ideas in minority movements and radical military mobilization, for example, are often found in Latin American socialist movements, varying with the context. The experiences of oligarchy and military dictatorship in more industrialized countries – Argentina, Chile, Peru and Venezuela, for example – have led to a more urban movement, including labour movements, while in some countries in Central America – Mexico, Nicaragua, Bolivia, for example – farmers' radical uprisings are significant.[5]

In contrast to some of our observations on East Asia, the Latin American experience as a whole shows overall a rather deeply conflictual relationship between state and civil society. Violent encounters occurred fairly frequently and the institutional way of formal politics was blocked by several military coups – and this against the background of persisting serious economic and social problems such as high unemployment, huge foreign debts, serious social inequality, high illiteracy rates and ethnic discrimination. While historically and culturally Latin America has shared similar political and religious orientations with Europe, it has suffered from strong dependency upon other economic powers in the global economy, and, has thus had to face the impact of world economic crises in a more intensive way than other regions. The cause for civil society action is strongly provided by this problematic situation, but the space for a fruitful impact remains rather limited.

In contrast, even though the capability of non-state actors in East Asia is still also rather small, South Korean civil society actors begin to show a possibility of effectively promoting democracy and the Japanese case unveils its own procedural and institutional dynamic. The limits here seem to be of a different kind. While there is some broad understanding of a common cause in Latin American civil society activities, evidence for which was provided by the pioneering role in the World Social Forum, the democratic actors in the East Asian region will not be able to treat many crucial political problems, including the issue of security, unless they strongly show international solidarity. In order to achieve this above all, the nationalist attitude in political discourses will need to be replaced by universal principles that cover national differences. However, different views may be held on the relationship between universal principles and cultural practices that are specifically effective and necessary for regional agendas. The East Asian discourse of civil society would need to focus on the elements with which the conceptual gap among the national, the regional and the universal is filled out.

Notes

1. The Latin American interpretation of the relationship between politics and religion could be a key element of the understanding of the region as one of a variety of modernities (Gill and Keshavarzian 1999).
2. See Furtado (1976) for a view on the underdevelopment of the Latin American economy and its structural dependency on the world economic system; and Galeano (1974) for an understanding of Latin America as the object of exploitation by the European and North American powers since the sixteenth century.
3. It is elucidating to compare this situation with the rapidly industrializing economies in East Asia after the Second World War, in terms of them changing industrial structures from light industries to automobiles and electronic products, through heavy and chemical industries, and their export strategies being closely linked to American industries.
4. It needs to be noted, though, that the Lula and Kirchner governments in Brazil and Argentina mark a turn. For the idea of policy reforms for the state in economic crisis, see Williamson (1994).
5. In Latin American studies, the idea of a correlation between (economic) modernization and (political) democracy has been a focus of critical scrutiny. In the observation of frequent military coups and the failure of maintaining and developing democratic formal politics, O'Donnell (1979, see also O'Donnell et al. 1986) suggests the model of 'bureaucratic authoritarianism', connecting Latin American states' political problems with dependent industrialization in the region. In studying some

states that sustain a relatively stable political development, Columbia, Costa Rica and Venezuela, for example, Peeler (1985) argues that the compromises of the elite in competition in formal politics helped political stability. See also Jung (1986) for the Nicaraguan experience and Troncoso and Burnett (1962) for early labour movements in the region.

Chapter 8

GLOBAL CIVIL SOCIETY: FROM DISSIDENT DISCOURSE TO WORLD BANK PARLANCE

Jody Jensen and Ferenc Miszlivetz

In a visionary article first published in 1986, Marc Nerfin provided a powerful and dynamic model to help in understanding the new interconnectedness of local and global social change and the emerging world-view coupled with it. According to Nerfin, the roots of the global crisis that unfolded in the 1980s was the growing gap between the perception of the world in 1945 when the UN was founded, and the second half of the 1980s when development policies proved ineffective vis-à-vis the growing anomalies of globalized capitalism. Developmental strategies essentially reflected a white, Western, Christian and elitist world-view and were based on the paradigm that developing societies '... have more often than not proved unable by themselves to offer solutions to the crisis and even less to contribute to the search for alternatives' (Nerfin 1987: 172).

The beginnings of this alternative-seeking and systemic approach go back to the late 1970s to a rather modest initiative of the International Foundation for Development Alternatives (IFDA), or the Third System Project which tried to offer an alternative to the UN International Development Strategy in the 1980s. There is a conscious reference in the concept of the Third System to the Third World, and even to Third Order which could be interpreted as a reference to the transcendence of the *ancien régime*. This struck a chord at the time by exposing a widespread social need and political sentiment. Although Nerfin never mentions civil society *expressis verbis*, this is *de facto* what he means when he elaborates the concept:

The third system is not coterminus with the people. It brings together only those among the people who are reaching a critical consciousness of the role they may play. It is not a party or an organization, but the movement of those associations or citizens who perceive that the essence of history is an endless effort for emancipation ... The third system does not seek governmental or economic power. On the contrary, its function is to help people to assert their own autonomous power *vis-à-vis* both Prince and Merchant. It endeavors to listen to those never or rarely heard and at least to offer a tribune to the unheard voices. (Nerfin 1987: 182)

Nerfin's definition takes particular account of the problems of people living in underdeveloped societies. His words echo many voices from the social movements of the 1970s and 1980s and are expressions of a new world-view emerging 'from below'. This powerful metaphor, the locally and globally self-organizing Citizen vis-à-vis the already well-organized financial and market forces of the Merchant and the states and governments of the Prince, became a rich source of linguistic and theoretical innovation and proliferation. Nerfin's model is neither static nor rigid. His 'third system' is a terrain of diverse and self-organizing movements, initiatives and associations. He mentions peace, women's liberation, human rights, environment, local self-reliance, alternative lifestyles, consumer defence, solidarity with the Third World, and new forms of trade unionism such as *Solidarnosc* among them. The new spirit is an obvious continuation of the social movements from the late 1960s and early 1970s, expressed in a vocabulary of a new and emerging global consciousness:

Citizens and their associations usually act in a determined space – local, regional, national, multinational, global – but also, and increasingly so, in several spaces simultaneously. Amnesty International ... acts in the global space through representations to the United Nations Commission on Human Rights, in the national space through pressure on governments, and in the local space through the many groups which 'adopt' a political prisoner and campaign for his/her liberation. (ibid.: 174)

Nerfin recognizes the important and powerful networking capacity of civil society. Civil society associations, NGOs and civic initiatives started to gather together at parallel summits already in the early 1980s. UN conferences opened new space for networking. This networking, which offers an alternative to the Prince and the Merchant's pyramidical and hierarchical organization with centre and periphery, is organized horizontally:

Their centres are everywhere, their peripheries nowhere. Networking simply means that a number of autonomous, equal and usually small groups link up to share knowledge, practice, solidarity or act jointly and/or simultaneously in different spaces. (ibid.: 186–87)

This ideal-type description of civil society networks certainly shaped the imagination of many NGOs during the past decades and served as a model for their activities. Nerfin's rich metaphor gave rise to a whole literature during the 1990s dealing with the 'third sector'. It strongly influenced the language of civil society organizations working in the fields of development, human rights and the environment and the formulation of a new world-view by global civil society networks and social movements.

From the mid-1990s there is an explosion in interpretation of the role of 'civil society' in democracy, democratization and development. The confusion about the meaning of the notion, however, has contributed to the abuse of the concept by players (mostly authorities, governments, transnational organizations and politicians) in whose interest it is to keep 'politically correct' discourse moving ahead, creating the impression of openness and readiness for change; but whose interests *de facto* lie somewhere else.[1] The phenomenal carrier of the notion in the last decade deserves not only attention, but also a careful and more detailed analysis. The language of civil society has become a crucial determinant of the game of 'who speaks to whom?' and on what terms? What definitions are adopted by donors and authorities (such as 'partners') of civil society organizations? Is there a genuine language of civil society to be heard from independent, grass-roots circles and social movements? Or can one no longer distinguish the real voices from below from the more sophisticated 'dear-friend'-type[2] of discourse emanating from above?

In order to 'measure' the real weight of civil society in particular political contexts, one has to be able to separate out genuine civil society talk from pseudo-civil society language. Hence critical discourse is the key to the survival of the meaning of civil society. This critique, however, presupposes a widespread consensus and readiness to fight for the realization of the 'common good' among constituting elements of civil society. What is understood as common good in a community depends, among other factors, on the cultural-political context and the existence of independent mediating institutions such as the media, the educational system and the availability and accessibility to channels of information, information technology and communication.

Civil Society and NGOs: Conceptual and Language Wars

Most authors agree that the meaning of the term 'civil society' has undergone significant change since the end of the Cold War. According to Mary Kaldor, at the core of what is new in the concept since 1989 is globalization. The prerequisite social contract between civil society and the state is seen in the constitution of 'a global system of rules, underpinned by overlapping inter-governmental, governmental and global authorities' (Kaldor 2003: 2). The fact that no concensus can be reached on the definition of civil society, its inherent ambiguity, says Kaldor, reveals one of its attractions. Habermas also points out that its 'rediscovery' today has placed it in 'wholly new historical constellations' (Habermas 1996). Civil society is no longer viewed as constituted by markets, capital and commodities, but rather encompasses 'nongovernmental and noneconomic connections and voluntary associations that anchor the communication structures of the public sphere in the society component of the lifeworld' (ibid.: 367). Civil society, as a network of associations, articulates and amplifies social problems of the private life spheres in the public sphere; and these associations are both egalitarian and open (ibid.: 367).

Civil society can express itself in a great variety of forms, from individual initiatives through social movements, clubs, associations, societies and other organizations. More importantly, however, it is embodied in a spirit of civic solidarity, civil courage and community *ethos*. This can manifest itself rather spontaneously and can take a wide variety of forms, from mild deliberation to strong protest. It is, therefore, never a mechanical sum total of existing or potential formations. To quote Alan Fowler, 'civil society is the location from where legitimacy must be obtained if one is to talk of a democratic political system' (Fowler 1996: 25). Civil society in this sense is more a philosophical concept than a set of organizations.

Civil society can be viewed as a potential – an ad hoc melting pot and battleground of diverse interests and actors, ranging from public individuals to international NGOs. It is the terrain of self-reflection, self-articulation and autonomy that inherently presupposes and necessitates a self-organizing public arena, where the critique, the control and containment of existing and prevailing power-monopolies (the state, the army, the police, multinational companies, intergovernmental institutions, local authorities, and so on) can be practiced. This public arena is not homogenous; it is constituted rather as a permanent regrouping and renegotiating process between and among new and old participants. Its non-constant social fabric and catalyzed interdependencies are built on the autonomous and voluntary will of the individual who actively takes part in social and political affairs.

The need for civil society stems from democracy's deficiencies. This special social space assumes a strong consciousness of being a citizen as well as citizen participation in social processes. Pure deliberative civil society is not enough, however, to strengthen democracy. Strong civil societies presuppose effective and enabling institutions along with legal guarantees. This interrelatedness between the individual, his/her associations and a larger framework of mediating institutions is the key to understanding civil society's added value to democracy as is emphasized in recent literature on civil society and NGOs. Lars Jorgensen, for example, envisions civil society as a 'meeting place for debate and common endeavour', acknowledging that 'the right of each individual to participate in the workings of society, and the recognition that periodical elections and referendums ... are not sufficient' (Jorgensen 1996: 36). In other words, there is nothing stable or mechanistic about civil society, especially not as far as its 'institutions' are concerned. Mary Kaldor suggests that 'the advantage of the language of civil society is precisely its political content, its implications for participation and citizenship' (Kaldor 1997: 23).

Those who do take up the challenge of reframing the conceptual discourse are conscious of the dangers of the lack of self-reflection on the part of NGOs and the lack of conceptual clarity on the part of intellectuals which has led to confusion in practice. Jenny Pearce asks simply: 'What and who is your practice for?' And she reminds us that the 'failure to ask such questions has led to the false linguistic consensus of the 1990s and ... to an intellectual lazy reliance on a handful of concepts and words as a substitute for thought' (Pearce 1993: 12). She continues by arguing that if we are not guided by praxis, theoretical clarity and ethical practices, words can be defined by whoever chooses for whatever purpose.[3] The danger is that civil society is turned into a project by Western donors, instead of being seen as a process of complex interactions among different players; and in the absence of self-reflection on their own side, NGOs end up simply implementing the vision of donors. Thus, there is not one model, one discourse or one correct definition of civil society. Its very essence lies in its diversity, difference, spontaneity and pluralism. Hence, a polished dialogue with Mr/Ms Civil Society, a wish often expressed by governments and politicians, will never be possible. This is what distinguishes the Citizen (and its public space) from the Merchant and the Prince. Civil society is multilingual and cannot be taught one exclusive and particular language.

The philosopher W.T. Jones, pondering on the often ineffective character of the dialogical processes taking place between interlocutors concerned with the same subject, demonstrated that discontinuities in communication can be described in terms of pre-rational axes of bias on the part of the participants or schools of thought. These differences can be reflected in, among other things, policy and action preferences, and also in the preferred style of discussion.[4] Differences in position among people along an axis give rise to discontinuity which is difficult to manage in a rational frame of reference. Some of these axes include preferences as listed in the following table:

PREFERENCES	
ORDER System, structure, conceptual clarity	DISORDER Fluidity, muddle, chaos
STATIC Changeless, eternal	DYNAMIC Movement, explanation in genetic and process terms
CONTINUITY Wholeness, unity	DISCRETENESS Plurality, diversity
PROCESS Explanations subject to laws, defineable processes	SPONTANEITY Change, freedom, accident

This model can be useful when comparing the internal discourse of civil society with and about itself to the external discourse of global and international institutions about civil society. The compulsion of institutions is to what some term 'colonize' the language of civil society – to objectify, normatively define and compartmentalize the concept, whereas civil society actors often see themselves and their activities rather as a dynamic and fluid process. In fact, much of the critique from international institutions, like the WTO and IMF, relating to the limitations of 'dialogue' with civil society, is focused on the perception that civil society is non-static, ungraspable and ultimately indefinable. Where is Mr/Ms Civil Society, they ask? Since no one seems to step forward, except for some self-appointed old apparatchiks from former communist countries, governments and politicians strive to carry out their own 'civil society' expressed by their own language of civil society. The construction of frames to compartmentalize NGOs and civil society organizations has ultimately led to selective exclusion of certain groups from participation at the global institutional level.

Institutional definitions tend to rely on the preferences of order, continuity and process. From an abundance of relative classifications related to the WTO we could mention below the following as characteristic:

Conformers: those who accept present trade discourse, as well as aims and activities of the WTO. **Reformers:** those who accept the need for a global trade regime, but seek changes to current theory, policy or procedures. **Radicals:** those who seek to extensively change the WTO's scope, powers or even existence. (Scholte 1999)

Reformists: those who seek minor reforms to the WTO for more openness, accountability and representation. **Stakeholders:** those who seek representation stakes for a wider range of view points or interests. **Cosmopolitans:** those who seek more direct democracy and participatory structures. (McGrew 1999)

Responsive globalists: those who accept globalization, trade liberalism and the WTO, but also accept the need for slightly wider input to and participation in WTO processes. **Participatory:** those who accept the above mentioned premises but want more participation for particular key changes; LINGOs (labour NGOs) typically take this view. **Reformists:** these groups vary in their degree of acceptance of globalization and the currently-constituted WTO, so they propose a wide range of changes to WTO's scope, subject matter, procedures, transparency, representativeness, and so on; most environmental NGOs and development NGOs fit this bill. **Radical critics:** those who fundamentally question the legitimacy of current trade and globalization mechanisms, thus proposing extensive changes to the present global order, without wanting abolition of all global trade or economic structures. (Dunkley 2000)

Non-institutional approaches to definition tend to embody the preferences of disorder, dynamism, discreteness and spontaneity. We were able to differentiate according to the user's attitude quite a few languages of civil society. Some of the most outstanding are:

The **'innovative':** the best example of this category is probably Anthony Judge, a language virtuoso. Other examples include John Keane, Jan Aart Scholte, Marc Nerfin, Ronnie Lipschutz and Manuel Castells.

The **'patronizing':** the 'civil society language' of most intergovernmental organizations belongs to this category. An outstanding example is the IMF-initiated newsletter 'Dear Friend ...' and the entire process of 'accrediting' civil society organizations as partners in dialogue. Guy Verhofstadt's open letter is another good example. (Verhofstadt 2001)

The **'radical':** those who refuse the patronizing language and demand real participation in dialogues and decision-making at the global level. The best examples are the movements and networks categorized by multilateral economic institutions (MEIs) as 'absolutists' such as *50 Years was Enough, Greenpeace, Jubilee 2000, Ruckus Society*, etc.

The **'global enthusiasts':** those who speak the 'pozzy' language of Anthony Judge. Edward Comor's 'global civil society progressives'; John Keane's 'civil society purists'.

'Civil society fakers': 'I am Mr/Ms Civil Society!' A lucrative job for benefactors of former authoritarian regimes who have the skills and networks to create fake coalitions that they represent at national, European or global fora. This is particularly evident in post-communist, feckless democracies.

The 'practical practitioners' of the 'third sector': they rarely talk civil society explicitly and show little enthusiasm for theoretical civil society debates.

'Theoreticians of civil society': academics who do the opposite of the practical practitioners.

The 'totalizing': from Aristotle to Alan Greenspan, 'the whole world is civil society' including, of course, uncivil society!

The 'empiricist': 'statistics please!' Only measurable NGOs count. The rest is fantasy. Representatives of American mainstream social sciences literature are leading this group. They would be labelled as 'neggies' in Anthony Judge's classification. Those who are always sceptical for good reason. They actually help detect the mistakes and failures of others in the civil society literature.

There are obviously many overlaps between the users of these ways of speaking and these categories can, of course, be extended. The different languages used by rather influential representatives of the above-mentioned categories are reflections of the significance of this peculiar term and the new social, political and economic terrains it occupies. In order to better understand the expanding worldwide usage of the term 'civil society' one needs to discover the less obvious reasons behind its usage. Besides pragmatic and prescriptive work on the one hand, and grand historical-theoretical analysis on the other, the proposal to see civil society as metaphor offers one of the most genuine and convincing discursive formulations of this issue.

In a recent publication, Hakan Seckinelgin (2002) makes a sharp distinction between the meaning and image of 'civil society' in the 1980s advocated by East Central European intellectuals dedicated to social change, and the most recent use of the term that attempts to involve people in the process of development. Seckinelgin incisively observes that one must recognize the 'aspirational formation' of the concept which maps an intellectual situation, based on experience elsewhere, onto a target context (Seckinelgin 2002: 357). What he detects is that the usage of the concept of civil society this way combines two meanings: one is real life experience, the other is an imagined and desired, 'would-be' reality. This general aspirational usage presupposes the reduction of different historic and political contexts to one ahistorical concept. This is related to Pearce's argument regarding the normative application of the concept. Seckinelgin defines the language of civil society employed by international development organizations and multilateral economic institutions (MEIs) as a metaphor. He argues that the process of involvement of civil society organizations by MEIs in the development context contributes to the spread of Western, neo-liberal social relations; in other words, it strengthens rather than changes the present state of affairs. The essential outcome of this process is the establishment of a 'new organizational culture based on Western sectoral divisions'.[5]

Moreover, Seckinelgin is adamant that each 'way of speaking *a civil society* ... reflects a way of distinct life and relations particular to that life' (Seckinelgin 2002: 359). Using the ahistorical concept of civil society as a metaphor can be seen as an invitation to participation by the 'sender' of the message. The accepted invitation might create the impression of similarity between fundamentally different participants of the linguistic game (sender/recipient), thereby acknowledging a similarity that creates the impression of community (see Cohen 1980, cited in Seckinelgin 2002: 361). A crucial point in Seckinelgin's argument is that the message sent by the metaphor of civil society is not necessarily understood by the recipient in its complexity and could result in 'unexpected consequences for those who are ascribed to be civil society' (ibid.: 359).

According to Seckinelgin, besides the general, aspirational metaphor of civil society, it also plays a major role in signifying the 'intended' participants of the civil society discourse.[6] Explicitly and implicitly, the mindset, the cognitive map and the interest of donors or the 'sender' of the metaphor are some of the determinants of reality. Choosing and selecting the NGOs who are supposed to represent civil society is an attempt to create a certain kind of civil society or, using Seckinelgin's phrase, an attempt to reformulate the space for civil society. Therefore, the particular language of civil society used by the reports has a transformative effect on the existing civil societies of the recipients. It is clear from their documents and programmes that the World Bank and other MEIs recognize and 'accredit' their own civil society organizations according to what fits their criteria. They build and advertise their civil society model upon that empirical base. The civil society – and the civil society language – created are not only problematic and ungenuine but also become a hotbed for further social, cultural and political tensions. International organizations have a great capacity to create and popularize concepts and images, especially by attracting the attention of the global media and influencing their member-governments in order to foster social changes and alter the way societies and their members function. Civil society is used, thus, as an attempt by international organizations to continue the 'process of civilization':

> By using civil society organizations, an attempt is made to bring long-term socio-political change on the basis of Western experience. Therefore, the seemingly technical recommendations made by these international organizations, in which the metaphor is an agent of change for the social functions,… are actually political interventions, insofar as they intervene in the entirety of society for a change implicitly encoded in the metaphor. (Seckinelgin 2002: 376)

However fine-tuned and precise it might be, this analysis encompasses only one part of the whole picture. Although conscious and unconscious attempts to further develop the process of Western civilization can be seen as powerful and potentially successful, the emerging post-national condition and information society/economy is profoundly different from the age of early capitalism. Influential international organizations, MEIs and others are seriously challenged by powerful social movements, ad hoc global alliances, and transnational networks of civil society. These new and old actors employ their own civil society language to shape reality, trying to carve out, occupy and dominate real and virtual social spaces with their own discourse and metaphors. The international or rather intergovernmental organizations – globalized representatives of the Prince and the Merchant – have formidable tools at their disposal, but lack the legitimacy of the nation state which played such a decisive role in the development of Western civilization. In many ways they are more defensive, trying to attract, seduce or convince their chosen civil society partners (and through them a larger global audience) of their good intentions, usefulness, and inevitability.

Global Civil Society and Global Citizenship

Vaclav Havel understands civil society as the universality of human rights that allow us to fulfill our potential in all of our roles: as members of our nation, our family, our region, our church, our community, profession, political party, and so on. In other words, by becoming citizens 'in the broadest and deepest sense of the word' (cited in Dahrendorf 1997: 58). Civil society, and the organically related concept of citizenship, therefore provide a protective umbrella, a guarantee of security, an experience of belonging, of home. Jeffrey Alexander voices a similar idea:

> Civil society should be conceived as a solidarity sphere in which a certain kind of universalising community exists, it is exhibited by 'public opinion', possesses its own cultural codes and narratives in a democratic idiom, is patterned by a set of peculiar institutions, most notably legal and journalistic ones, and is visible in historically distinctive sets of interactional practices like civility, equality, criticism, and respect. This kind of civil community can never exist as such; it can exist only 'to one degree or another'. (Alexander 1998: 58)

In our understanding, the key actor of civil society is the Citizen, the sovereign individual who possesses rights and responsibilities and is ready to accept the rules of cooperation for the good of him/herself and the community, in this way sacrificing a part of his/her own sovereignty. However, there is no complete, strong and efficient civil society without the universal status of citizenship. It is the set of rights and capacities related to citizenship that guarantees a defence against *anomie* and protects against an over-indulgent market of turbo-capitalism. Dahrendorf characterizes citizenship as the epitome of freedom, and civil society as the medium through which this freedom is projected, boosted and dispersed. It thus constitutes the home of the Citizen:

> ... citizenship and civil society go one important step further than elections and markets. They are goals to strive for rather than dangers to avoid. In this sense they are moral objectives ...(Dahrendorf 1997: 60)

Alexander calls our attention to the fact that although civil society is dependent on other spheres, the sphere of solidarity still enjoys relative autonomy (and as such should be studied independently). He reminds us that civil society cannot be reduced to the realm of institutions. The world of civil society is also the world of structured, socially constructed conscience, 'a network of understandings that operates beneath and above explicit institutions' (ibid.: 97). Alexander points out that the world created by the discourse is polarized. It offers the image of open society in contrast to the model of a closed, secretive, conspiratorial world. The symbolic characteristics on the positive side can guarantee the preservation of society; the networks of solidarity on the negative side serve the purpose of undermining mutual respect and destroying social integration.

Language, therefore, carries with it the danger of polarization and the creation of enemy images. The questions are always the same: Who is it that speaks in the name of civil society? Who delineates the 'insiders' and the 'outsiders'? Who distinguishes the 'good guys' from the 'bad guys'? Who has access to the necessary resources to sustain civil society? In societies that are in the early stages of democratic development, the danger is especially great. On the one hand, new enemies are created through the use of language and, on the other hand, the discourse of civil or open society can be kidnapped in a way that is not civil, not open, and not democratic.

For a long time analysis of the impact of civil society on citizenship remained within national boundaries and more recently within the European Union (see Callahan 1996: 1–25; Castells 1998; Davidson 1997: 33–56; De Swaan 1997: 561–75; Heater 1996; Huntington 1993: 22–49; Hutchings 1996; Walzer 1995). Theoretical and empirical analysis of the emerging global civil society was sporadic in the 1990s and started to accumulate only around the turn of the century (see Lipschutz 1992: 389–420; Edwards 2002: 71–76; Falk 1995; Falk 1998: 99–111; Florini 2000; Kaldor 2003; Keane 2003; Magone 2000; Scholte 2002: 281–304). Most authors agree with Michael Muetzelfeldt and Gary Smith that analysing global civil society presupposes the analysis of global governance and the democratic deficit on the global level. They draw a parallel between nation-states and global institutions concerning their treatment of their corresponding civil society partners.

> Just as states may facilitate or obstruct the emergence and development of national civil society, so too, global governance institutions may facilitate or obstruct an emerging global civil society. (Muetzelfeldt and Smith 2002: 56; see chapter 6)

The 'mutually emergent approach' focuses on the interdependence among the major players in the global arena. Their main question, whether civil society is able to extend its reach 'in step with the globalization of markets and systems of governance, and with what effects?'(ibid.: 59) again echoes Nerfin's model and the most recent literature on global civil society.

Institutions of an emerging global governance such as the World Bank, the IMF and the WTO, focused both in their activities and their language on pursuing their original aim of developing and supporting global finance and trade markets. This socially and politically rather one-sided approach and behaviour went through a significant change during the second half of the 1990s. First the World Bank, then the IMF and the WTO recognized that they could not achieve their objectives any longer without trying to create some harmony between the economic, social and political aspects of global development. In order to do so, they had to convince some major players (INGOs and social movements) about the correctness of their activities. In other words, they had to enter a structured and regular dialogue with identifiable actors of global civil society. This has opened a new period of intermediate interfaces that gave impetus for both political debates and social scientific analysis.

Since the mid-1990s, there is a growing consensus among global civil society representatives that their activity can be instrumental in solving transnational issues which individual governments or intergovernmental organizations are unable to solve by themselves. This new optimism has been reflected in the recent literature on global civil society. Lester Salamon's (1994) phrase, 'associational revolution', whose significance equals for the author the emergence of the nation state, is a good example of the academic/activist optimism which provoked more support than contempt. As John Keane (2003) and others repeatedly point out, this optimism is often unfounded and reflects the growing desire of many intellectuals to identify actors who are able to solve the mounting problems of the world. By the same token, it is hard to deny that there is an unprecedented shift on the global stage in activities and organizational capacities and as a consequence in achievements of global networks, movements and organizations, including ad hoc initiatives. Although the distinction between ungrounded and therefore sometimes irresponsible optimism from real progress and civil society empowerment is difficult to sustain, it nevertheless presents social science with one of its major tasks.

Jan Aart Scholte seems to be moving towards this direction and his challenging theory of civil society is largely based on an acute awareness of the need to cast doubt on traditional conceptual schemata. His starting point is that global civil society played an important role in recasting politics in the late twentieth century, since it offered new chances for the enhancement of security, equity and democracy in the contemporary world (Scholte 1999). Along with other authors, Scholte understands civil society to reside outside the boundaries of the market, yet he is aware of overlaps and interfaces. Dissatisfied with the negative definition of non-governmental organizations and the non-profit sector, he provides a more focused and practical definition, according to which '... civil society exists when people make concerted efforts through voluntary associations to mould rules' (ibid.: 7). 'Moreover', he continues 'a distinction is drawn between *civil society* which is seen as the collective noun and *civic groups*, organizations etc. [that] are [seen as being] the individual elements within civil society' (ibid.: 4). More explicitly put, 'civil society exists whenever people mobilize through voluntary associations in initiatives to shape the social order' (ibid.: 7). He believes, that further generalization is difficult since really existing civil societies are greatly varied and diverse.

Even if the history of transnational or international organizations goes back to the ninettenth century, global civil society is a relatively new phenomenon and global civil society 'talk' emerged only in the early 1990s (see Falk 1992: 219–39; Lipschutz 1992; *Citizens Strengthening Global Civil Society* 1994; Shaw 1994: 647–67). Global civil society surfaced with many related terms, such as international non-governmental organizations, transnational advocacy networks, global social movements, new multilateralism, and so on, heralding not only an associational but also a linguistic revolution. Scholte observes that among the different meanings associated with the new phenomenon of globality (internationalisation, universalization, Westernization, Americanization and deterritorialization), only deterritorialization can be seen as a distinctive trend which signals a turning point. Deterritorialization means that territorial locations, distance, borders, and so on, no longer have a determining influence. 'In global space, "place" is not territorially fixed, territorial distance is covered in effectively no time, and territorial frontiers present no particular impediment. Thus global relations have what could be called a "supraterritorial", "transborder" or "transworld" character' (Scholte 1999: 7). Deterritorialization does not mean, however, that territorial geography has lost all of its relevance and, as Scholte emphasizes, 'we inhibit a globalizing rather than a completely globalized world' (ibid.: 9).

Territoriality and non-territoriality, as demonstrated in the case of the European Union and European integration, exist in a rich amalgamation and interdependence (Tunander et al. 1997). This coexistence, however, does not blur the fact that we are at the beginning of a new epoch where although 'territoriality may continue to be important, globalization has brought an end to territorialism' (Scholte 1999: 9). Inventing and introducing a new vocabulary, Scholte identifies globality as supraterritoriality and constructs his notion of global civil society accordingly:

> If we identify globality as supraterritoriality, then what does global civil society involve? In short, global civil society encompasses civic activity that: (a) addresses transworld issues; (b) involves transborder communication; (c) has a global organisation; (d) works on a premise of supraterritorial solidarity. Often these four attributes go hand in hand, but civic associations can also have a global character in only one or several of these four respects. For example, a localised group that campaigns on supraterritorial problems like climate change could be considered part of global civil society even though the association lacks a transborder organization and indeed might only rarely communicate with civic groups elsewhere in the world. Conversely, global civic networks might mobilise around a local development like the 1994 genocide in Rwanda. (ibid.: 10)

What are those new conditions that can be seen as responsible for the expansion of the vocabulary, the horizon and the further development of the language of civil society? And what are the causes of such an enormous change? First of all, there is the worldwide restructuration of power-relations, that is the rise of the postnational constellation, the emergence of new transnational units, cross-border frameworks and regional institutions. Scholte admits that civic associations operate regionally and in global spaces as well as locally and nationally, and consequently our notions of 'civil society need to be recast to reflect these changed circumstances' (ibid.: 285).

This conclusion is based on the recognition that we have reached a new epoch of global civil society development which is highly relevant for students as well as activists and clients (partners, interlocutors) of civil society organizations. The new vocabulary is a reflection of diversified meanings and, as a consequence, the language of civil society has gone through significant change: a new epoch gave birth to a new discourse. This does not mean, however, that the remarkable intellectual and political history of civil society theory has become obsolete or irrelevant. Instead, the linguistically expanded development in civil society discourse throws new light on previous concepts and conceptualizations. Retrospectively, it is becoming clearer why the term had such rich potential from the very moment of its resurfacing in the second half of the 1970s in Latin America and East Central Europe (see chapters 6 and 7 above). This potential has been unfolding in present political and academic debates on global, transnational, European, and regional civil society, and is manifested in the 4.2 million shots on the Internet search of the different categories of civil society. The table below represents one type of categorization by subject. The breadth and variety available under the heading 'civil society' is impressive.

	Google.com	*Questia.com*	*Amazon.com*	*EBSCO*
European civil society	1.270.000	29.176	29	105
Trans-national civil society	229.000	213	1	52
Democracy + civil society	1.070.000	110	149	377
Language of civil society	1.280.000	32.556	22	29
Public spheres + civil society	143.000	7	0	9
Citizenship + civil society	388.000	49	68	98
Globalization + civil society	370.000	2	17	106
Development + civil society	2.170.000	34	74	461
Citizenship + civil society	388.000	49	68	98
Social movement + civil society	994.000	93	25	96
Networks + civil society	823.000	5	17	43
Governance + civil society	797.000	4	25	124
Media + civil society	1.630.000	21	25	86
Civic discourse + civil society	40.900	4	4	6

This result does not simply provide a *post festum* justification of the ongoing civil society debate in academia. It is rather an attempt to explain the perseverance and proliferation of the concept, on the one hand, and the growing demand of the market of ideas and intellectual innovations, on the other. It is a reflection of a broader and more fundamental social need and an expression of interest by various groups and associations in society to find the proper way to create a common denominator so their voices will be heard.

Civil society literature began to grow from the late 1980s and, with certain ups and downs, continued to accelerate through the 1990s. In the early 1990s there was a stronger tendency of scepticism about the usefulness of civil society as a social scientific category. Some authors expressed strong opinions about the uselessness and inadequacy of the category, in the first place mentioning its blurred character and its normative and political-ideological loadedness (see, for example, Seligman 1992; Kumar 1994: 127–30; Gáspár 1994: 205–22). Many political and academic analyses in the 1990s revealed that it was a necessary but outdated and romantic expression of the heroic decade when the struggle was waged against weakening dictatorships and authoritarian regimes. Since – the argument goes – that epoch is over, we no longer need unclear, overstretched, value-loaded categories to describe or analyse economic transition and social democratization. These analyses believe that democracy and market economy sufficiently serve intellectual and analytical demands.

This assumption, however, proved to be wrong. As a result, from the mid-1990s onwards, we can observe a somewhat surprising growth and expansion of interest in the concept, both in the fields of praxis and in theory-building, as the abundance of literature shows. The old concept of civil society does, however, need restructuring since its meaning has gone through significant change. Scholte argues that consequently other related categories – first of all democracy – need to be reconceptualized under the radically new political-economic constellation, which Habermas (2000) calls postnational for good reason. Both democracy and civil society (not to speak of even broader categories, such as society) belonged to the era of modernity which overlaps with that of the modern nation state. Within this era, the natural unit of both political life and social analysis used to be the universally perceived nation state.

The nation state paradigm dominated throughout the nineteenth and twentieth centuries, but the two world wars fundamentally undermined its claim of absolute sovereignty and relativized its practical usefulness. Although this constellation has significantly changed since the end of – and even during – the Second World War, the domination of the nation state paradigm has survived fundamental changes and transition towards crossborder, trans- and supranational and even global structures first in the economic then in the political and social realms. The belatedness of the social-scientific world to grasp this fundamental restructuration is partly due to the rigidity and conservative character of our system of knowledge production and its institutions. This time lag in perception of changing realities contributed to the present cacophony of social scientific interpretations.

Already in 1992, Ronnie Lipschutz reasoned that 'the growth of global civil society represents an ongoing project of civil society to reconstruct, re-imagine, or re-map world politics' (Lipschutz 1992: 391). The emergence of global civil society at this particular juncture has been seen as a response to the 'leaking away of sovereignty from the state both upwards, to supranational institutions, and downwards, to subnational ones' and therefore as a 'functional response to the decreasing ability and willingness of governments to undertake a variety of welfare functions' (Lipschutz 1992: 399). The state, we should be reminded, had its origins not in the desire to provide welfare service, but rather to sell protection whether it was wanted or not. The Second World War destroyed the pact between society and the state because in its pursuit of security the state was willing to sacrifice millions of people. state incompetence with regard to managing highly complex problems (like global mass media, environmental problems, illegal arms trade), rather than the traditional ones of war and finance, has led to increasing the need for societal competence (ibid.: 399).

Integration, as in the case of the EU, has loosened the links between territory and collective destiny. Transborder solidarity networks were already strengthening during the 1970s and 1980s; and cosmopolitan bonds have been developing for centuries. The meaning of 'people' has certainly lost its unequivocal or predominantly nation state-oriented character. Globalization, the process of European integration and the re-emergence of historic regions along with new crossborder Euroregions, are making claims for their own 'public'. Crossborder cooperation also strengthens 'supraterritorial networks' which provide new loyalties and regional identities. As a consequence, there is a shift in the 'geography of values' which supports the argument for an emerging global civil society. Identification with the nation state as the primary social grouping has begun to wither in some places. At the same time, identity based on consumption and the market was insufficient for establishing new identities. Therefore we have seen a rise in new forms of collective identities, new nationalisms in some places but also the creation of cosmopolitan identities and a global consciousness (Scholte 2002: 287):

> Democracy is constructed in relation to context and should be reconstructed when that context changes.... Contemporary globalization constitutes the sort of change of situation that requires new approaches to democracy. (ibid.: 285)

Scholte recognizes the democratic deficit on the level of global governance, and wonders whether and how civil society can contribute to reducing it, dynamizing the process of global democratization. More precisely, he is concerned with the role civil society could play in the context for a reconfigured democracy for global governance. In this approach, the distinctive feature of globalization is deterritorialization, in the rise of 'supraterritoriality':

> Globality refers to a particular kind of social space ... a realm, that substantially transcends the confines of territorial place, territorial distance and territorial borders. Whereas territorial spaces are mapped in terms of longitude, latitude and altitude, global relations transpire in the world as a

single place, as one more or less seamless realm. Globality in this sense has a 'transworld' or 'transborder' quality. A supraterritorial phenomenon can appear simultaneously at any location on earth. (ibid.: 286)

This theorization of the postnational constellation or 'supranationality' does not deny the continuity and significance of territoriality and its institutions and geographic as well as metaphoric identities. Scholte and others emphasize that globality has not taken over territoriality but territoriality no longer has the monopoly on social geography. One can argue about the unequal character of globalization along the faultlines of assymetrical dichotomies such as urban–rural, South–North, affluent–poor, male–female categories, but 'globality' is an undeniable and significant phenomenon that has significant consequences for the social sciences, political praxis and social relations.

Global Civil Society and Global Governance

As the wide literature on European integration has emphasized in the last decade, 'governance' involves many more layers than the state; and in contemporary multilevel (multicentred) governance civil society should play a significant role. Global governance, however, is not an embryonic form of a world government modelled after the modern nation-state. It appears that global relations are regulated without a single centre of authority. As a consequence, the governance of supraterritorial spaces is characterized by democratic deficit, since 'global governance is not democratically legitimate' (Scholte 2002: 292). Civil society, therefore, serves a different function than in the previous epoch and has to find new ways for establishing itself within this new global, postnational constellation. Many authors talk about the democratic promise of globalizing civil society which can give voice to stakeholders and even empower them, and by doing so enhancing participation on the global level; can contribute to the quality and scope of public education since the complexities and rapidly changing 'realities' of globalized information societies need permanent learning and education; can foster discussions about actual challenges of global governance – locally as well as on the supranational level; can contribute to enhancing the transparency of global governance; and can increase accountability. Altogether these opportunities, if realized, would give legitimacy both for global governance and for civil society actors playing on the global stage. Likewise, the engagement 'between civil society and regulatory mechanisms can … enhance the respect that citizens accord to global governance' (ibid.: 294).[7]

During the 1990s, both the engagement and the representation of civil society organizations and networks shifted from monitoring to active participation in governance (see Foster 2001; Edwards 2002). Benjamin Barber (2001) speaks about 'signs of an emerging internationalism' around transnational civil institutions, global social movements, and a world public opinion. There is a growing agreement in recent literature that an 'associational revolution' took place during the 1990s on all possible levels – global, regional, local. Although the development of social movements, NGOs and civil society organizations is uneven worldwide, their 'growth in number and reach around the world is unquestioned' (Salamon 1994: 113).

The move from monitoring to governing (actively shaping decision-making and participating in confrontative dialogues with decision-makers) is partly a result of the dramatically changed global economic and political constellations which led the UN to initiate a series of world conferences on the most contested issues, such as the environment, human rights, gender, and global economic policies. This opened up rather closed intergovernmental organizations or MEIs such as the World Bank, the IMF, and the WTO towards dialogue and cooperation. It is also the result of a growing global consciousness and global sense of responsibility. It represents the changing values of an unprecedented and growing number of citizens who not only protest, gather and organize themselves across frontiers, but who are also consciously developing their networks of networks on a more or less permanent basis. Consequently, the World Conferences of the 1990s resulted in a cumulative vision of a desired future.

This growing discrepancy between words and deeds, between the civil society language used by representatives of the Merchant and the Prince on the one hand, and a genuine civil society discourse of self-organizing Citizens on the other, proved to be a creative confrontation and an expression of the growing role of civil society in settling global matters. Looking at the rewards of subsequent parallel summits and significant changes in global issues as a result of protest and structured criticism, Foster's claim that the associational revolution is extended by an organizational revolution on the side of civil society is strong.

Manuel Castells in *The Rise of the Network Society* (Castells 2000) offers other challenging and comprehensive conceptual tools of analysis. His main argument is that networks are the 'critical sources of domination and change in our society' (ibid.: 500) and consequently social morphology enjoys pre-eminence vis-à-vis social action.

> … this networking logic includes a social determination of a higher level than that of the specific social interests expressed through the networks: the power of flows takes precedence over the flows of power. (ibid.: 500)

Castells sees the network society as a dynamic and open system that can innovate without undermining itself. The rise of the network society has fundamental consequences for social relations, structures and institutions and redefines the dimensions, scope and boundaries of social action. In this continuously reshaped and radically new reality, it becomes increasingly difficult to understand the different roles of old and new actors, their inter-relatedness, interfaces and overlaps.

It is an open question whether civil society in its globalized, but still fragmented forms reflecting global inequalities in terms of participation and accessibility to technology, is capable or not of creating meaningful links of interdependence between individuals and social groups. The attempt is clearly present. The humanized aims of a global future are formulated, while the vocabulary of a global and local civil society is growing. However, different languages are spoken at one and the same time and the institutionalized forms and frames for a more systematic and structured dialogue are still missing. It is too early to tell whether emerging transnational, European and global publics and civil networks will be able to deliver enabling frameworks, institutions and fora which will be powerful and persistent enough to shape a new order of regional and transnational publics and contribute to what we could call 'global governance' with global civil society.

Intergovernmental institutions like the IMF, WTO, and World Bank have come under increasing pressure from criticism by a coalition of civil society networks with regard to their decision-making process and operations. This has resulted in attempts by each of these organizations to address in a variety of ways, with more or less success and sincerity, to engage elements of what they define as civil society actors in their discourse. Increasingly vocal and concerted criticism that fostered weaker and stronger attempts at dialogue can be reviewed in the framework of a general mistrust of organizations that operate in a culture of secrecy, and who are viewed as having destabilized and undermined economic development in developing countries for decades to the benefit of developed countries. The lack of transparency and exclusionary decision-making processes evidenced in their operations, and the human and social costs of their implemented programmes erupted in violent protests against these institutions in an unprecedented manner – unprecedented because of the cross-issue, transnational character of civil society's response. The message to the WTO, for example, by the Seattle to Brussels Network (a pan-European network of ninety-nine associations) was 'Shrink or Sink!'

The WTO, in its Marrakesh Agreement, provides the potential for relationships with NGOs in Article V (2):

> The General Council may make appropriate arrangements for consultation and co-operation with non-governmental organisations concerned with matters related to those of the WTO.[8]

However, further guidelines adopted by the General Council of the WTO state:

> ... there is currently a broadly held view that it would not be possible for NGOs to be directly involved in the work of the WTO or its meetings. Closer consultation and cooperation with NGOs can also be met constructively through appropriate processes at the national level where lies primary responsibility for taking into account the different elements of public interest which are brought to bear on trade policy-making.

This expresses a typical argument against NGO observership as representatives of national interest groups whose concerns should be met at national levels. Another argument runs that the WTO is a forum for negotiations between governments not societies and a third, practical argument relates to the increased demand for physical space required by NGO presence and involvement. Smaller WTO members would then fear that most negotiations would be held in private, marginalizing them, and the sessions of WTO bodies would become mere public relations exercises. The IMF has also been reticent to open up its policy-making process to what they may observe as undisciplined if not openly hostile representatives of civil society.

In the contemporary context it seems evident that there will be increasing probability of conflicts between such institutions as the WTO, IMF and WB and the societies in which they work. More challenges to the system will be made, including the questioning of power relations. The challenge to these institutions takes the form of questioning their democratic structure and decision-making processes, their lack of transparency, legitimacy and capacity to deal with an increasing range of complex, interrelated and divisive issues. Besides securing better access to information emanating from the agencies which would increase the possibility of building public trust in their operations, inclusion of civil society promotes accountability at the global level. In the emerging arena of global governance, NGO-nized civil society has an important role to play (see Willetts 2002).[9] This new force on the global stage may be expected to increasingly influence the global agenda, decision-making and policy implementation.

Although the United Nations led in the engagement of civil groups in its proceedings,[10] today the World Bank, among the mentioned institutions, has made the most assertive attempt to speak the language of civil society with a high profile at least with regard to appearance. Its relatively new (as of 28 May 2003) website (www.worldbank.org/civilsociety) could be taken as a model for the new discourse and resultant organizational restructuring. The World Bank boasts a Civil Society Team (CST), the Civil Society Group (CSG) and over eighty Civil Society Country Staff (CSC). The stated purpose of these new structures and the website is 'to provide CSOs with

COMPARATIVE TABLES OF NGO PARTICIPATION IN A SELECTION OF INTERNATIONAL BODIES

	WTO	ITO	ECOSOC (UN)	UNCTAD (UN)	CBD Convention on Biodiversity	UNCED (UN)	NGO-World Bank Committee	OECD	JPAC (NAFTA)
Who selects the NGOs?	Secretarial + Member States consent	Member States on rec. of the Secretariat	Member States on rec. of a Cite on NGOs composed of Member States	Member States on rec. of the Secretariat	Member States on rec. of the Secretariat	Member States on rec. of the Secretariat	The NGOs themselves	Member States on rec. of the Secretariat	Member States individually
Main criteria for selection	NGOs 'concerned with matters related to those of the WTO'	Expertise ECOSOC accreditation	Expertise Representivity NGO supports UN's work and principles Democratic structure Accountability	Expertise Representivity NGO supports UNCTAD's work and principles International structure	Expertise May be admitted unless 1/3 of the Parties present object	Expertise Representivity NGO supports UN's work and principles Organic structure ECOSOC accreditation	NGOs elected by regional assemblies of NGOWB Expertise Geographical representivity International/ National structure	Expertise Representivity International structure	Criteria set by Member States individually
Form of participation	Ad hoc consultation	Ad hoc consultation + Advisory Committee	Consultative Status (General, Special, Roster)	Consultative Status (General, Special, Register)	Consultative Status	Consultative Status	NGO Advisory Committee at global and regional levels	NGO Advisory Committee – obs status at some meetings	NGO Advisory Committee
Who administers NGO participation	Secretariat	Director General	Secretariat (NGLS, UN Department of Public Info., etc.)	Secretariat (NGLS, UN Department of Public Info., etc.)	Secretariat (NGLS, UN Department of Public Info., etc.)	Secretariat (NGLS, UN Department of Public Info., etc.)	NGOs and Bank staff	Secretary-General + Liaison Committee with NGOs	JPAC Member + Council

	WTO	ITO	ECOSOC (UN)	UNCTAD (UN)	CBD Convention on Biodiversity	UNCED (UN)	NGO-World Bank Committee	OECD	JPAC (NAFTA)
Access to meetings of the org.	None except Ministerial Conferences	None except Ministerial Conferences	Yes	Yes	Yes	Yes	No	No	No
Can propose agenda items	No	Only for the Annual Conference	Yes	Yes	No	No	No	No	No
Can speak at some meetings	No	No	Yes	Yes	Yes	Yes	No	Yes	No
Circ. Written statements	No	No	Yes	Yes	Yes	Yes	No	Yes	Yes
Access to information	NGOs only have access to derestricted documents	Receive copies of all unrestricted documents	The Secretariat is authorised to distribute docs as appropriate in its judgement	The Secretariat is authorised to distribute docs as appropriate in its judgement	NGOs have access to official documents	NGOs have access to official documents	The Bank may distribute docs as appropriate in its judgement	The Secretariat is authorised to distribute docs as appropriate in its judgement	Members may receive information including confidential doc from the Secretariat, the Council and the Parties

Source: ICTSD, *Accreditation Schemes and Other Arrangements for Public Participation in International Fora*, International Centre for Trade and Sustainable Development, Geneva, November 1999.

information and materials on the World Bank's evolving relationship with civil society throughout the world'. This is taken in response to what the WB sees as the significant growth of civil society involvement in the area of international development which has lead to partnerships that effectively reduce poverty and achieve sustainable development.

Even its strongest proponents acknowledge that the actual reality and the progressive potential of global civil society are very far from each other. Michael Edwards, who talks enthusiastically about the positive impact of global social movements on decision-making and their ability to reduce the democratic deficit of global governance, also soberly warns that the outcome of civil society involvement depends, among other factors, on whose voices are heard in global debates, and on 'whether civil groups are effective in playing the roles assigned to them in the evolving international system' (Edwards 2002: 72). The danger he sees is real: in the absence of accepted rules of the game, the loudest, the strongest, and the best connected groups will dominate the discourse.

Another often cited criticism is the lack of legitimacy and/or transparency on the side of global civil society actors. This claim may be exaggerated, since they represent their own views and values and should be judged upon their achievements and activities compared to their mission statements. There is, however, a strong tendency among internationally recognized, efficient and well-funded NGOs to develop a neo-liberal, bureaucratized 'professional' language, reproducing thereby power relations and hierarchies. Doubling the contested world is a self-generating way of co-optation.

Stanley Hoffmann provides an even bleaker view when he says that global civil society is still embryonic, and that NGOs have little independence from governments (Hoffmann 2002: 109). In addition, what we call 'global governance' is partial and weak, 'at a time when economic globalization deprives many states of independent monetary and fiscal policies, or it obliges them to make cruel choices between economic competitiveness and the preservation of social safety nets' (ibid.: 110). In contrast to Scholte and others, Hoffmann does not see the rise of a collective global consciousness or solidarity and as a consequence a sense of world citizenship, but he rather insists that in opposition to economic life, 'human identity remains national' (ibid.: 111).

The EU is viewed as rather weak in terms of institutions where the emergence of a supranational identity has just begun (see also chapter 6 above), and the United States as a hegemon unable to resist the temptation of unilateralism:

> We live in a world where a society of uneven and often virtual states overlaps with a global society burdened by weak public institutions and underdeveloped civil society. A single power dominates but its economy could become unmanageable or disrupted by future terrorist attacks. (ibid.: 114)

Edward Comor, another critic of global civil society enthusiasm, directs his attention not so much to the structural unevenness of the processes of globalization, but rather to what he calls the 'GCS progressives' lack of understanding, misinterpretation or superficial analysis of global communication, communication technologies and the deeper interrelatedness between information and knowledge. He stresses that most of the 'GCS progressives' neglect to see how information becomes knowledge and as a consequence they fall into the trap of Internet-fascination. Comor certainly brings an important insight into the global civil society debate, in arguing that

> Human beings ... do not process information in ... necessarily 'rational' or instrumental ways. Instead, our mediating conceptual systems are shaped by lifestyles, work experiences, customs, language, mythologies – by cultures. (Comor 2001: 395)

Although it can be said that 'GCS progressives' have some intimation of the importance of culture, Comor rightly stresses that

> ... GCS literature generally tends to overestimate our collective capacity to be resocialized directly through communications and ideas, the power of individuals and groups to overcome the structural conditions of their lives, and the importance of spatial integration despite the related dismantling of time. (ibid.: 405)

Although Comor does not deny the significance of the new role of communication technologies, and their strategic usefulness as organizational tools, he warns that '... paradoxically they also weaken the reflexive capabilities of collectives, inspiring rapid mobilization but leaving little time for critical reflection' (ibid.: 405). Consequently, if global civil society is going to develop its own genuine language, it cannot be exclusively that of the Internet.

Expanding and Narrowing Horizons of Civil Society

Even if much of the criticism mentioned earlier is well taken, it is hard to deny that an 'organizational revolution' is taking place beyond the surface of public events, street confrontations, and at parallel summits that one-sidedly attract the media. It is expressed by the expanding impact of the Internet (information, communication, shrinking of time-space); by growing networking among a great number and variety of locales; and by the re-emergence of transnational social movements, including civil society networks, and so on (Foster 2001: 6).

Beyond the teargas, riot police and the violence of a small group of protesters (often coupled with police brutality), movements and broad alliances of NGOs, CSOs and concerned individuals have started to reshape global 'realities' and introduced new habits in dealing with world affairs. The worldwide civic movement against landmines, initiated by Jody Williams, enacted a treaty subscribed to by most nations; Jubilee 2000, an anti-debt movement, achieved putting international debt on the agenda of world leaders; a rapidly growing number of NGOs and CSOs are creating new alliances and gathering in transnational organizations such as the World Forum on Democracy, People's Summits at the WTO, or Summits of the Americas, and so on. Far from being 'one-issue movements', as were many of their predecessors from the 1970s and 1980s, these new social movements not only protest, network and raise a critical voice against outstanding injustices, inequalities or power monopolies, they have also begun work on 'alternative futures' (ibid.: 6), and for that they have started to create and develop alternative, transnational publics.

As Michael Edwards, the director of Governance and Civil Society at the Ford Foundation, reports, more than 49 million people joined the 'Hemispheric Social Alliance' to control the Free Trade Agreements of the Americas, and more than 30 thousand INGOs are active on the world stage, along with 20 thousand transnational civil society networks (Edwards 2002: 77). Edwards gives a clear answer to why civil society should be involved:

> In theory ... civil society can make two contributions to effective global governance: First, improving the quality of debate and decision-making by injecting more information, transparency and accountability into the international system, based on a recognition that government and business have no monopoly of ideas or expertise. The Jubilee 2000 movement created enormous pressure for debt relief, but it also put new models and policy suggestions on the table that gradually worked their way into the international establishment.
>
> Second, strengthening the legitimacy and effectiveness of decisions ... by providing a broader spectrum of those whose support is required to make them work. Governments can confer authority on decisions but rarely a complete sense of legitimacy, especially in a 'wired world' ... In this scenario, the weight of public pressure will be felt much more keenly by decision-makers ... and support from non-actors will be crucial in ensuring that decisions are actually implemented ... This was part of the rationale behind the success, for example, of the landmines campaign in 1997, the international certification of the diamond trade in 2000, and concessions at the Doha world trade talks in 2001 around intellectual property rights. (ibid.: 77)

All of these civil engagements and crossborder, transnational networking activities, combined with a growing civic responsibility on the one hand,

and a growing global democratic deficit on the other, lead to strengthening the global representation of civil society. This occurs simultaneously with the articulation of common – globally shared – visions, goals and proposals.

From the early 1980s, when the concept was reintroduced by small circles of East Central European and Latin American dissident intellectuals, to the first decade of the third Millenium, civil society has travelled a long way. Myriads of networks, local, regional, global movements, NGOs, INGOs, and also donors, intergovernmental agencies, multilateral economic institutions and governments, are using it in their everyday parlance in order to attract a sceptical or reluctant audience and sell their policies as 'socially and politically correct'. It seemed for a while that after the relative success of the Velvet Revolutions of 1989, the concept would be forgotten and rendered useless by academia and politics as part of a heroic and short-lived period in East European and Latin American history.

These expectations have partially been realized. Indeed, the mobilizing energies under the banner of civil society, together with East-West dialogue, began to evaporate in East Central Europe by the early 1990s. This left behind a vacuum and frustration. But the concept of civil society proved to be more durable and resilient than the movements of East European intellectuals. It found new places, spaces, forms and languages for its development. Against forecasts and expectations, it not only popped up in an East-West European form and perspective, but in more remote areas like Africa and Asia where it has become part of everyday language and research programs. Although many valid arguments can be made about the adequate or inadequate usage of the concept and its Western bias and origin (and we do need more social scientific, interdisciplinary analysis of its widespread usage and proliferating languages), it seems nothing can halt its linguistic and public expansion. In fact, this is the manifestation of a great need to reinterpret and partly replace the nineteenth century concepts of political and scientific analysis. Civil society, with its elasticity and 'in-betweenness' has proved to be the metaphor for fulfilling needs that come from different and sometimes opposite corners of our rapidly globalizing and evaporating realities. It can represent generically different social contents and political intentions and still offers a promising, deliberative framework for protest, compromise and legitimacy.

We conclude that the tension between the different languages of civil society and its users is inevitable. But, in fact, the very essence of the concept lies exactly in the creative potential conflicts among the different definitions and interpretations. The long chain of interpretations, reinterpretations, and subsequent emerging of new aspects and domains of civil society stem from the discourse generated by these conflicts and are valuable contributions to the crystallization of a new understanding. This newly emerging understanding is a reflection of a rapidly changing reality which is fundamentally different from the realities which gave birth to theories of civil society in the eighteenth and later in the twentieth centuries.

Notes

1. Nerfin warns that the UN considers 'NGOs as conveyor belts of intergovernmental or bureaucratic wisdom distilled from above, to the public which is seen as a passive receptacle' and believes that only 'full accountability' will help the third system to avoid the traps of bureaucratization and cooptation (Nerfin 1987: 189).

2. See the IMF approach in Dawson and Bhatt (2001: 11).

3. 'The use of the term as a normative concept, that is, what we would like civil society to be or what we think it ought to be, is often confused with an empirical description … the constant slippage between the two in the development literature and in the practice of multilateral agencies, governments, and NGOs has contributed to a technical and depoliticising approach to the strengthening of civil society which ultimately has had political implications' (Pearce 1993: 14).

4. 'Global Strategies Project – Notes and Commentaries' in *Encyclopedia of World Problems and Human Potential*, http://www. uia.be/strategies/stratcom_bodies.php.

5. The author's strategy in order to 'unpack' this language and to understand the implied meaning 'beyond the veil of ahistorical aspirational form' (Seckinelgin 2002: 358) involves the analysis of two reports, one by the British Department for International Development (DfID 2001 – available online at http://www.dfid.gov.uk/Pubs/files/tsp_government.pdf) and one by the World Bank (2001). Both reports, whose major goal is to find efficient ways and tools to fight poverty, identify civil society with the sum-total of NGOs. The reports present 'Ngo-nized' civil society as a strategic ally of the private sector that 'can promote political empowerment of poor people, pressuring the state to better serve their interest' (World Bank 2001: 99–102).

6. 'The metaphor of civil society organizations is not a coincidence or an accidental construction. It is produced within a particular cultural context and it fits a certain understanding of civil society. It is clear that the reports posit a particular relationship between civil society organizations, the market and the state for the effective governance of people and their issues. Furthermore, they explicitly attribute an already decided role to the civil society organizations' (Seckinelgin 2002: 365).

7. Scholte is very explicit about the role of civil society in global governance: civil society can offer a means for affected publics to affirm that global governance arrangements should guide – and where necessary, constrain – their behaviour. Likewise, civil society can also provide a space for the expression of discontent and the pursuit of change when existing governance arrangements are regarded as illegitimate (ibid.: 294).

8. This should be compared to the text of Article 71 of the UN Charter: 'The Economic and Social Council may make suitable arrangements for consultation with non-governmental organizations which are concerned with matters within its competence'. In fact, comparison of the texts suggests that the WTO's inclusion of the word 'co-operation' reveals a more positive attitude had the article been implemented, which it has not. There are no consultative arrangements between the WTO and NGOs to date (see Willetts 2002).

9. Other successes can be found as well including the role of civil society in raising awareness of global environmental crises (global warming, protection of biodiversity)

which has been instrumental in bringing governments together to attempt to address these issues. Also, in Doha, NGOs and developing countries successfully united to confront pharmaceutical companies on the issue of patents against the objections of countries like the US, Germany and the UK (see Ritchie 2001).

10. Participation of NGOs in the UN system are characterized as: (1) unstructured, open access, (2) structured, open access, (3) indirect, open access through a network, (4) external campaigning by a network, (5) limited access to the secretariat, (6) limited access to delegations (see Willetts 2002).

Chapter 9

THE CRITIQUE OF ORGANIZED MODERNITY

Jean Terrier and Peter Wagner

After the end of the Second World War and the defeat of Nazism, the restoration of democracy in West Central Europe was first informed by a revival of individualist liberalism. This political philosophy with its emphasis on negative liberty, translated into human and civic rights and the rule of law, seemed best suited to prevent the re-emergence of the totalitarian projects of creating political and societal homogeneity. Gradually, however, the observation that these democracies were restored on broadly the same grounds as before the war gave rise to the insight that they may be as vulnerable to deteriorations of the political situation as the interwar polities, and that historically more long-term developments and conceptually more profound flaws in the liberal-democratic view of the modern polity had been in the background of the institutional breakdown.

Even though the term 'civil society' was mostly not central to them, a fact that in itself is telling about the decline of the concept from the middle of the nineteenth to the middle of the twentieth century, the diagnoses of what we call organized modernity that were increasingly proposed from the late 1950s onwards, are related, topic-wise, to the eighteenth-century debate on 'civil society' which we briefly summarized in chapter 1. These diagnoses took basically two forms, mirroring in their critical reflection indeed the relation between the sociology and the political theory of mass society from the first half of the twentieth century (see chapter 4). An approach that retained the idea that an analysis of the structure of social configurations would provide the key to the transformation of the political forms of modern society grew out of the critical theory of the Frankfurt School. Alternatively, an approach that emphasized the transformations in the self-understanding of the political forms and precisely criticized the attempts at sociologically determining the viability of political forms linked up directly to the political philosophies of the interwar period, even though gradually the work of reconstructing the political created longer intellectual linkages, to Tocqueville and other post-revolutionary thinkers, to Machiavelli and the republican tradition and to ancient Greece and the origins of democracy. Important representatives of these approaches are Jürgen Habermas for the former and Hannah Arendt as well as Cornelius Castoriadis and Claude Lefort for the latter.

Jürgen Habermas and the Critical Analysis of the Decline of Civil Society: the Rise of Technocratic Thinking

In chapter 4 we discussed some aspects of Habermas's *Transformation of the Public Sphere*, published in the early 1960s. In subsequent writings, Habermas developed in more detail that which had remained the point of conclusion only in his historical analysis of the public sphere, namely a theoretically guided diagnosis of contemporary society. Initially radicalizing his diagnosis of the decline of the public sphere, and by implication of civil society, he linked his thinking to the analysis offered by the founding generation of the Frankfurt School, famous for its description of the post-war social configuration as an administered society (*verwaltete Gesellschaft*). Dealing in more detail than Adorno and Horkheimer with the operating modes of contemporary science, politics and administration, Habermas offered in *Technik und Wissenschaft als 'Ideologie'* (Habermas 1974) perhaps the most telling description of such a system. In the essays gathered under that title (and especially in the piece on 'technique on science itself', but also in the one on 'scientization of politics and public opinion' – Habermas 1971b), Habermas discusses the rise of a new understanding of the relationship between science and politics. In this understanding, science is given the task not only of furnishing technical advice to political actors; it is also taken to be capable of delivering positive indications about the ends that need to be pursued. Habermas uses the term *technocracy* for this 'positivistic' political arrangement. Technocratic societies are societies in which the activity of government proper has ceased to be prevalent to give rise to mere social engineering:

> Insofar as government action is directed toward the economic system's stability and growth, politics now takes on a peculiarly negative character. For it is oriented toward the elimination of dysfunctions and the avoidance of risks that

threaten the system: not, in other words, toward the *realization of practical goals* but toward the *solution of technical problems*. (Habermas 1971b: 102–03)

Technology and Science as 'Ideology' represents, to a certain extent, a move away from the economic determinism of the *Structural Transformations of the Public Sphere*. Habermas pays greater attention to the social and political tensions to which the technocratic system is a provisional response. He argues that the challenge of post-war Western societies was to bind 'the masses' loyalty' (ibid.: 102) to the capitalist system of production. This was achieved via the establishment of massive material rewards [*Entschädigungen* – literally: compensations] conceded to wage-earning workers:

> It was on the basis of the capitalist mode of production that the struggle of social classes as such was first constituted, thereby creating an objective situation from which the class structure of traditional society, with its immediately political constitutions, could be *recognized* in retrospect. State-regulated capitalism, which emerged from a reaction against the dangers to the system produced by open class antagonism, suspends class conflict. The system of advanced capitalism is so defined by a policy of securing the loyalty of the wage-earning masses through rewards, that is by avoiding conflict … (ibid.: 107–08)

This incompatibility between the technocratic arrangement and civil society is well described by Habermas:

> The permanent regulation of the economic process by means of state intervention arose as a defense mechanism against the dysfunctional tendencies, which threaten the system, that capitalism generates when left to itself. Capitalism's actual development manifestly contradicted its own idea of a civil society [*seiner eigenen Idee einer bürgerlichen Gesellschaft*], emancipated from domination, in which power is neutralized. (ibid.: 101 – the parenthesis is ours)[1]

Even while this view may entail a relative shift from an 'economic' to a 'political' explanation in Habermas's diagnosis, he does not go as far as explicating in detail the twofold politico-theoretical assumption that lies at the core of the technocratic system. He emphasizes the fact that the mechanisms of collective deliberation are deprecated under the technocratic regime, and that they are replaced by sheer instrumental rationality. Habermas argues that, under technocratic conditions, instrumental rationality (although in an intrinsically unstable way) not only presides over the identification of efficient means to efficiently pursue political goals, but also dictates the political goals themselves. For this to occur, however, one would need to understand how instrumental rationality, which is classically defined, for instance by Max Weber, as a mere procedure to evaluate the relative efficacy of different available means, suddenly turns into a technology for the setting of final goals.[2]

In our understanding, instrumental rationality remains deprived of its capacity to decide over means under technical arrangements. What changes in the post-war era is less instrumental rationality itself than the general understanding of what social individuals are. Social engineering assumes that individuals have clearly identifiable, at least groupwise similar and roughly constant preferences. On the stable ground created by this first assumption the idea emerges that the social world is objectively comprehensible and graspable by the human mind, insofar as it is ruled by an identifiable set of invariable laws. Scientific government establishes itself as a set of objective techniques to satisfy these individual preferences. Social engineering, to phrase it slightly differently, makes use of a set of anthropological assumptions to determine average individual preferences and aggregate them into a manageable compound – which is in turn (to borrow here the vocabulary of systemism, very influential at the time) delivered to the political system as its primary input.

It readily appears that the anthropological and methodological assumptions in question can only be extremely basic, and we can indeed describe them as a mixture of Hobbesianism and utilitarianism. Methodologically, the analysis starts with individuals and arrives at 'society' by mere means of aggregation. To arrive at findings that are applicable to the 'engineering' of such society, preferences must be sufficiently alike to relate to a very high number of individuals. Thus, anthropological assumptions are – mostly implicitly – added. Individuals are taken to have a priori strong preferences for social peace (this is the Hobbesian dimension), and for the maximal satisfaction of material needs (for the more utilitarian dimension).[3] Faced with such an input, the output produced by the social engineers who composed public administration was rather similar in most European countries: mechanisms for the redistribution of wealth were put to work as a way to guarantee social peace; indirect income enhanced consumption as a tool to achieve material satisfaction; lastly, the monitoring of the economy through the state (be it in the form of mere incentives or in the form of its direct intervention by way of nationalized companies) ensured the permanence and steadiness of supply.

To come back to the central question raised in this paper, it now becomes obvious that the technocratic arrangement leaves little space for a debate similar to the one conducted under the heading of 'civil society' in other historical periods. Technocracy represents a response to the modern problématique of legitimate institutionalisation, but the response it gives leaves no space for the deliberative processes which lay at the core of civil society, as defined in the first chapter of this volume. This is because legitimate institutions are established not as products of an active agreement between different individuals, but as necessary results of the a priori identification of the preferences of largely identical individuals.

While we follow Habermas in many of his remarks on post-war political arrangements, we think nonetheless that he tended to overemphasize their overall stability and coherence. In particular, he tended to overlook that other principles of legitimation were still in place, whose importance should not be underestimated. The post-war arrangements were complex, tension-ridden entities: they 'were indeed not based on the pure proceduralism of individualist liberalism, but showed signs of a compromise between liberal justifications and those of both a linguistic-cultural and a social nature, and tied those justifications together by recourse to an empirical science of politics and society, the employment of which was never free of technocratic undertones' (Friese and Wagner 1999: 40). Even though it is arguable that the post-war era was characterized by a decrease of what we might call national energies,[4] certain institutions, such as the school system, remained nonetheless to a large extent organized along national lines. Similarly, in spite of the increasing importance of political technology, the full substitution of the 'government of men' by the 'administration of things', as Marx would have it, never occurred. While many pages could be devoted to the transformation of parliamentary politics in the post-war era, it remains undeniable that the principles of democratic sovereignty were not seriously put at risk in most Western countries.

Grasping these tensions is important insofar as it enables us to understand how the technocratic arrangement entered into crisis in the 1980s. Emphasising stability and coherence, Habermas overestimated the success of the technocratic system in enforcing the de-politicisation of the masses. He thought that under technocracy the politics of compensation and social pacification managed to keep 'latent' the central conflict of the capitalist mode of production, namely that between dependent workers, on the one hand, and the owners of the instruments of production, on the other: 'the conflict still built into the structure of society in virtue of the private mode of capital utilization is the very area of conflict which has the greatest possibility of remaining latent' (ibid.: 108). Borrowing his ideas from the writings of Claus Offe, Habermas concludes that, as a consequence of this, only the less harmful among the various forms of conflict could find a direct expression in Western post-war societies. Habermas predicted that only peripheral conflicts (that is, conflicts induced by an incapacity of state power to deliver compensations evenly across the whole national territory) might continue to exist in late capitalist societies.

At the time of writing *Technology and Science as 'Ideology'*, Habermas was still caught in the classical Marxist conception of a centrality of class conflict. What Habermas describes as peripheral conflicts actually powerfully contributed to undermining the foundation of the post-war social arrangements. Under technocratic conditions, the 'system-endangering' critique (to use Habermas's apt formulation) did not take the form of demands for a further institutionalisation of welfare, as he seemed to suggest. It rather took the form of a vindication of self-organisation and autonomy (see Boltanski and Chiapello 1999). In this sense, the principal bearers of critique under technocratic conditions were not institutionalized parties (such at communist parties) and their respective intelligentsias, either in the 'organic' or the *'compagnon de route'* form. The bearers of critique were those who sympathized with the cultural utopias of the 1960s and 1970s, which advocated a series of 'ends': the end of work, the end of bureaucracy, the end of growth, the end of politics, the end of war, and the like. In replacement of the 'myth' of technological progress and economic growth, these critics were trying to restore a conception of society as a direct of product of human action, thus connecting back (sometimes explicitly) to the eighteenth-century debate on civil society.[5]

The Triumph of Labour and the Decline of Civic Action: Hannah Arendt

While changes in the structure of society were the prime cause in Habermas's version of the diagnosis of decline of civil society, as we phrase the issue here, the work of political thinkers such as Hannah Arendt or Cornelius Castoriadis focused on changing conceptions of the political. These thinkers advocated a radical transformation of our understanding of democratic politics which can be interpreted as an attempt at restoring the conditions of possibility of civil society.

Of particular relevance for the present discussion is Arendt's book of 1958, *The Human Condition*. It is interesting to note that the themes touched upon by Arendt in this work, such as the description of the distinctive features of modern societies in comparison with those of ancient times, the discussion of the effects of economic activities upon civic life or the insistence upon the communicative dimension of human action, are clearly reminiscent of those that we found in Ferguson's and Tocqueville's writings.

Arendt started by distinguishing between two main ways that human beings have to relate to the world. The first one is not, strictly speaking, an activity, insofar as it is characterized by a *passive* attitude of reception, of openness to the inputs coming from the environing world. Arendt called this attitude 'contemplation'. In contemplative life, one usually retreats from social life and devotes oneself to philosophical reflection or religious meditation, expecting the blessings of revelation. Certain societies, or at least certain communities within these societies, have placed contemplative life on top of the hierarchy of their values. This is the case for instance, argued Arendt, of the religious communities of the Middle Ages.

In modernity, by contrast, the passivity that is characteristic of contemplative life was increasingly rejected in favour of more active attitudes. As is well known, Arendt distinguished between three types of activity: labour, work and action. *Labour* is the instrumental activity which aims to satisfy needs. *Work*, by contrast, is a kind of activity whose purpose is the production of goods; thus, the archetypal worker, according to Arendt, is the artisan, the craftsman. Lastly, Arendt defined *action* as that kind of activity which is characterized by the fact that individuals enter in relation with one another by the mediation of language (Arendt, 1998: 179) – action, in other words (like civil society in Ferguson) is essentially made of communicative fluxes. It is thus a highly interactive activity, as we shall see more precisely below: '[t]he revelatory quality of speech and action comes to the fore where people are *with* others and neither for nor against them – that is, in sheer human togetherness' (ibid.: 180). Educational tasks, artistic activities, as well as political involvement, all fall under the category of action.

While it escapes the narrow realm of sheer necessity, action is nonetheless extremely important: in action, one produces meaning, norms, representations, whose significance and validity derive from the fact that they are elaborated collectively. Action therefore provides a shared background to the life of individuals, on the basis of which (or in confrontation to which) they can elaborate their own way to inhabit the world. As Arendt wrote, 'without a space of appearance and without trusting in action and speech as a mode of being together, neither the reality of one's self, of one's own identity, nor the reality of the surrounding world can be established beyond doubt' (ibid.: 208).

The Human Condition is, among other things, a narration of the long process by which modernity has moved away from contemplative life to emphasize first the importance of work, before giving centrality to labour. In other words, one major type of activity is absent from the modern condition – namely *action*.

According to Arendt, the deprecation of contemplative life started in the early seventeenth century with the diffusion of new epistemological conceptions. We have already suggested that the major assumption of *vita contemplativa* is that knowledge can be gathered by adopting an attitude of openness in front of the world: certainty is taken to be revealed, instead of actively acquired. To show the limits of the contemplative conception is, according to Arendt, the sense of the Cartesian project. Descartes rejected the idea that sense data or mere contemplation could, as such, lead to the acquisition of certain knowledge. This is because, as the Cartesian reasoning went, one can indeed never be sure that a *malin génie* is not instilling false conceptions into our passive minds. Instead, certainty can be reached only by way of following precise rules – those discovered and exposed, precisely, in the *Discours de la méthode*, as Descartes's treatise is quite appropriately entitled (ibid.: 273–80).

This transformation, argued Arendt, in the conception of the ways of acquiring knowledge is a good illustration of a more general shift of emphasis from *vita contemplativa* to *vita activa*. The rise of experimental methods in the natural sciences is a good indicator of the importance increasingly taken by the idea that the objects of social life (in this case: knowledge) are the result of a process of *production* which implies a continuous use of *tools*. This inaugurated the era of *homo faber*, understood here as the active individual, the fabricator, the producer of objects. By an interesting historical twist, however, *homo faber* underwent a thorough reinterpretation during the eighteenth century, under the influence of the idea of happiness (ibid.: 305–13).

Products were mainly seen by *homo faber* under the perspective of their utility – in the sense of what could be achieved by using them. But the redefinition of the notion of utility by the materialists of the Enlightenment and, prominently, by early nineteenth-century utilitarian thinkers suggested that utility had to be rephrased in different terms: the utility of a given object was best measured, according to them, by the pleasures it gave to the individual user. This is the first step towards a general redefinition of objects as being, primarily, not products but commodities. In such a context, individuals lose their identity of producers (which they also are) and tend to become consumers, that is, mere calculators of pleasure and pain.

It is no surprise that this evolution occurs in a parallel to the development of commerce. Thus, like Ferguson, Arendt took the rise of commercial society, and of the imaginary that is connected with it, as representing a major historical break. The triumph of the labourer, indeed, brings us to a situation which is at the extreme opposite of contemplative life: human thought itself, which was taken to be the supreme 'channel' through which the truth of the universe could be revealed, is reduced to a mere instrument for the hierarchization of preferences and the evaluation of the relative quality of pleasures (ibid.: 321–22). On the other hand, as social contract theories suggest, society was redefined as a tool in the hands of individuals to increase the efficiency of human labour and thus to gain access to a higher number of goods: 'Society is the form in which the fact of mutual dependence for the sake of life and nothing else assumes public significance and where the activities connected with sheer survival are permitted to appear in public' (ibid.: 46).

There is a paradox in these developments. While utilitarianism could prima facie appear as an individualistic theory (insofar as it emphasizes individual preferences), its influence actually led to a uniformization of society.[6] This is because utilitarianism was the philosophy which accompanied the reduction of individuals to primary wants and needs, as we have seen. Now these primary wants and needs are, by and large, shared by most individuals:[7] we understand, thus, how society was progressively turned into an ensemble of individuals who were at the same time isolated and similar: 'society expects from each of its members a certain kind of behavior, imposes innumerable and various rules, all of which tend to "normalize" its members, to make them behave, to exclude spontaneous action and outstanding achievement' (ibid.: 40).

Not incidentally, the connection between isolation and conformism was described already by Tocqueville. In Tocqueville this took the name of 'individualism', which he understood as a retreat from public involvement and civil life and a concentration upon private business and petty passions. The isolation induced by individualism, he argued, was the consequence of the levelling of conditions which characterized democratic times:

> As social equality spreads there are more and more people who, though neither rich nor powerful enough to have much hold over others, have gained or kept enough wealth and enough understanding to look after their own needs. Such folk owe no man anything and hardly expect anything from anybody. They form the habit of thinking themselves in isolation and imagine that their whole destiny is in their own hands. (de Tocqueville 1994: pt II, chap. 2: 508)

According to Tocqueville, precisely this individualism could give birth to a new form of despotism: because of their abandonment of any interest in public affairs, democratic individuals tended to overlook that centralized forms of power were emerging that were capable of keeping societies under tight control.

Arendt had similar concerns. As we have seen, she thought that among the various types of activities available to the human, one had taken momentum in the nineteenth century at the cost of all others: it was labour, which supplanted work and action. Now in labour tasks are coordinated, if at all, by way of very simple communicative processes. In other words, labour is a purely instrumental activity which neither produces a shared world nor requires its existence. In the society of labour, as in Tocqueville's democratic society, individuals are isolated from each other, thus paving the way to tyranny:

> Montesquieu realized that the outstanding characteristic of tyranny was that it rested on isolation – on the isolation of the tyrant from his subjects and the isolation of the subjects from each other through mutual fear and suspicion – and hence that tyranny was not one form of government among others but contradicted the essential human condition of plurality, the acting and

speaking together, which is the condition of all forms of political organization. (Arendt 1995: 202)[8]

In such a context, logically concluded Arendt, the only way to avoid isolation and the nefarious political consequences which come along with it is the restoration of the linguistic bond – that is, the restoration of action and speech. She looked for inspiration on how to achieve such a goal in ancient Greece, whose citizens, she argued, lived a life which came close to a pure life of action. In ancient civic life individuals overcame their isolation by gathering onto the *agora* – which can be interpreted not only as a physical square but also as a virtual space of linguistic exchange.

Thus, as we see, there are some links between the preoccupations of Arendt and those of authors such as Ferguson and Tocqueville. There are also differences: Arendt insisted perhaps more than her predecessors (and, for that matter, definitely more than Habermas) upon the fact that the public space is not only a formal place of deliberation where individual relations are marked by the obligation of conformity to an argumentative model. For Arendt the public space is also defined as an ontological space of appearance, in which 'agonal' relations provide recognition and carve individual identities. In spite of these differences, however, it seems to us that Arendt can legitimately be taken as a 'continuator' of the political tradition which sees civil society and its corollaries (namely, first and foremost, the involvement in deliberative processes with a view to decide upon politically desirable measures and institutions) as the only way to save liberty from the threat represented by the development of commercial society. Liberty is indeed understood by Arendt, in a way which is again reminiscent of the two classical authors, as a collective achievement – it can be enjoyed only against the background of a common world and as such, it needs to be defended against the worldlessness resulting from the development of commercial relationships.

The Advocacy of Radical Self-governance: Cornelius Castoriadis

Like other authors already encountered, Cornelius Castoriadis started by rejecting the liberal idea of a completely asocial, isolated individual. He argued instead that individuals are socially constituted: 'Outside society ... the human being is neither beast nor God (as Aristotle said) but quite simply is not and cannot exist either physically or, what is more, psychically. Radically unfit for life ... the newborn human baby must be humanized; and this process of humanization is its socialization, the labour of society mediated and instrumented by the infants's immediate entourage' (Castoriadis 1997: 2). This process of socialization had the effect, according to Castoriadis, of diffusing shared meanings among the members of the collectivity considered, thus constituting a specific form of life. He also, however, thought that socialization could never be complete.

As Habermas (1987) critically noted, Castoriadis postulated the existence of a pre-social psychic core which would escape any taming. This pre-social psyche was, argued Castoriadis, the seat of what he called the 'radical imaginary': while most new phenomena occurring in the world are the result of an innovative combination of existing elements, the radical imaginary, instead, was described as an instance of pure, *ex nihilo* creation. Of course, the radical imaginary rarely operates alone: if it is an impulse, a push (*poussée*) towards the questioning and re-elaboration of arbitrarily existing forms of life, it is nonetheless always mediated and channelled by conscious reflection, and only then can become the ground for deliberate activity (Kalyvlas 2001: 9). Without assuming the existence of the radical imaginary, however, one could not account for social changes, let alone deep ruptures in the course of history (Castoriadis 1975). In Castoriadis's ontology the radical imaginary constituted the core of his attempt at redefining Being in terms of indeterminacy – against a substantial part of the modern philosophical tradition for which Being is Being-determined-to-be (Kalyvas 2001: 5).

Society, for Castoriadis, is a collection of institutions – understood in a quasi Durkheimian sense of 'any solidified set of practices or representations'. No society can do without them, since socialization would be impossible without some institutional frame of reference common to the members of large groups, which are to be inculcated to the newborn child. For instance, as Castoriadis repeatedly insisted (like Habermas, incidentally, also did), no socialization can occur outside of language, and language is a social institution (Castoriadis 1997: 2).

However, this collection of institutions can take two distinct forms. On the one hand, heteronomous societies are characterized by the fact that they hide from themselves their capacity for self-institution. Instead, they attribute their origins (and, by way of consequence, explain and legitimate their current shape) to non-human, that is transcendent, factors – such as the action of a god or the specificity of their physical constitution. On the other hand, Castoriadis called autonomous these societies which were aware of the fact that their past, current and future shape depended mainly of the joint actions of their members – these societies, in Castoriadis's own terms, knew that their 'institutions depend on the conscious and explicit activity of the collectivity' (ibid.: 4). In other words, an autonomous society is a society in which 'the question of what are the good (or best) institutions' is 'open' (ibid.). The most prominent examples of societies of this type are, according to Castoriadis, Ancient Greece and modern society.

Castoriadis's more historically-oriented work (such as his reflection on totalitarianism or on the workers' movement) can be understood as an attempt to understand why, in spite of the existence of the radical imaginary, instituted schemes often tend to prevail over instituting moments. In other words his question is: how is it possible that the instituted imaginary (the institution in the sense of solidified practices and representations) is a more permanent feature of social life than the instituting imaginary (the institution in the sense of a creation of practices and representations)?

There are two answers to this question. First of all, by definition, inherited institutions have a status of taken-for-grantedness and thus naturally tend to perpetuate themselves in the minds of social agents. Furthermore, insofar as some sort of institution is necessary for fundamental processes, such as that of socialization to occur, their radical questioning always appears as presenting a risk of social disaggregation.

On the other hand, one needs to bring power games into the picture. Instituted heteronomy can thus be understood as one of the many sides of political hegemony. It is obviously more than that, since heteronomy takes the form, as we have noted, of a set of inherited institutions whose stability and solidity are incommensurable with the flexibility of power interests. To phrase this differently, it is not sufficient to say – it would even be, to a certain extent, self-contradictory – that heteronomous institutions are a political product and that heteronomy is coterminous with manipulation. It remains true, however, that politics is marked by a struggle around collective significations; therefore, the defence of, or the indifference towards, the existence of inherited institutions is necessarily a political stance. It serves the individuals and groups who, in the situation of heteronomy, benefit from the greatest advantages. In other words, if heteronomous institutions are not necessarily direct products of political will, it is nonetheless arguable that their existence serves specific interests.

On these theoretical bases, Castoriadis elaborated a critique of organized modernity. As we have seen, organized modernity is characterized by the fact that it promotes a relatively tight closure of the social space. The idea of a functional integration of the different spheres of social life, very widespread at the time, contains the notion that certain global equilibria must be left untouched for the sake of societal stability and efficiency: for instance, as Castoriadis noted, capitalism rested upon the antidemocratic assumption of a necessary separation of the tasks of management and those of execution. These general prescriptions, however, obviously represented a limitation of the capacities of action of society upon itself. They also constituted a justification, as it readily appears, for the uneven repartition of political power which characterized the capitalist mode of production.

In his critique, however, Castoriadis did not target only state bureaucracies and capitalist structures. In the guise of the political activist involved in the debates and actions of the French radical left from the 1950s to the 1970s, Castoriadis drew heavily on his social theory to criticize the dominant understanding of how oppositional politics should be conducted. He defended the idea that the traditional Leninist conception of the vanguard party, endowed with the task of guiding an unenlightened proletariat, did not do justice to the endogenous political capacities of the working class. He suggested, thus, that the task of the political organization was not one of guidance, but of mere theoretical accompaniment and logistic support to struggles which tended to emerge spontaneously. There was indeed an 'autonomous development of the proletariat towards socialism' (Castoriadis 1974.: 138). This fundamental conviction led Castoriadis to target equally, in his critique of organized modernity, Western state bureaucracies, the traditional organizations of the working class, most importantly the various communist parties, and the states that claimed to represent the working class's interests and future, namely those of the Soviet block. According to him, these communist parties had degenerated and become integral part of the capitalist exploitation system (ibid.: 141–42), insofar as they reproduced the typically capitalist distinction between execution and management (p. 143), thus negating and betraying proletarian autonomy. Lastly, and for roughly the same reasons, Castoriadis articulated one of the earliest and fiercest left-wing critiques of the Soviet Union, which he defined as 'bureaucratic state capitalism', thus rejecting the definition of the Soviet system as socialist – be it, in Trotskyite fashion, a degenerated socialism.

Castoriadis paid a close attention to the manifestations of proletarian autonomy. Analysing in detail the insurrectional moments of 1917 in Russia, 1918 in Germany, and 1956 in Hungary (as well as the way in which spontaneous strikes were conducted in Western countries), he concluded that the proletariat's primary task during all these events was to set up independent workers' councils. He interpreted this as an attempt, made by the workers themselves, to create a political space in which deliberative fluxes could be unleashed, thus allowing for a deployment of the radical imaginary and a reopening of the collective reflection upon desirable institutions. The experience of councils corresponded, in short, to a moment of restoration of the instituting imaginary against inherited institutions.

It is striking that we find in Castoriadis, once again, the very themes that we have identified as belonging to the tradition of reflection on civil society. Especially interesting in his work, perhaps, is the attention he paid to the question of the self-institution of society – thus speaking of human collectivities as social configurations in search of a political form. In his reasoning, Castoriadis pointed at a paradox of social life – which is not thinkable without institutions enforcing collective decisions,[9] but which cannot be told free if these institutions are locatetd without reach of the individuals who make up the collectivity. Castoriadis's answer to this tension lies in his insistence upon the importance of social and political participation, which he called 'autogestion' ('self-governance', Castoriadis 1997: 5). This is another element that binds Castoriadis to the tradition of reflection on civil society, in the sense we have given to this term. A society marked by 'autogestion' is a radically democratic society, in which all political decisions are mediated by participatory processes. But it goes further than this, in that 'autogestion' is applicable not only to the political spheres *stricto sensu*, but to all spheres of social life: factories, firms, and schools should also move towards a disappearance of the hierarchical social relations they contain to give way to mutual help and collaborative processes. In turn, societal 'autogestion' is also the condition for 'autogestion' in individual life, understood as a situation in which one organizes one's existence autonomously, free of any constraint except those upon which one has had an explicit say.

Notes

1. We have altered the translation. *Bürgerliche Gesellschaft* was translated as 'bourgeois society'.
2. For a related analysis of a shift in the meaning of efficiency in development policy, see Karagiannis 2004. Significantly, though, this analysis focused on the period from the 1970s to the 1990s, thus explores the movement from an understanding in which means were subject to politically set goals and efficiency defined in terms of the best such means to one in which efficiency becomes itself the goal.
3. Note the similarity to classical economic liberalism, in our earlier discussion in chapter 1, in as far as the latter was seen as a political theory.
4. In the sense that nations were no longer objects of collective passion. This is what Marshall means when he ironically writes, in *Class, Citizenship, and Social Development* that '[w]e still use those typically eighteenth-century songs "God save the King" and "Rule Britannia", but we omit the passages which would offend our modern, and more modest, sensibilities' (Marshall 1977: 102).
5. For the sake of brevity, we add just a short note on *The Theory of Communicative Action*, arguably Habermas's major oeuvre. There, he complemented the Marx-inspired critical analysis of capitalism by a Parsons-inspired idea of society as a set of spheres, which potentially can be in (normative) balance, but in which the risk of colonization of life-world-based arrangements by systemic arrangements remains omnipresent. In this approach, a well-defined and limited place is reserved for 'civil society', which was absent in the intermediate writings on technocracy.
6. Taking the collective good in terms of an aggregation of individual goods as the ultimate measure, utilitarianism is indeed in some way a collectivistic theory.
7. This idea, according to Arendt, is best expressed by Bentham: his 'basic assumption [is that] what all men have in common is not the world but the sameness of their nature, which manifests itself in the sameness of calculation and the sameness of being affected by pain and pleasure' (ibid.: 309).

8. This emphasis was inspired by the insights derived from her analysis of the historical decline of nation-states based on the ideas of commercial freedom and popular sovereignty in *The Origins of Totalitarianism* (Arendt 1951).

9. '[T]here is a need for explicitly instituted instances or agencies that can make sanction-bearing decisions about what is to be done and not to be done, that can legislate, "execute" decisions, settle points of litigation, and govern' (Castoriadis 1997: 3).

PART IV

Concluding

Chapter 10

THE RETURN OF CIVIL SOCIETY AND THE REOPENING OF THE POLITICAL PROBLÉMATIQUE

Jean Terrier and Peter Wagner

Varieties of Responses to the Crisis of Organized Democracy

As has been observed many times, over the past two decades the notion of civil society has made an important return in the social and political sciences as well as in public debate. Set in the framework of the narrative of fall and rise of the concept, as indicated at the beginning of this volume, it may sometimes seem as if the time for the realization of the promise of civil society, as originally sketched in the seventeenth and eighteenth century, has finally come. However, to succumb to any temptation to analyse this return in terms of a restoration of an unjustly forgotten concept would mean to lose sense of the specificity of the contexts in which the concept was put forward, largely withdrawn, and now revived. Once again, we need to take care to see precisely how the political problématique of modernity was phrased during the 1960s and 1970s and what rephrasing the return of the concept of civil society claims to offer. Fundamentally, our argument is that the re-emergence of the notion of civil society is directly linked with the erosion of the social setting which predominantly characterized organized modernity. Such an erosion reopened a space in which the notion of civil society could appear as an important resource for agents trying to find a way to respond to a situation of increased contingency.

The starting observation for this final part of our analysis, therefore, is that the relatively consolidated arrangement of the post-war era eroded in the 1980s. The apparent failure of the traditional, Keynesian techniques of economic steering, the difficulties encountered by the countries of the Soviet bloc, the development of what Ulrich Beck (1986) calls *risk* (unpredictable events to which no immediate solution can be found, if at all, such as pandemics or natural disasters) triggered a general reflection on the shortcomings of the myth of a scientifically administered society.[1] For Western Europe, we have characterized this arrangement as a largely technocratic management of the lines of socio-political cleavage, broadly set into the framework of a compromise between individualist-liberal, cultural-communitarian and social-solidaristic political commitments (see chapter 9). Similar elements were in use in other societies, even though the balance of justifications was often highly different. In the U.S., the individualist-liberal component was certainly much stronger than anywhere else, whereas in the 'peoples' democracies' the commitment to solidarity based on a strong notion of class community was implemented in a decidedly non-liberal way (see chapter 5 for the G.D.R. and chapter 6 for East Central Europe). In Latin America, the degree of merely formal or substantial democracy varies over time and across countries; and in East Asia, the degree of cultural commonality has only recently been newly debated after the grip of both the authoritarian regimes that flourished with U.S. support and the socialist regimes has been loosened so that other modes of societal integration became more clearly visible (see chapter 7).

Despite this variety of social configurations and political forms, what all these socio-political settings had in common was a relatively high degree of consolidation, stabilized not least also by the 'frozen' world-political context of the Cold War. And even though the precise reasons and forms of recent change also vary considerably, hardly any of these societies has escaped the reopening of the specifically modern question of the establishment of legitimate institutions. It is in this context of the reopening of the question of the political legitimacy of institutional forms that the new debate on civil society emerged, but we have to emphasize that this discourse does not provide the only response to this reopening, by a long way. Three different, and largely incompatible, responses to this question emerged in the 1980s and 1990s. None of them was entirely novel, even though in all of them more or less sustained attempts were made to elaborate an existing position of political thinking in the light of the contemporary observation.

The first response is that of *economic liberalism*, which now appears in the guise of neo-liberalism, but continues to rely on the basic assumptions of neo-classical economics and revives those elements of a rudimentary political philosophy that marked its origins as political economy in the eighteenth century. As we have seen, this conception states that the social is capable of self-regulation thanks to the intrinsic qualities of market mechanisms. This response was enormously successful in the 1990s, giving birth to a whole tendency to downsize state institutions and to dismantle welfare mechanisms in order to give way to market-driven self-regulation.

The second response borrows a lot from the nineteenth-century idea of *social homogeneity*, which should rise to prominence in the critique of classical liberalism around and after the turn of that century. The idea at stake here is that our societies can be conceived as resting on shared identities, in which inspiration for the successful establishment of legitimate institutions can be found. Many recent debates can be understood against such a background, such as that around communitarianism, that around the question of a 'European identity' (Passerini 2003), or the 'clash of civilisations' debate (Terrier 2002). This response appears to be currently acquiring momentum, as the revival of nationalist rhetoric in the context of the recent wars suggests.

In both of these responses the crisis of organized modernity leads towards an abdication of the commitment to collective self-determination on the basis of a deliberation among the free members of a political collectivity. In the first response, individual self-determination is considered to be a sufficient basis for a peaceful and efficient organization of social life. As we have seen before, this approach needs to make assumptions about the nature of the human being and about social relations that stand in tension, to say the least, with any moderately complex concept of liberty. In the second response, on the other hand, the need for collective self-determination is fully acknowledged, and its significance is even underlined under conditions of current 'globalization' given that its realization has become more difficult. However, the conceptual solution found here lies in the assumption of the existence of fully constituted cultural-political collectivities, to which human beings clearly identifiably belong. In many respects, this second response is not only a response to the crisis of organized democracy, but also a response to the first response, to the rise of neo-liberalism which threatens the coherence of such collectivities. Thus, we find here some historico-conceptual affinities to the rise of aggressive nationalism and fascism, on the one hand, and communism, on the other, in the face of the devastating impact of nineteenth-century economic liberalism and imperialism, the historical term for 'globalization', on the configuration of social relations (Polanyi 1980). Islamism, for instance, seems to be best understood as an alternative such collectivist thinking after the failure of both secular nationalism and communism in the Islamic-Arab world (Eisenstadt 1999).

It is only in the third response that an attempt is made to see the problems with organized democracy not as a sign of failure of the project of collective self–determination *tout court*, but as the occasion to revive some of the conceptual and normative concerns that stood at the outset of this project and to revise them under conditions of a novel configuration of social relations. The lively debates on republicanism, on deliberative democracy, and so on. which took place in the 1990s are a good indicator of the restoration of the problématique of deliberation. The return of the notion of civil society must be understood as belonging to the same general trend. Beyond the conceptual work in academic and public debate, it has also shown its vibrancy in political life, most visibly probably in the transformation of East European socialism (see chapter 6) as well as in the increasing activity of non-governmental organizations. Most recently – and, as we shall argue conceptually below, possibly also most significantly – the new, globalization-oriented social movements, which have formed from the late 1990s onwards, can indeed be interpreted as the contemporary bearers of the deliberative inspiration that stands in the background of the civil society debate.

If our observation of this plurality of mutually incompatible proposals to exit from organized democracy is correct, however, then we cannot take for granted that civil society will establish itself as the central principle of the new political arrangements which are currently taking shape. While a space of possibilities is open in which the idea of civil society has its place, as the continuing debate on the question shows, it is far from certain that we shall not be faced, in the very near future, with a tight new closure of the social space in the form of the first or the second response outlined above. One of the preconditions for avoiding such an outcome of the current socio-political restructuring is an elaboration of the third response, the one focusing on a concept of civil society, in such a way that it effectively addresses the political problématique of contemporary modernity in a convincing way. The last reflections of our reasoning shall thus be devoted to what we see as shortcomings of the current debate in the light of our preceding attempt at historico-conceptual retrieval.

Civil Society, Associations, State: Shortcomings of the Recent Debate

First of all, it is useful to recall that the debate on civil society started as an attempt to conceptually understand and support the resistance to illegitimate state-power or to the emptying out of the substance of democracy from the 1980s onwards (see chapters 6 to 9). Depending on the political situation, the precise meaning and use of the concept varied considerably. During this period, in the Eastern European setting, institutions largely autonomous from state control, and often clandestine, were put in place, with a view to restore the capacity of society to act upon itself, in a context, typical of authoritarian settings, of sheer alienation of state and society: this first line of analysis posits civil society as a principle of opposition to state power. In the U.S., in turn, civil society debates focused on the existence and/or creation of social bonds in an otherwise highly individualized and commodified society. Here, the concept moved in vicinity to terms such as 'social capital' (Robert Putnam) or 'embeddedness' (Mark Granovetter) of economic action, thus signalling that its main line of resistance was not towards the state but towards the prevalence of market relations as the main characteristic of the overall configuration of social relations. Significantly, it was also inscribed into the common opposition between instrumental and value-based action, and thus often referred more to the language of moral philosophy than to the one of political philosophy (Robert Bellah, Alan Wolfe). In Western European social configurations – in between the other two settings in more than a geographical sense – civil society was often seen as a third (or fourth) major realm of social life, complementing and balancing the workings of state and economy (and family). The line of thinking that reached from Hegel to Habermas remained influential, even though the precise conceptual proposals differed often considerably from those made in these theoretical edifices. As useful as the debate was in many cases to support a line of resistance in these settings, for the very same reason of pointing negatively towards the working of existing institutions, the nature of civil society remained often underspecified – or where it was specified, the understanding was often too much derived from the given context to provide a basis for a more general conceptual elaboration. Two issues appear to us here of critical relevance: first, the tendency to equate civil society with a rich associative life; and second, the way in which the relation between civil society and state was conceptualized.

It is often argued that the rise of civil society can be witnessed in the birth of an increasing number and density of 'middle-range' social institutions that take an intermediate position between citizens and society as a whole, such as local assemblies in which political debates can take place, interest groups, or associations of citizens bound together by common objectives or preferences. For John Keane (1998b: 6), for instance, civil society 'both describes and envisages a complex and dynamic ensemble of legally protected non-governmental institutions that tend to be non-violent, self-organizing, self-reflexive, and permanently in tension with each other and with the state institutions that "frame", constrict and enable their activities'. However, in the light of the conceptual trajectory that we sketched in this volume, the mere existence of associational life or intermediary institutions is far from being a sufficient indicator of the existence of civil society. In asserting that civil society is essentially a series of intermediary institutions (such as non-governmental organisations, political parties, independent media, and the like) one is at risk of overlooking the tension between the configuration of social relations and the form of the polity, a tension that is constitutive of the problématique that the concept civil society historically aimed to address.

The emphasis on associative life is an important source of confusion, for instance, in as far as it renders the distinction between very dissimilar social situations almost impossible. Political arrangements in which the deliberative and communicative inspiration of civil society is absent, but in which intermediary institutions exist, are perfectly imaginable. For instance, authoritarian regimes usually allow (obviously within strictly defined limits) for a certain self-organisation of social life which escapes the direct control of political power.[2] At the same time, they try to limit as much as possible the deployment of deliberation and the questioning of political forms, which could further erode the fragile legitimacy of existing institutions. Similarly, we can perfectly think of political situations in which associational life is strictly kept under the control of the state, but from which elements of a civil society *in statu nascendi* are not absent: many situations of the former Soviet bloc were close to this description, insofar as a clandestine flux of deliberation on desirable institutions existed. In some cases, this process of underground deliberation managed to give birth to an equally clandestine set of materialisations, such as independent trade-unions, an unofficial press, and the like.

The problem of the identification of civil society in the sense delineated above with associative life has obviously not gone unnoticed in the recent debate. One of its expressions can be found indeed in the rising concern about the lack of representativity of non-governmental organizations, as well as the one about their co-optation by established institutions (see chapters 6 and 8). In cases where such organizations have declared themselves to be the true spokespersons for a cause and for a group of concerned people and have captured public attention on the basis of a moral-political claim, they may force elected politicians to address their claims without, though, themselves having any institutional legitimacy. Such observations have led civil society theorists to become more explicitly concerned with questions of representation and legitimacy, thus implicitly returning to the debate that ensued after the democratic revolutions.

As a consequence, though, parts of the debate have become too inclined to tie civil society closely to the state and to law. There is a tendency then to argue that civil society and the state should not be taken as separate entities, but as two necessary elements of any functioning democratic society. While speaking of the rediscovery of civil society in non-democratic settings and describing it as a principle of struggle against a certain conception of the overarching, 'bureaucratic-authoritarian' state, of the state 'as the bearer of an ethical project bent on reshaping or reordering the identity of its inhabitants', John Keane (1998b: 24, 33), for instance, repeatedly insists upon the importance of state power in guaranteeing the existence of the institutions of civil society.[3] His perspective understands 'democracy as a special type of political system in which civil society and state institutions tend to function as two necessary moments, separate but contiguous, distinct but interdependent' (ibid. p. 8). Targeting primarily the work of Gramsci, he thus argues against what he sees as the vacuity of the anarchist *rêverie* of a civil society without a state.

There are, however, several problems with such an argument. First of all, the establishment of a tight link between civil society and the state complicates the interpretation of classical texts on these matters. It is noteworthy, for instance, recalling the beginning of our analysis above, that the question of state power is left untouched by Adam Ferguson; its importance in Tocquevillean thought, similarly, is only very relative. In contrast, the work of Hegel (who is often presented as the inventor of a conception of civil society which is still prevalent today: namely civil society as intermediary institutions)[4] gives a central role to the state, as distinct from civil society. In Hegel's *Rechtsphilosophie*, however, as we have seen, civil society is not primarily conceived as a deliberative body. It is rather a surface of contact between citizens and the state which allows for a deeper penetration of state principles into the social, which amount to a negation of civil society as the primary locus of political power (Terrier 2001).[5]

These considerations force us to revise a common understanding of civil society as characterized by its dialectical relationship with state institutions. To hold this conception is the best way to overlook the permanent *problem* of the creation of an adequate relation between a configuration of social relations and the form of the polity under conditions of political modernity. And this is what we take to be the problem of civil society. We do not want to be misunderstood as saying that a collectivity of human beings could consist solely of the deliberative flux of civil society (if this is what the anarchist *rêverie* is about); we think, on the contrary, as we tried to suggest above, that what we might call the institutional tension is a central component of the idea of civil society. However, we wish to deny the fact that the state, and especially the state in its contemporary Western understanding, can be the only possible form of addressing the thus understood problem of civil society.[6] Or, to phrase it differently, we think that the error in this reasoning consists in taking a historical compromise between civil society and the state, whereby civil society takes the state as the instrument of its realization, as the only possible way of solving the problem of the institutionalization of the deliberations of civil society. Such a *raccourci*, to give one further example, can also be found in the work of Jürgen Habermas.

In *Between Facts and Norms* Habermas proposes a kind of transcendental deduction of fundamental rights (*Grundrechte*) which takes the following shape: in the context of social association, individuals are confronted with the problem of the coordination of their action. Deliberation, suggests Habermas, is the procedure which lies most evidently at hand when a collection of individuals must find an agreement about what is to be done. In turn, deliberation can be taken to give birth to decisions enjoying universal acceptance only if it follows some basic rules which guarantee the fairness of the deliberative process. These rules are none other than the *Grundrechte* themselves: any individual, if she is to take part in the deliberative process, must be able to count on the respect of all other members of the collectivity for her right to live, to have her physical integrity respected, to express her opinion, and so on. Habermas, however, thinks that the *Grundrechte* must be guaranteed by a special body which enforces their respect:

> the self-referential act that legally institutionalizes civic autonomy is still incomplete in essential respects; in cannot stabilize itself. The moment of a reciprocal conferral or rights remains a metaphorical event. It can perhaps be recalled and ritualized, but it cannot become permanent unless state power is established and put to work. If the interpenetration of private and public autonomy brought about in the system of rights is to be rendered permanent, then the process of juridification must not limit itself to the liberty of private persons and the communicative freedom of citizens. It must extend immediately to that political power *already presupposed* with the medium of law, a power to which the making as well as the enforcing of law owe their binding character. The co-original constitution and conceptual interpenetration of law and political power call for a more extensive legitimation, one requiring legal channels for the sanctioning , organizing, and executive powers of the state itself. This is the idea of government by law [*Rechtsstaat*]. (Habermas 2001: 132–33)

In this quote there appears to be an ambiguity. Habermas touches upon the problem of self-realization of civil society: the problem of a consolidation and enforcement of its contingent decisions. He rightly points out that only a political *institution* ('political power') can play this role. The fact that this institution must necessarily be a state, however, is a mere assumption whose origins ('already presupposed') and form are left out of the argumentation.

The question of an institutionalisation of civil society is certainly absolutely central. It is equally central, however, to think about this question in *problematic* terms. Civil society's need for institutions opens possibilities to which the already constituted contemporary state is only one of the many responses.

Towards a Conceptual Reappraisal:
Expanding Normative Horizons in the Wake
of the Crisis of Organized Democracy

At this point, therefore, our reflections have to move backwards, in a literal-temporal and in a figurative sense. After having aimed at a contextual reconstruction of the conceptual development throughout this volume, we now need to decontextualize the findings with a view to provide the broadest possible understanding of 'civil society', one that can capture a large variety of different socio-political situations. In our view, this approach will lead to two basic assumptions without which any debate on civil society would have with little meaning. On the one hand, one needs to assume that human beings are diverse, because otherwise the problématique of political modernity and, thus, of civil society, would not exist; on the other hand, one needs to assume that collective deliberation is the best, if not the only, way to establish and maintain a collectivity under conditions of individual diversity.[7] These assumptions express nothing else than the idea that 'civil society' is a way of addressing the political problématique of modernity, namely the question of relating by means of collective self-determination a configuration of social relations to a political form. More empirically speaking, we can say that social arrangements take the form of 'civil society' when a large portion of the members of a collectivity show interest in, and take part in, collective debates on social institutions with a view to decide upon their desirability, and to establish or modify them accordingly.

Modernity is not to be understood here as describing merely a historical moment, but rather an imaginary configuration in which the idea of the intrinsic contingency of social order takes it rise. Thus, modernity must be taken here to mean a historical condition in which the social is predominantly conceived as a series of institutions deriving from the conscious action of a collection of human beings. Under modern conditions, society is not perceived as a heteronomous given, but as the endogenous product of human will. Civil society incarnates the political problématique of modernity in the sense that, first, the latter is fundamentally that of the self-institution of society; and that, second, civil society can be interpreted as a response to the question of self-institution insofar as it promotes a principle of institutional legitimacy.

The social is the totality of actual and potential actions performed, and representations held, by a collection of agents who are aware of the fact that their actions have an effect on other agents. Modernity is the consciousness of the contingency of social order. Lastly, institutions play the role of guidelines for social agents insofar as their role is to ease the coordination of action by building up a common background of 'taken-for-grantedness'. The question posed to the social by modernity, thus, is the following: on what *endogenous* basis are *legitimate* institutions going to be established? Civil society is an incarnation of modernity insofar as it proposes an answer to this interrogation, and its answer is: the basis of legitimate institutionalisation can be based on nothing but *communication and consent*.

Communication and agreement are thinkable only if there is something to communicate about and agree upon and someone to communicate and agree with. In slightly more technical terms, we can say that civil society is possible only if two further conditions are fulfilled, one epistemological, the other ontological. First, civil society can exist only if a specific epistemology is widely diffused, which claims that what we call truth in social and political matters is not determined externally or heteronomously, but through series of statements that benefit from a broad explicit consensus. Second, civil society is dependent upon a specific social ontology which emphasizes the autonomy of singular human beings (and not merely of society as a whole).[8] Without the perception of human beings as capable of autonomous reasoning and, as a consequence thereof, of autonomous action, the possibility of active deliberation and subsequent agreement is lost, and civil society is deprived of its foundation. Such view, however, does not in turn necessarily ascribe autonomy to atomistic individuals, as both economic and political liberalism tended to do in most of their variants. If human beings are seen as 'social animals', then they always already exist in social relations. A concept of civil society that starts out from configurations of social relations is thus necessary, and as such it paves the way, sociologically, to a conception of society as a non-homogeneous whole. The assumption of individual autonomy translates into strong expectations about a possible divergence of opinions within a given social space.[9]

At this point it should have become clear why, in our understanding, the notion of civil society bears some strong conceptual affinities with that of democracy as its political form, namely as expressive of the modern political commitment to collective self-determination. However, we conceive of democracy essentially as an institutional setting, precisely a political form, while civil society is for us, first and foremost, a virtual space of deliberation that contains a plurality of yet undecided possibilities.[10]

The concept of civil society in this understanding is of particular importance in the current moment for two reasons. First, many existing polities have undergone and keep undergoing a process of de-institutionalization. This process was in many, even though by far not all cases, at least partially brought about by civil society activities in quest for a stronger form of democracy. The debate about, and the activities of, civil society aim at a restructuring of political spaces in light of such democratic quest.

However, de-institutionalization was also brought about, or is accompanied by, transformations in the configurations of social relations. Economic 'globalization' under the sign of neo-liberalism has extended and expanded the commercial linkages between human beings; and, partly in response to such 'thinning out' of the social bond, cultural 'globalization' has led to a new emphasis on strong cultural ties to others that are seen as pre-existing singular human beings and that are related to the renewed quest for culturally defined polities. In both of these tendencies, the communicative link between human beings as constitutive of the polity tends to be underestimated in its conceptual importance and weakened in the course of ongoing social transformations.

In such a global situation, the quest for democracy as voiced from civil society cannot rest content with the attempt to restructure the spaces of existing polities. What seems at stake is the broader quest for a new instituting of society and polity. Such as a re-constituting under conditions of crisis of organized democracy and of 'globalization' would need to aim at expanding the normative horizons of democracy beyond organized modernity. In the sense that civil society as a configuration of social relations will always relate to a political form, this instituting process may in Europe possibly be seen in the creation of a European polity through a European civil society – or at least this is one of the yet undecided possibilities of civil society today that is in need of exploration.

Notes

1. The work of Lyotard (1989) is very revealing in this respect.
2. This element, by the way, is the best way to differentiate between authoritarian and totalitarian regimes, which aim at a total mobilisation of the collectivity and thus re-incorporate any intermediary organisation into the direct sphere of influence of the bearers of social power (who usually also control state institution). Castoriadis proposed an analysis of the passage of the Soviet Union from totalitarian to authoritarian rule, the differences between the former and the latter being 'the end of the attempt of establishing a total ideological *control*' and 'an officially promoted process of privatization' (Castoriadis 1986: 253–56).

234 • *Jean Terrier and Peter Wagner*

3. A similar tendency can also be felt in the recent contribution of Khilnani (2001) to the subject.

4. See Riedel 1984, and to a certain extent Bobbio 1976, as examples of this kind of argumentation.

5. This is another way of saying that the (arguably quite tempting) idea of defining the modern reflection on civil society as characterized by its positing a threefold distinction of the social (the household, the state, civil society) has some weaknesses. This definition is perfectly compatible with a conception of civil society as a collection of intermediary institutions; it is much less compatible with our own perspective, which emphasizes the deliberative dimension of civil society and thus addresses more centrally the political problématique of modernity, though.

6. This is not at all an easy task. Khilnani, for instance, similarly insists upon the necessity of avoiding any unconditional linkage between civil society and historically existing political forms (e.g., liberal democracy). In spite of this, however, he ends up arguing that civil society cannot thrive without a certain set of precise institutions, which are: a 'legal structure of propriety rights', a 'system of markets where such rights can be exchanged', and a 'legal recognition of political associations and voluntary agencies' (Khilnani 2001: 30). Independent organizations, a separate legal system, a market: the author's efforts to complicate our understanding of civil society by insisting that it can exist under very different kinds of political arrangements ends with describing an institutional setting that seems to be nothing but the typical liberal-Western polity.

7. We may just recall that the elements we have just described as core components of the idea of civil society can be found in an especially clear form in the writings of those two authors whom we for those reasons take to offer the most fruitful approaches to civil society, namely Adam Ferguson (*An Essay on the History of Civil Society*) and Alexis de Tocqueville (*Democracy in America*). We note explicitly that this assumption gives priority to *communication* as a type of social relations between members of a polity, or, in other words, that it does not have any a priori faith in the assumption that other types of social relations – with the relation through *commerce* as the most prominent one in the history of ideas – would lead to an understanding of common matters without communication.

8. As was shown before, it is indeed possible to conceive of society as an autonomous whole composed of non-autonomous parts, this conception having been fairly widespread in the nineteenth century, with organicism as its clearest example and the varieties of nationalist expressions as the predominant political interpretation.

9. There are some similarities between the approach proposed here and the recent contribution of Khilnani to the subject. Khilnani also discusses the conditions of possibility of civil society, which are, according to him: a set of 'human *capacities*, moral and political' (Khilnani 2001: 25), i.e., a specific conception of the self, 'one that is mutable, able to conceive of interests as transient, and able to change and to choose political loyalties and public affiliations' (ibid.: 28); an arrangement of the political as an 'arena or set of practices which is subject to regular and punctual publicity' (p. 26); an 'institutionalized dispersal of social power' (p. 30), etc. Our impression is, however, as briefly stated above, that Khilnani fails to distinguish clearly enough between what belongs to the fundamental ontological and epistemological prerequisites of civil society, on the one hand, and the mere historical contingencies of its incarnations.

10. In the vocabulary of Cornelius Castoriadis, we may say that civil society is the place in which the *instituting imaginary* deploys itself, while democracy falls on the side of the *instituted imaginary* (Castoriadis 1975).

NOTES ON CONTRIBUTORS

Peter Hallberg, is a Research Professor at Stockholm University and the Swedish Collegium for Advanced Study in the Social Sciences (SCASSS). He specializes in theories and histories of democracy. In his historical works, he focuses on the ways in which concepts emerge, change meaning and come to serve different ideological purposes, chiefly in eighteenth-century political discourse. He teaches courses on Political Theory and Human Rights.

Jody Jensen is a Research Fellow at the Institute of Political Science at the Hungarian Academy of Sciences. She is a Jean Monnet course holder in European Studies at the Institute for Social and European Studies (ISES) and the director of international relations for ISES. She has written books and articles on transition and social innovation in East and Central Europe, and Europe and the Balkans.

Ferenc Miszlivetz was a leading figure in the democratic opposition movement in Hungary. He is a sociologist and Senior Research Fellow at the Institute of Political Science at the Hungarian Academy of Sciences and is the author of several books in English and Hungarian as well as numerous articles in professional journals. In 2005 he was awarded the Knights Cross by the Hungarian president for his work on civil society and European integration.

Jay Rowell is a Research Fellow in sociology at the Centre National de Recherche Scientifique, Groupe de Sociologie Politique Européenne at the Université Robert Schuman in Strasburg. His fields of research include the sociology of the communist state, the history of housing and urbanism in Germany and France, methods in comparative historical and sociological enquiry and more recently the construction of public problems in the European Union. His book entitled *Le régime totalitaire au concret* is forthcoming.

Shin, Jong-Hwa is Research Professor at the Institute of Social Research, Korea University in Korea. He holds a Ph.D. from the University of Warwick where he completed a doctoral thesis on the Historical Formation of

Modernity in Korea. He continues to publish articles on Korean modernity in comparative perspective, his current research concerning modernity and civil society in comparative historical sociology.

Jean Terrier is a Mellon Fellow at the Society of Fellows in the Humanities and a lecturer at Columbia University. He holds a Ph.D. in Social and Political Science from the European University Institute in Florence, with a dissertation on the notion of national character in late nineteenth-century France. His interests range from the history of the social sciences and the history of political thought to political sociology and contemporary political theory.

Peter Wagner is Professor of Social and Political Theory at the European University Institute and Professor of Sociology at the University of Warwick. His current research focuses on a re-assessment of European modernity in comparative-historical and politico-philosophical perspective and on the relation between historical sociology and political philosophy in general.

Björn Wittrock is University Professor at Uppsala University and Principal of the Swedish Collegium for Advanced Study in the Social Sciences, Uppsala. Formerly Lars Hierta Professor of Government at Stockholm University, he has published extensively in the fields of intellectual history, historical social science and social theory. He is President of the *International Institute of Sociology* (founded in 1893) and a Member of the *Academia Europaea*. He is also a member of the editorial board of *Academia Europaea*'s journal, *European Review*.

Bénédicte Zimmermann is Maître de conférences at the Ecole des Hautes Etudes en Sciences Sociales, Paris. Her main research interests are in the history and sociology of work and categories of social organization. Her recent publications include: *La constitution du chômage en Allemagne. Entre professions et territoires* (Paris, Ed. Maison des Sciences de l'Homme, 2001); *Les sciences sociales à l'épreuve de l'action. Le savant, le politique et l'Europe* (Paris, Ed. Maison des Sciences de l'Homme, 2004); *De la comparaison à l'histoire croisée* (ed. with M. Werner, Paris, Seuil, 2004).

BIBLIOGRAPHY

Abensour, Miguel. 1997. *La démocratie contre l'Etat. Marx et le moment machiavélien*. Paris: Presses universitaires de France.

Adorno, Theodor W. 1986 [1951]. 'Individuum und Staat', *Gesammelte Schriften 20/1: Vermischte Schriften* I. Frankfurt: Suhrkamp, 287–92.

Alexander, Jeffrey C. 1998. *Real Civil Socieities – Dilemmas of Institutionalization*. London: Sage.

Andræ, Carl Göran. 1980. 'Om lärda sammanslutningar'. *Historisk tidskrift* 1–2.

Aquinas, St Thomas. 2002. *Political Writings*. Cambridge: Cambridge University Press.

Arato, Andrew and Jean L. Cohen. 1992. *Civil Society and Political Theory*. Cambridge: MIT Press.

Arendt, Hannah. 1951. *The Origins of Totalitarianism*. New York: Harcourt, Brace, Jovanovich.

———. 1965. *On Revolution*. New York: Viking.

———. 1998 [1958]. *The Human Condition*. Chicago: The University of Chicago Press.

Aristotle. 1492. *Politicorum libri* VIII. Rome: Silber.

———. 1996. *The Politics and The Constitution of Athens*. Cambridge: Cambridge University Press.

Armfeldt, Carl Henric. 1765. *Afhandling, om Medel, At Förekomma Borgerliga Seders Almenna Fördärf*. Åbo: Frenckell.

Armstrong, Charles K., ed. 2002. *Korean Society: Civil Society, Democracy and the State*. London: Routledge.

Arnason, Johann P. 2003. *Civilizations in Dispute*. Leiden, Brill.

———. 2004. 'The Axial Age and Its Interpreters: Reopening a Debate'. In J.P. Arnason, S.N. Eisenstadt and B. Wittrock (eds), *Axial Civilizations and World History*. Leiden-Boston: Brill.

Assmann, Jan. 2004. 'Axial "Breakthroughs" and Semantic "Relocations" in Ancient Egypt and Israel'. In J.P. Arnason, S.N. Eisenstadt and B. Wittrock (eds), *Axial Civilizations and World History*. Leiden-Boston: Brill.

Baker, Keith Michael. 1990. *Inventing the French Revolution: Essays on French Political Culture in the Eighteenth Century*. Cambridge: Cambridge University Press.

———. 2001. 'Enlightenment and the Institution of Society: Notes for a Conceptual History'. In Sudipta Kaviraj and Sunil Khilnani (eds), *Civil Society: History and Possibilities*. Cambridge: Cambridge University Press, pp. 84–104.

Ball, Terence, James Farr, and Russell L. Hanson. 1989. 'Editors' Introduction'. In Terence Ball, James Farr and Russell L. Hanson (eds), *Political Innovation and Conceptual Change*. Cambridge: Cambridge University Press.

Barber, Benjamin. 2001. *Globalization Nightmare or Global Civil Society?* [online] Freedom in the World. Available at: http://freedomhouse.org/research/freeworld/2001/essay2text.htm.

Barker, Ernest. 1946. *The Politics of Aristotle*. Oxford: Oxford University Press.

Baron, Hans. 1966. *The Crisis of the Early Italian Renaissance. Civic Humanism and Republican Liberty in an Age of Classicism and Tyranny*. Princeton: Princeton University Press.

———. 1988. *In Search of Florentine Civic Humanism. Essays on the Transition from Medieval to Modern Thought*, vol. 2. Princeton: Princeton University Press.

Beck, Ulrich. 1986. *Risikogesellschaft*. Frankfurt: Suhrkamp.

Bennich-Björkman, Bo. 1998. 'Eliternas gata och handeln på broar och marknader. Systemen för spridning av böcker i Sverige 1600–1850'. In Jan-Erik Pettersson (ed.), *Bokens vägar: Seelig & Co 150 år*. Solna: Seelig.

Bernhard, Michael. 1996. 'Civil Society after the First Transition'. *Communist and Post-Communist Studies* 29(3): 309–30.

Berquist, Charles. 1986. *Labor in Latin America: Comparative Essays on Chile, Argentina, Venezuela, and Colombia*. Stanford: Stanford University Press.

Birnbaum, Pierre. 1982. *La logique de l'Etat*. Paris: Fayard.

Black, Antony 1992. *Political Thought in Europe 1250–1450*. Cambridge: Cambridge University Press.

Blythe, James M. 1986. 'The Mixed Constitution and the Distinction between Regal and Political Power in the Work of Thomas Aquinas'. *Journal of the History of Ideas* 47(4): 547–65.

Bobbio, Norberto. 1976. *Gramsci e la concezione della società civile*. Milan: Feltrinelli, Opuscoli marxisti.

———. 1981. *Studi hegeliani*. Turin: Einaudi.

Bolgar, R.R. 1954. *The Classical Heritage and its Beneficiaries*. Cambridge: Cambridge University Press.

Bolsinger, Eckard. 2001. *The Autonomy of the Political. Carl Schmitt's and Lenin's Political Realism*. Westport, CT: Greenwood.

Boltanski, Luc and Eve Chiapello. 1999. *Le nouvel esprit du capitalisme*. Paris, Gallimard.

Boltanski, Luc and Laurent Thévenot. 1991. *De la justification. Les économies de la grandeur*. Paris: Gallimard.

Botin, Anders af. 1757–64. *Utkast till svenska folkets historia*. 4 vols. Stockholm: Salvius.

Bourdieu, Pierre. 1980. *Le sens pratique*. Paris: Minuit.

Bozóki, András and Miklós Sükösd. 1993. 'Civil Society and Populism in the Eastern European Democratic Transitions'. *Praxis International* 13: 224–41.

Bruni, Leonardo. 1968. *Laudatio Florentinae Urbis* in Hans Baron (ed.), *From Petrarch to Leonardo Bruni*. Chicago: University of Chicago Press.

Budiman, A. 1990. *State and Civil Society in Indonesia*. Clayton, Victoria: Centre of South East Asian Studies, Monash University.

Butterfield, Jim and Marcia A. Weigle. 1992. 'Civil Society in Reforming Communist Regimes: the Logic of Emergence'. *Comparative Politics* 25(1): 1–2.

Butterworth, Charles 1996. 'Averroes, Precursor of the Enlightenment?'. *Alif: Journal of Comparative Poetics* 16.

Callahan, W.A. 1996. 'Rescripting East/West Relations, Rethinking Asian Democracy'. *Pacifica Review* 8: 1–25.

Callon, Michel, Pierre Lascoumes and Yannick Barthes. 2001. *Agir dans un monde incertain. Essai sur la démocratie technique*. Paris: Editions du Seuil.

Callus, D.A. 1947. 'The Date of Grosseteste's Translations and Commentaries on Pseudo-Dionysius and the *Nicomachean Ethics*'. *Recherches de théologie ancienne et médiévale* 14.

Carlsson, Sten. 1962. *Bonde – präst – ämbetsman: svensk ståndscirkulation från 1680 till våra dagar*. 2nd edn. Stockholm: Prisma.

Carlsson, Sten, and Jerker Rosén. 1961. *Svensk historia: Tiden efter 1718*, vol. 2. Stockholm: Bonnier.

———. 1980. *Svensk historia: Tiden efter 1718*. Stockholm: Esselte studium.

Castel, Robert. 1995. *Les Métamorphoses de la question sociale. Une chronique du salariat*. Paris: Fayard.

Castel, Robert and Claudine Haroche. 2001. *Propriété privé, propriété sociale, propriété de soi*. Paris: Fayard.

Castells, Manuel. 1998. *The End of the Millennium*. London: Blackwell.

———. 2000. *The Rise of the Network Society*, 2nd edn. Oxford: Blackwell.

Castoriadis, Cornelius. 1974. *L'expérience du mouvement ouvrier. Prolétariat et organisation* II. Paris: 10/18.

———. 1975. *L'institution imaginaire de la société*. Paris: Seuil.

———. 1986 [1981]. 'Les destinées du totalitarisme', in *Domaines de l'homme. Les carrefours du labyrinthe* 2. Paris: Seuil (Points).

———. 1997. 'Democracy as Procedure and Democracy as Regime'. *Constellations* 4(1).

Chakrabarty, Dipesh. 2000. *Provincializing Europe: Postcolonial Thought and Historical Difference*. Princeton: Princeton University Press.

Chartier, Roger. 1987. 'From Texts to Manners. A Concept and Its Books: Civilité between Aristocratic Distinction and Popular Appropriation'. In Lydia G. Cochrane (trans.), *The Cultural Uses of Print in Early Modern France*. Princeton: Princeton University Press, pp. 71–109.

Cho, Hein. 1997. 'The Historical Origin of Civil Society in Korea'. *Korea Journal* 37(2) (Summer): 24–41.

Christensson, Jakob. 1996. *Lyckoriket: studier i svensk upplysning*. Stockholm: Atlantis.

Chryssochoou, Dimitris. 2001. *Towards a Civic Conception of the European Polity*. Working Paper 33, University of Exeter.

Citizens Strengthening Global Civil Society. 1994. Washington, CIVICUS World Alliance for Citizen Participation.

Clayton, Andrew (ed.). 1996. *NGO's, Civil Society and the State: Building Democracy in Transitional Societies*. Oxford: Intrac.

Cochrane, Eric. 1981. *Historians and Historiography in the Italian Renaissance*. Chicago: Chicago University Press.

Cohen, T. 1980. 'Metaphor and the Cultivation of Intimacy'. In Sheldon Sacks (ed.) *On Metaphor*. Chicago: University of Chicago Press.

Colas, Dominique. 1991, *Le Glaive et le Fléau. Genèse du fanatisme et de la société civile*. Paris: Grasset.

———. 1997. *Civil Society and Fanaticism: Conjoined Histories*. Stanford: Stanford University Press.

Collier, Ruth Berins. 1982. 'Popular Incorporation and Political Supremacy: Regime Evolution in Brazil and Mexico'. In Sylvia Ann Hewlett and Richard S. Weinert (eds), *Brazil and Mexico: Patterns in Late Development*. Philadelphia: Institute for the Study of Human Issues, pp. 57–109.

Colliot-Thélène, Catherine and Jean-François Kervégan (eds). 2002. *De la société à la sociologie*. Paris: ENS Editions (Theoria).

Commission of the European Communities 2001. *European Governance: A White Paper*. Brussels: Commission of the European Communities. Available from: http://europa.eu.int/eur-lex/en/com/cnc/2001/com2001_0428en01.pdf

Common Europe. Available from: http://www.common.org.pl/.

Comor, Edward. 2001. 'The Role of Communication in Global Civil Society: Forces Processes, Prospects'. *International Studies Quarterly* 45(1): 395.

Conniff, James. 1978–1979. 'Hume on Political Parties: the Case for Hume as a Whig'. *Eighteenth-Century Studies* 12(2): 150–73.

Constant, Benjamin. 1988a [1819]. 'The Liberty of the Ancients Compared with That of the Moderns'. *Political Writings*. Cambridge: Cambridge University Press.

———. 1988b [1815]. *Principles of Politics Applicable to All Representative Governments*. In *Political Writings*. Cambridge: Cambridge University Press.

———. 2003 [1806]. *Principles of Politics Applicable to All Governments*. Indianapolis: Liberty Fund.

Coraggio, Jose Luis. 1986. 'Economic and Politics in the Transition to Socialism: Reflections on the Nicaragua Experience'. In Richard Fagan, Carmen Diana Deere and Jose Luis Coraggio (eds) *Transition and Development: Problems of Third World Development*. New York: Monthly Review Press, pp. 143–70.

Cumberland, Charles C. 1968. *Mexico: The Struggle for Modernity*. Oxford: Oxford University Press.

Daedalus. 1998. Early Modernities.

Daedalus. 2000. Multiple Modernities.

Dahrendorf, Ralph. 1997. *After 1989: Morals, Revolution and Civil Society*. Basingstoke, Macmillan in association with St. Anthony College, Oxford.

Dalin, Olof von. 1749. *Tal vid praesidii afläggande om Sverige i sit ämne och Sverige i sin upodling, hållit i kongl. svenska vetenskaps academien, den 29. apr. 1749*. Stockholm: Salvius.

d'Arcy, François and Guy Saez. 1985. De la représentation, in François d'Arcy (ed.), *La représentation*. Paris: Economica, pp. 7–31.

Darcy de Oliveira, Miguel and Rajesh Tandon. 1994. *Citizens Strengthening Global Civil Society*. Washington: CIVICUS World Alliance for Citizen Participation.

Davidson, A. 1997. 'Regional Politics: The European Union and Citizenship'. *Citizenship Studies* 1: 33–56.

Davis, Harold Eugene. 1972. *Latin American Thought: Historical Introduction*. Baton Rouge: Louisiana State University Press.

Dawson, Thomas C. and Gita Bhatt. 2001. 'The IMF and Civil Society Organizations: Striking a Balance'. *IMF Policy Discussion Paper*, PDP01/2. International Monetary Fund.

De La Porte, Caroline and Philippe Pochet (eds). 2002. *Building Social Europe through the Open Method of Coordination*. Brussels: PIE-Peter Lang.

Delblanc, Sven. 1965. *Ära och minne: studier kring ett motivkomplex i 1700–talets litteratur*. Stockholm: Bonnier.

Department for International Development. 2001. *Making Government Work for Poor People – Building State Capability*. Available from: http://www.dfid.gov.uk/Pubs/files/tsp_government.pdf..

Derrida, Jacques. 1986. 'Declarations of Independence'. *New Political Science* 15: 7–13.

Desrosières, Alain. 1993. *La politique des grands nombres. Histoire de la raison statistique*. Paris: La découverte.

De Swaan, Abram. 1997. 'The Receding Prospects for Transnational Social Policy'. *Theory and Society* 26: 561–75.

Dix, Robert H. 1985. 'Populism: Authoritarian and Democratic'. *Latin American Research Review* 20(2): 29–52.

Dod, Bernard G. 1982. 'Aristoteles Latinus,' in Norman Kretzmann, Anthony Kenny and Jan Pinborg (eds), *The Cambridge History of Later Medieval Philosophy*. Cambridge: Cambridge University Press.

Draft Treaty Establishing a Constitution for Europe 2003. CONV 850/03, 18 July.

Dragovic, J, Liebich, A, Warner, D. 1995. *Citizenship, East and West*. London: Kegan Paul International.

Dunbabin, Jean 1982. 'The Reception and Interpretation of Aristotle's *Politics*'. In Norman Kretzmann, Anthony Kenny and Jan Pinborg (eds), *The Cambridge History of Later Medieval Philosophy*. Cambridge: Cambridge University Press.

Dunkley, Graham. 2000. 'INGOs, LINGOs, DINGOs and TRINGOs Trade, the WTO and the Interest of Civil Society'. In *Conference on International Trade, Education and Research, 26–27 October 2000, Melbourne*. Available from: http://www.arts.monash.edu.au/ausapec/dunkley.pdf.

Durkheim, Emile. 1973 [1894]. *De la division du travail social*. Paris: PUF.

Dyson, R.W. 2002. 'Introduction'. In St. Thomas Aquinas, *Political Writings*. Cambridge: Cambridge University Press.

Edwards, Michael. 2002. 'Herding Cats? Civil Society and Global Governance'. *New Economy* 9(2): 71–76.

Edwards, Sebastian. 1985. 'Stabilization with Liberalization: An Evaluation of Ten Years of Chile's Experiment with Free-Market Policies'. *Economic Development and Cultural Changes* 33(2): 223–54.

Ehrenpreus, Carl Didrik. 1748. *Tal om den förmån och nytta som fria konster och handa-slögder tilskyndas af historien, hållit för kongl. vetensk. academien af … Carl Ehrenpreus, då han lade af sit praesidium den 23 april 1748*. Stockholm: Salvius.

Eisenstadt, Shmuel N. 1999. *Fundamentalism, sectarianism, and revolution. The Jacobin dimension of modernity*. Cambridge: Cambridge University Press.

Ekedahl, Nils. 1999. *Det svenska Israel: myt och retorik i Haquin Spegels predikokonst*. Uppsala: Gidlund.

Elander, I. and M. Gustafsson. 1995. 'The Re-emergence of Local Self-Government in Central Europe: Some Notes of the First Experience'. *European Journal of Political Research* 23(3): 295–322.

Elvius, Pehr. 1746. 'Svar.' In Carl Gustaf Tessin's, *Kårt tal om svenska språkets rykt och upodlande, hållit för kongl. svenska vetenskaps academien, af … Carl Gustaf Tessin, då han afträdde sit praesidium d. 10. januarii 1746*. Stockholm: Salvius.

———. 1748. 'Svar.' In *Tal om den förmån och nytta som fria konster och handa-slögder tilskyndas af historien, hållit för kongl. vetensk. academien af … Carl Ehrenpreus, då han lade af sit praesidium den 23 april 1748*. Stockholm: Salvius.

Engels, Friedrich. 1872. *Zur Wohnungsfrage*. Leipzig: Volksstaat.

Everson, Stephen. 1996. 'Introduction'. In Aristotle, *The Politics and The Constitution of Athens*, ed. Stephen Everson. Cambridge: Cambridge University Press.

Ewald, François. 1986. *L'Etat providence*. Paris: Grasset.

Faggot, Jacob. 1743. 'Svar.' In Hindric Jacob Wrede, *Tal om et borgerligit samhälles eller et land ock rikes rätta styrka, samt sätt ock utvägar at komma där til, hållit för kongl. svenska vetenskaps academien den 26 januarii år 1743*. Stockholm: Salvius.

Falk, Richard A. 1992. 'The Infancy of Global Civil Society'. In G. Lundestad and
O.A. Westad (eds), *Beyond the Cold War: New Dimensions in International
Relations.* Oslo: Scandinavian University Press, pp. 219–39.
———. 1995. *On Humane Governance: Toward a New Global Politics. The World
Order Models Project Report on the Global Civilizational Initiative.* Cambridge:
Polity Press.
———. 1998. 'Global Civil Society: Perspectives, Initiatives, Movements'. *Oxford
Development Studies* 26(1): 99–111.
Fay, Bernard. 1932. 'Learned Societies in Europe and America in the Eighteenth
Century'. *The American Historical Review* 37(2): 255–66.
Ferguson, Adam. 1995 [1767]. *An Essay on the History of Civil Society.* Cambridge,
Cambridge University Press.
Florini, Ann M. ed. 2000. *The Third Force. The Rise of Transnational Civil Society.*
Washington DC: Carnegie Endowment for International Peace.
Foster, John. 2001. *Knowing Ourselves: A Brief History of Emerging Civil Society.*
Washington, DC: 4th CIVICUS World Assembly.
Fowler, Alan. 1996. 'Strengthening Civil Society in Transition Economies'. In
Andrew Clapton (ed.), *NGOs, Civil Society and the State, Building Democracy in
Transitional Societies.* Oxford: INTRAC.
Fox, Elizabeth (ed.). 1988. *Media and Politics in Latin America.* London: SAGE.
Frängsmyr, Tore. 1972. *Wolffianismens genombrott i. Uppsala: frihetstida.
universitetsfilosofi till 1700–talets mitt.* Uppsala: Uppsala universitet/Almqvist &
Wiksell.
Fredenstierna, Adam. 1769. *Presidentens uti kongl. maj:ts och riksens Swea hof-rätt
Adam Fredenstiernas Memorialer, angående finance-werket och lagarnes
wärkställighet. Ingifne hos högl. ridderskapet och adelen den 18 nov. 1769, och 6
oct. 1766.* Stockholm: Wennberg och Nordström.
Friese, Heidrun and Peter Wagner. 1999. 'Inescapability and Attainability in the
Sociology of Modernity. A Note on the Variety of Modes of Social Theorizing'.
European Journal of Social Theory 2(1): 27–44.
Fuentes, Carlos. 1999. *The Buried Mirror: Reflections on Spain and the New World.*
Boston: Houghton Miffin.
Furtado, Celoso. 1976. *Economic Development of Latin America: Historical Background
and Contemporary Problems.* 2nd edn, Cambridge: Cambridge University Press.
Galeano, Eduardo. 1974. *Open Veins of Latin America: Five Centuries of the Pillage of
a Continent.* New York: Monthly Review Press.
Garton Ash, Timothy. 1998. 'Europe's Endangered Liberal Order'. *Foreign Affairs,*
March–April 1998: 51–65.
Gáspár, Miklós Tamás. 1994. 'A Disquisition on Civil Society'. *Social Research*
61(2): 205–22.
Giddens, Anthony. 1984. *The Constitution of Society.* Cambridge: Polity.
———. 1998. *The Third Way: The Renewal of Social Democracy.* Cambridge: Polity.
Gill, Anthony and Aran Keshavarzian. 1999. 'State Building and Religious
Resources: An Institutional Theory of Church-State Relations in Iran and
Mexico'. *Politics and Society* 27(3): 431–46.
Gillespie, Paul and John Palmer. 2001. *The Mission and Values of the Europe We
Need* [online]. Available from http://europa.eu.int/futurum/documents/
other/oth200901_2_en.pdf. The European Policy Centre (20 September 2001).
Glenn, John K. 2001. *Framing Democracy: Civil Society and Civic Movements in
Eastern Europe.* Stanford: Stanford University Press.

Global Strategies Project – Notes and Commentaries, in *Encyclopedia of World Problems and Human Potential.* Available from: http://www.uia.be/strategies/stratcom_bodies.php

Goffman, Erving. 1974. *Frame Analysis. An Essay of the Organization of Experience.* New York: Harper and Row.

Goodman, Dena. 1994. *The Republic of Letters: A Cultural History of the French Enlightenment.* Ithaca: Cornell University Press.

Gosewinkel, Dieter and Sven Reichardt (eds). 2004. *Ambivalenzen der Zivilgesellschaft. Gegenbegriffe, Gewalt und Macht.* Berlin: WZB, Discussion paper n°SP IV 2004–501.

Habermas, Jürgen. 1971a. 'The Scientization of Politics and Public Opinion'. In *Toward a Rational Society. Student Protest, Science, and Politics.* Boston: Beacon Press.

———. 1971b. 'Technology and Science as "Ideology"'. In *Toward a Rational Society. Student Protest, Science, and Politics.* Boston: Beacon Press.

———. 1974 [1968]. *Technik und Wissenschaft als 'Ideologie'.* Frankfurt: Suhrkamp.

———. 1981. *Theorie des kommunikativen Handelns.* Frankfurt: Suhrkamp.

———. 1987. *The Philosophical Discourse of Modernity.* Cambridge: Polity.

———. 1989 [1962]. *The Structural Transformations of the Public Sphere.* London: Polity Press.

———. 1992. *Faktizität und Geltung. Beiträge zur Diskurstheorie des Rechts und des demokratischen Rechtsstaats.* Frankfurt: Suhrkamp.

———. 1996. 'Civil Society and the Public Sphere'. In *Between Facts and Norms. Contribution to a Discourse Theory of Law and Democracy.* Cambridge, MA: MIT Press.

———. 1997. *Droit et démocratie. Entre faits et norms.* Paris: Gallimard.

———. 2000. *The Post-National Constellation: Political Essays.* Cambridge: Polity Press.

———. 2001. 'Why Europe Needs a Constitution?'. *New Left Review* 11 (September–October 2001): 16.

———. 2001. *Between Facts and Norms, Contributions to a Discourse Theory of Law and Democracy.* Cambridge, MA: MIT Press.

Haboush, JaHyun Kim. 1994. 'Academies and Civil Society in Choson Korea'. *Etudes Thematiques: La Societe Civile Face a l'Etat dans Les Traditions Chinoise, Japonaise, Coreenne et Vietnaiennnes* 3: 383–92.

Hacking, Ian. 1999. *The Social Construction of What?* Cambridge, MA: Harvard University Press.

Hall, John A. (ed.). 1995. *Civil Society: Theory, History, Comparison.* Cambridge: Polity Press.

Hall, Peter and David Soskice (eds). 2001. *Varieties of Capitalism.* Oxford: Oxford University Press.

Hallberg, Peter. 2003. *Ages of Liberty: Social Upheaval, History Writing and the New Public Sphere in Sweden, 1740–1792.* Stockholm: Stockholm University.

Hankins, James. 2000a. 'Introduction'. In James Hankins (ed.), *Renaissance Civic Humanism: Reappraisals and Reflections.* Cambridge: Cambridge University Press.

———. 2000b. 'The Civic Panegyrics of Leonardo Bruni,' in James Hankins (ed.), *Renaissance Civic Humanism: Reappraisals and Reflections.* Cambridge: Cambridge University Press.

Hannesdóttir, Anna Helga. 1998. *Lexikografihistorisk spegel: den enspråkiga svenska lexikografins utveckling ur den tvåspråkiga.* Göteborg: Göteborgs universitet.

———. 2002. In *Nationalism och nationell identitet i 1700–talets Sverige*, vol. 27, eds Bo Lindberg and Åsa Karlsson. Uppsala: Opuscula historica Upsaliensia, pp. 87–100.

Hartz, Louis.1964. *The Founding of New Societies*. New York: Harcout, Brace and World.

Haupt, Georges, Michaël Löwy and Claude Weill (eds). 1997. *Les marxistes et la question nationale. 1848–1914*. Paris: L'Harmattan.

Heater, D. 1996. *World Citizenship and Government: Cosmopolitan Ideas in the History of Western Political Thought*. London: Macmillan.

Hegel, G.W.F. 1991 [1821]. *Elements of the Philosophy of Right*. Cambridge: Cambridge University Press.

Heilbron, Johan. 1995. *The Rise of Social Theory*. Cambridge: Polity.

Hennis, Wilhelm. 1987. *Max Webers Fragestellung*. Tübingen: Mohr.

Hernlund, Hugo, ed. 1892. *Bidrag till den svenska skollagstiftningens historia under partitidehvarfvet 1718–1809, I:B. Öfversigter och öfriga bilagor, Bilaga IV*. Stockholm: Isaac Marcus' boktryckeri.

Hessler, Carl Arvid. 1943. '"Aristokratifördömandet". En riktning i svensk historieskrivning.' *Scandia* 15: 209–66.

Hirschman, Albert O. 1970. *Exit, Voice and Loyalty*. Cambridge, MA: Harvard University Press.

———. 1977. *The Passions and the Interests. Arguments for Capitalism before Its Triumph*. Princeton: Princeton University Press.

———. 1993. 'Exit, Voice and the Fate of the German Democratic Republic'. *World Politics* 45(2): 173–202.

Hoffmann, Stanley. 2002. 'Clash of Globalizations'. *Foreign Affairs* 81(4): 109.

Honig, Bonnie. 1991. 'Declarations of Independence: Arendt and Derrida on the Problem of Founding a Republic'. *American Political Science Review* 85(1): 97–113.

Honneth, Axel. 1992. *Kampf um Anerkennung*. Frankfurt: Suhrkamp (Engl. trans. 1996).

———. 2001. *Leiden an Unbestimmtheit. Eine Reaktualisierung der Hegelschen Rechtsphilosophie*. Stuttgart: Reclam.

Hont, Istvan and Michael Ignatieff. 1983. 'Needs and Justice in the "Wealth of Nations"'. In Istvan Hont, Michael Ignatieff (eds), *Wealth and Virtue. The Shaping of Political Economy in the Scottish Enlightenment*. Cambridge: Cambridge University Press.

Howell, Jude and Jenny Pearce. 2001. *Civil Society and Development: A Critical Exploration*. Boulder: Lynne Rienner.

Huber, Victor Aimé. 1857. *Die Wohnungsnot der kleinen Leute in den grossen Städten*. Leipzig.

Hübner, Peter. 1994. *Konsens, Konflikt und Kompromis*. Berlin: Akademie Verlag.

Huinink, Johannes and Karl-Ulrich Mayer (eds). 1995. *Kollektiv und Eigensinn: Lebensverläufe in der DDR und danach*. Berlin: Akademie Verlag.

Hume, David. 1964. *The Philosophical Works*, vol. 3: *Essays Moral, Political, and Literary*. Darmstadt: Aalen Scientia Verlag.

———. 1987. *Essays, Moral, Political, and Literary*, Indianapolis: Liberty Classics.

Huntington, Samuel P. 1993. 'The Clash of Civilizations'. *Foreign Affairs* 72: 22–49.

Hutchings, Kimberley. 1996. 'The Idea of International Citizenship'. In B. Holden (ed.), *The Ethical Dimensions of Global Change*. London: Macmillan.

Jackson, Howard. 2002. *Lexicography: An Introduction*. New York: Routledge.

Janvry, Alain de. 1981. *The Agrarian Question and Reformism in Latin America*. Baltimore, MD: Johns Hopkins University Press.

Jensen, Jody and Ferenc Miszlivetz. 1998a. 'An Emerging Paradox: Civil Society from Above?'. In Dietrich and Marilyn Rueschemeyer and Björn Wittrock (eds), *Participation and Democracy – East and West. Comparisons and Interpretations*. Armonk, New York: M.E. Sharpe, pp. 83–98.

———. 1998b. 'A civil társadalom metamorfózisa 1988–1998'. In Ferenc Miszlivetz (ed.), *Közép-európai változások*. Szombathely: Savaria University Press, pp. 141–70.

Joas, Hans. 1992. *Die Kreativität des Handelns*. Frankfurt: Suhrkamp (Engl. trans. 1996).

Jobert, Bruno. 2003. 'Le mythe de la gouvernance dépolitisée'. In Pierre Favre, Jack Hayward and Yves Schemeil (eds), *tre gouverné*. Paris: Presses de Sciences Po., pp. 273–86.

Jorgensen, Lars. 1996. 'What are NGOs Doing in Civil Society?' In Andrew Clayton (ed.), *NGOs, Civil Society and the State: Building Democracy in Transnational Societies*. Oxford: INTRAC.

Jung, Myung-Gi. 1986. *The History of Nicaraguan Revolution*. Seoul: Hanmadang.

Kaelble, Hartmut. 2003. 'Gibt es eine europäische Zivilgesellschaft?'. In Gosewinkel Dieter, Dieter Rucht, Wolfgang van den Daele and Jürgen Kocka (eds), *Zivilgesellschaft. National und transnational*. Berlin: Sigma (*WZB Jahrbuch*), pp. 267–84.

Kaldor, Mary. 1991. *Europe from Below*. London: Verso.

———. 1997. 'Transnational Civil Society'. ms., Brighton: Sussex European Institute.

———. 2003. *Global Civil Society: An Answer to War*. Cambridge: Polity Press.

Kalyvas, Andreas. 2001. 'The Politics of Autonomy and the Challenge of Deliberation: Castoriadis contra Habermas'. *Thesis Eleven* 64(February).

Karagiannis, Nathalie. 2004. *Avoiding Responsibility. The Politics and Discourse of European Development Policy*. London, Pluto.

Kaviraj, Sudipta and Sunil Khilnani. 2001. 'Introduction: Ideas of Civil Society'. In Sudipta Kaviraj and Sunil Khilnani (eds), *Civil Society. History and Possibilities*. Cambridge: Cambridge University Press.

Keane, John. 1988. 'Introduction', in John Keane (ed.), *Civil Society and the State. New European Perspectives*. London: Verso.

———. ed. 1998a. *Civil Society and the State. New European Perspectives*. London: University of Westminster Press.

———. 1998b. *Civil Society. Old Images, New Visions*. Cambridge: Polity Press.

———. 1998c. *Democracy and Civil Society*. London: The University of Westminster Press.

———. 2003. *Global Civil Society?* Cambridge: Cambridge University Press.

Khilnani, Sunil. 2001. 'The Development of Civil Society'. In Sudipta Kaviraj and Sunil Khilnani (eds), *Civil Society. History and Possibilities*. Cambridge: Cambridge University Press.

Kim, Jun-Ho (ed.). 2002. *Social Movements and Social Change*. Seoul: Nanam (in Korean).

Kim, Woo-Taek (ed.). 2003. *The History of Latin America and Its Culture*. Seoul: Sohwa.

Kocka, Jürgen. 1996. *The Difficult Rise of Civil Society*. Berlin: Free University of Berlin.

———. 1999. 'The G.D.R.: A Special Kind of Modern Dictatorship'. In Konrad Jarausch (ed.), *Dictatorship as Experience: Towards a Socio-Cultural History of the GDR*. New York: Berghahn Books, 17–26.

———. 2004. 'Civil Society from a Historical Perspective'. *European Review* 12(1): 65–79.

Kongl. maj:ts nådigste stadfästelse på svenska vetenskaps academiens grund-reglor. Gifven Stockholm i råd-cammaren den 31. martii. 1741. Stockholm: Kongliga tryckeriet/Momma.

Koo, Hagen. 1993. *State and Society in Contemporary Korea*. Ithaca: Cornell University Press.

Koselleck, Reinhart. 1988. *Critique and Crisis: Enlightenment and the Pathogenesis of Modern Society*. Cambridge, MA.: MIT Press.

———. 2002. 'Three Bürgerliche Worlds? Preliminary Theoretical-Historical Remarks on the Comparative Semantics of Civil Society in Germany, England, and France'. In Reinhart Koselleck and Todd Samuel Presner (eds), *The Practice of Conceptual History: Timing History, Spacing Concepts*. Stanford: Stanford University Press.

Koselleck, Reinhart and Klaus Schreiner. 1994. 'Einleitung. Von der alteuropäischen zur neuzeitlichen Bürgerschaft. Ihr politisch-sozialer Wandel im Medium von Begriff-, Wirkungs- und Rezeptionsgeschichten'. In Reinhart Koselleck and Klaus Schreiner (eds), *Bürgerschaft. Rezeption und Innovation der Begrifflichkeit vom Hohen Mittelalter bis ins 19. Jahrhundert*. Stuttgart: Klett-Cotta.

Kott, Sandrine. 1995. *L'Etat social allemand. Représentations et pratiques*. Paris: Belin.

———. 2001. *Le communisme au quotidien. Les entreprises d'Etat dans la société est-allemande*. Paris: Belin.

Krygier, Martin. 1997. 'Virtuous Circles: Antipodean Reflections on Power, Institutions, and Civil Society'. *East European Politics and Societies* 11(1): 36–88.

Kumar, Krishan. 1994. 'Civil Society: a Reply to Christopher Bryant's Social Self-organization, Civility and Sociology'. *British Journal of Sociology* 45(1): 127–30.

Lagerroth, Fredrik. 1915. *Frihetstidens författning: en studie i den svenska konstitutionalismens historia*. Stockholm: Bonnier.

Lamberti, Jean-Claude. 1989. *Tocqueville and the Two Democracies*. Cambridge, MA and London: Harvard University Press.

Lärda Tidningar. 1745–73. Stockholm: Salvius.

Larrain, Jorge. 2000. *Identity and Modernity in Latin America*. Cambridge: Polity.

———. 2006. 'Latin American Varieties of Modernity'. In Nathalie Karagiannis and Peter Wagner, *Varieties of World-making: Beyond Globalization*. Liverpool: Liverpool University Press.

Laslett, Peter. 1969. 'Introduction'. In John Locke's, *Two Treaties of Government*, 2nd edn. Cambridge: Cambridge University Press.

Le Bon, Gustave. 1906 [1894]. *Les lois psychologiques de l'évolution des peuples*. Paris: Alcan.

———. 1958 [1895]. *The Crowd. A Study of the Popular Mind*. London: Ernest Benn.

———. 1975 [1895]. *La psychologie des foules*. Paris: Retz-C.E.P.L.

Lefort, Claude. 1992. *Ecrire à l'épreuve du politique*. Paris: Calmann-Lévy.

Legnér, Mattias. 2002. 'Geografin i fosterlandets tjänst. De ekonomiska ortsbeskrivningarna i Sverige cirka 1740–1790'. *Historiska och litteraturhistoriska studier* 77.

Lindberg, Bo. 1976. *Naturrätten i Uppsala 1655–1720*. Uppsala: Almqvist & Wiksell.

Lindenberger, Thomas (ed.). 1999. *Herrschaft und Eigen-Sinn in der Diktatur.* Köln, Weimar, Wien: Böhlau Verlag.

Lindroth, Sten. 1978–81. *Svensk lärdomshistoria* vol. 3, Frihetstiden, vol 4: Gustavianska tiden. Stockholm: Norstedt.

Lipschutz, Ronnie D. 1992. 'Reconstructing World Politics: the Emergence of Global Civil Society'. *Millenium: Journal of International Studies* 21(3): 389–420.

Locke, John. 1726. *Johan Lockes Oförgripelige tankar om werldslig regerings rätta ursprung, gräntsor och ändamål*, trans. by Hans Harmens. Stockholm: Kongliga tryckeriet.

———. 1969 [1690]. *Two Treaties of Government*, 2nd edn. Cambridge: Cambridge University Press.

Lowenthal, David. 1997. *The Past is a Foreign Country.* Cambridge: Cambridge University Press.

Lyotard, Jean-François. 1989 [1978]. *La condition postmoderne.* Paris: Minuit.

Magnusson, Lars, Johan Heilbron and Björn Wittrock (eds). 1998. *The Rise of the Social Sciences and the Formation of Modernity: Conceptual Change in Context, 1750–1850.* Dordrecht: Kluwer.

Magone, José M. 2000. *The Modern World System and European Civil Society: A Reconstruction of the Long Dureé of Modernity in the New Millenium.* Copenhagen: University of Copenhagen.

Maier, Hans. 1980 [1965]. *Die ältere deutsche Staats- und Verwaltungslehre.* München, Beck.

Manent, Pierre. 2001. *Cours familier de philosophie politique.* Paris, Fayard.

Marshall, Thomas H. 1950. *Citizenship and Social Class and Other Essays.* Cambridge: Cambridge University Press.

———. 1977 [1947] *Class, Citizenship, and Social Development.* Chicago and London: University of Chicago Press.

McClellan, James E. 1985. *Science Reorganized: Scientific Societies in the Eighteenth Century.* New York: Columbia University Press.

McGrew, T. 1999. 'The World Trade Organisation: Technocracy or Banana Republic?'. In A. Taylor and C. Thomas (eds), *Global Trade and Global Social Issues.* London and New York: Routledge.

Meier, Christian. 1990 [1980]. *The Greek Discovery of Politics.* Cambridge, MA: Harvard University Press.

Mennander, Carl Fredric. 1756. *Tal om bok-handelen i Sverige, hållit för kongl. vetenskaps academien vid praesidii afläggande, den 8 maji, 1756.* Stockholm: Salvius.

Meuschel, Sigrid. 1992. *Legitimation und Parteiherrschaft. Zum Paradox von Stabilität und Revolution in der DDR.* Frankfurt: Suhrkamp.

Michnik, Adam. 1985. *Letters from Prison and Other Essays.* Berkeley and Los Angeles: University of California Press.

Mill, John Stuart. 1995 [1861]. 'Considerations on Representative Government'. In *Utilitarianism, On Liberty, Considerations on Representative Government.* London: Everyman.

Möller, Levin. 1745. *Nouveau dictionaire françois-svedois et svedois-françois. En ny frantzösk och swensk samt swensk och frantzösk lexicon, eller orda-bok.* Stockholm and Uppsala: Gottfried Kiesewetter.

Moulakis, Athanasios 2000. 'Realist Consitutionalism'. In James Hankins (ed.), *Renaissance Civic Humanism: Reappraisals and Reflections.* Cambridge: Cambridge University Press.

Muetzelfeldt, Michael and Gary Smith, 2002. 'Civil Society and Global Governance: the Possibilities for Global Citizenship'. *Citizenship Studies* 6(1): 58.

Munck, Ronald. 1984. *Politics and Dependency in the Third World: the Case of Latin America*. London: Zed.

Nerfin, Marc. 1987. 'Neither Prince, nor Merchant: The Citizen. An Introduction to the Third System'. *Development Dialogue*: 170–95. First published in 1986 as 'Neither Prince nor Merchant: Citizen – An Introduction to the Third System'. *IFDA Dossier* 56 (November–December 1986): 3–29.

Nilsén, Per. 2000. *Att stoppa munnen till på bespottare och underrätta andra: den akademiska undervisningen i svensk statsrätt under frihetstiden*. Lund: Juridiska fakulteten.

Nipperdey, Thomas. 1986. *Nachdenken über die deutsche Geschichte: Essays*. München: C.H. Beck.

Noda, Pamela J., ed. 1998. *Globalization, Governance, and Civil Society*. Tokyo: Japan Center for International Exchange.

Nordin, Jonas. 2000. *Ett fattigt men fritt folk: nationell och politisk självbild i Sverige från sen stormaktstid till slutet av frihetstiden*. Eslöv: Symposion.

Nye, Robert A. 2000. *The Origins of Crowd Psychology. Gustave Le Bon and the Crisis of Mass Democracy in the Third Republic*. London: Sage.

O'Brien, Karen. 1997. *Narratives of Enlightenment: Cosmopolitan History From Voltaire to Gibbon*. Cambridge: Cambridge University Press.

O'Donnell, Guillermo. 1979. 'Tensions in the Bureaucratic-Authoritarianism State and the Question of Democracy'. In David Collier (ed.), *The New Authoritarianism in Latin America*. Princeton: Princeton University Press, pp. 285–318.

O'Donnell, Guillermo, Philippe C. Schmitter and Laurence Whitehead. 1986. *Transitions from Authoritarian Rule: Latin America*. Baltimore: Johns Hopkins University Press.

Oscarsson, Ingemar. 2000. 'Med tryckfrihet som tidig tradition (1732–1809)'. In Karl Erik Gustafsson and Per Rydén (eds), *Den svenska pressens historia: I begynnelsen (tiden före 1830)*, vol. 1. Stockholm: Ekerlid.

Outhwaite, William. 2000. 'Towards a European Civil Society'. *Soundings* 16(November 2000): 135–36.

Oz-Salzberger, Fania. 1995. 'Introduction'. In Adam Ferguson, *An Essay on the History of Civil Society*. Cambridge: Cambridge University Press.

Pankoke, Eckart. 1972. 'Soziale Selbstverwaltung. Zur Problemgeschichte sozial-liberaler Gesellschaftspolitik'. *Archiv für Sozialgeschichte*: 185–203.

Pareto, Vilfredo. 1966 [1921]. *La trasformazione della democrazia*. In *Scritti sociologici minori*. Torino: UTET.

Passerini, Luisa (ed.). 2003. *Figures d'Europe, Images and Myths for Europe*. Bern: Lang.

Pateman, Carol. 1988. 'The Fraternal Social Contract'. In John Keane (ed.), *Civil Society and the State. New European Perspectives*. London: Verso.

Pearce, Jenny. 1993. 'NGOs and Social Change: Agents or Facilitators?'. *Development in Practice* 3(3): 12.

Peeler, John A. 1985. *Latin American Democracies: Colombia, Costa Rica, Venezuela*. Chapel Hill: University of North Carolina Press.

Pérez-Diaz, Victor. 1998. 'The Public Sphere and a European Civil Society'. In Jeffrey C. Alexander (ed.), *Real Civil Societies*. London: Sage, pp. 211–38.

Petras, James F. and Frank T. Fitzgerald. 1988. 'Authoritarianism and Democracy in the Transition to Socialism'. *Latin American Perspectives* 15(1): 93–111.

Pocock, J.G.A. 1975. *The Machiavellian Moment: Florentine Political Thought and the Atlantic Republican Tradition*. Princeton: Princeton University Press.

———. 1983. 'Cambridge Paradigms and Scotch Philosophers: a Study of the Relations between the Civic Humanist and the Civil Jurisprudential Interpretation of Eighteenth Century Social Thought'. In Istvan Hont and Michael Ignatieff (eds), *Wealth and Virtue. The Shaping of Political Economy in the Scottish Enlightenment*. Cambridge: Cambridge University Press.

———. 1987. 'The Concept of Language and the Métier d'historien: Some Considerations of Practice'. In Anthony Pagden (ed.), *The Languages of Political Theory in Early Modern Europe*. Cambridge: Cambridge University Press.

Polanyi, Karl. 1980 [1944]. *The Great Transformation*. New York: Beacon Press.

Polhem, Christopher. 1745. *Tal öfver den vigtiga frågan: hvad som vårt kära fädernesland hafver nu mäst af nöden til sin ständiga förkofring i längden? Hållit för kongl. svenska vetenskaps academien, af Christofher Polhem, vid praesidii afläggande den 13 octob.: 1745*. Stockholm: Grefing.

Pufendorf, Samuel von. 1747. *Friherren Samuel Pufendorffs Twenne böcker om menniskians lefnads och samlefnads plicht, förswenskade och jemförde med Sweriges lag, beslut och förordningar, b. Pufendorffs Jure naturae & gentium samt några lärda mäns skrifter*. Stockholm: Historiographi regni tryckerij/Koch.

Putnam, Robert (ed.). 2002. *Democracies in Flux. The Evolution of Social Capital in Contemporary Society*. Oxford: Oxford University Press.

Ray, James Lee. 1983. 'The Cuban Path to Dependency Reversal'. In Charles Doran, George Modelski and Cal Clark (eds), *North/South Relations*. New York: Praeger, pp. 223–38.

Renan, Ernest. 1996. *Qu'est-ce qu'une nation et autres écrits politiques*. Paris: Imprimerie nationale.

Reulecke, Jürgen. 1997. 'Die Mobilisierung der 'Kräfte und Kapitales': der Wandel der Lebensverhältnisse im Gefolge von Industrialisierung und Verstädterung'. In Jürgen Reulecke (ed.), *Geschichte des Wohnens, 1800–1918, Das bürgerliche Zeitalter*. Stuttgart: Deutsche Verlags-Anstalt, pp. 15–144.

Rhee, Sung-Hyong (ed.). 1999. *Latin American History and Thoughts*, Seoul: Kachi [in Korean].

———. 2002. *Latin America: The Permanent Crisis of Political Economy*. Seoul: Yeoksa Bipyong [in Korean].

Riedel, Manfred. 1975. 'Gesellschaft, Bürgerliche'. In Otto Brunner, Werner Conze and Reinhart Koselleck (eds), *Geschichtliche Grundbegriffe. Historisches Lexikon zur politisch-sozialen Sprache in Deutschland*, vol. 2. Stuttgart: Ernst Klett Verlag.

———. 1984. *Between Tradition and Revolution: The Hegelian Transformation of Political Philosophy*. Cambridge: Cambridge University Press.

Ritchie, Mark. 2001. 'Fighting to a Draw in Doha'. *Agribusiness Examiner* [online], no. 134. Available from: http://www.organicconsumers.org/corp/doha112601.cfm [Accessed 26 November 2001].

Roberts, Michael. 1986. *The Age of Liberty: Sweden, 1719–1772*. Cambridge: Cambridge University Press.

Robertson, John. 1983. 'The Scottish Enlightenment and the Limits of the Civic Tradition'. In Istvan Hont and Michael Ignatieff (eds), *Wealth and Virtue. The Shaping of Political Economy in the Scottish Enlightenment*. Cambridge: Cambridge University Press.

Robinson, James Harvey. 1904. *Readings in European History: a Collection of Extracts from the Sources Chosen with the Purpose of Illustrating the Progress of*

Culture in Western Europe since the German Invasions, vol. 2. Boston and New York: Ginn and Company.

Rorty, Richard. 1989. *Contingency, Irony, Solidarity.* Cambridge: Cambridge University Press.

Rowell, Jay. 2002. 'Le pouvoir périphérique et le "centralisme démocratique" en RDA'. *Revue d'histoire moderne et contemporaine* 2: 102–24.

———. 2004a. 'Wohnungspolitik'. In Dirk Hoffmann and Michael Schwartz (eds), *Geschichte der Sozialpolitik in Deutschland: 1949–1961 Deutsche Demokratische Republik: Im Zeichen des Aufbaus des Sozialismus*, vol. 8. Baden-Baden: Nomos Verlag.

———. 2004b. 'L'ouverture bureaucratique comme mode de domination rapprochée: les paradoxes de l'Etat local en RDA', *Sociétés contemporaines*.

Rubinstein, Nicolai. 1987. 'The History of the Word *Politicus*'. In Anthony Pagden (ed.), *The Languages of Political Theory in Early-Modern Europe*. Cambridge: Cambridge University Press.

———. 1990. 'Machiavelli and Florentine Republican Experience'. In Gisela Bock, Quentin Skinner and Maurizio Viroli (eds), *Machiavelli and Republicanism*. Cambridge: Cambridge University Press.

Rueschemeyer, Dietrich, Marylin Rueschemeyer and Björn Wittrock. 1998. *Participation and Democracy – East and West. Comparisons and Interpretations.* London and New York: M.E. Sharpe.

Saastamoinen, Kari. 1999. 'Political Vocabularies in Early Modern Sweden'. Paper presented at the History of Concepts – The Finnish Project in European Context Conference, 15–18 September, at Tampere.

Sahlstedt, Abraham M. 1769. *Dictionarium psevdo-svecanum, det är: ord-lista på främmande i swenska språket förekommande ord.* Västerås: J. L. Horrn.

———. 1773. *Swensk ordbok med latinsk uttolkning.* Stockholm: Carl Stolpe.

Salamon, Lester M. 1994. 'The Rise of the Non-profit Sector'. *Foreign Affairs* 73: 108–22.

Sandels, Samuel. 1771. *Tal, om kongl. svenska vetenskaps academiens inrättning och dess fortgång til närvarande tid, hållit för kongl. vetensk. academien, vid praesidii nedläggande, den 6 november 1771.* Stockholm: Salvius.

Scheffer, Carl Fredric. 1755. *Tal, hållit för kongl. vetenskaps academien vid praesidii afläggande, den 2 augusti, år 1755.* Stockholm: Salvius.

Schiera, Pierangelo. 1992. *Laboratorium der bürgerlichen Welt. Deutsche Wissenschaft im 19. Jahrhundert.* Frankfurt: Suhrkamp.

Schluchter, Wolfgang. 1996. *Paradoxes of Modernity: Culture and Conduct in the Theory of Max Weber.* Stanford: Stanford University Press.

Schmitt, Carl. 1985 [1923]. *Die geistesgeschichtliche Lage des heutigen Parlamentarismus.* Berlin, Duncker and Humblot (English trans. 2000. *The Crisis of Parliamentary Democracy*, Cambridge, MA and London: MIT Press).

Schmoller, Gustav. 1865. 'Die Arbeiterfrage'. *Preussische Jahrbücher*, vol. 15: 32–65.

———. 1918. *Die soziale Frage. Klassenbildung, Arbeiterfrage, Klassenkampf.* Munich: Duncker and Humblot.

Scholte, Jan Aart. 1999. *Global Civil Society: Changing the World?* Centre for the Study of Globalization and Regionalisation, Working Paper no. 31. Coventry: University of Warwick.

———. 2002. 'Civil Society and Democracy in Global Governance'. *Global Governance* 8: 281–304.

Seckinelgin, Hakan. 2002. 'Civil Society as a Metaphor for Western Liberalism'. *Global Civil Society* 16(4).

Segerstedt, Torgny T. 1971. *Den akademiska friheten under frihetstiden: en sammanställning*. Uppsala: Almqvist and Wiksell.

Seidman, Steven. 1983. *Liberalism and the Origins of European Social Theory*. Berkeley, CA: University of California Press.

Seigel, J.E. 1966. '"Civic Humanism" or Ciceronian Rhetoric? The Culture of Petrarch and Bruni'. *Past and Present* 34.

Seligman, Adam B. 1992. *The Idea of Civil Society*. Princeton: Princeton University Press.

Sellberg, Jan Lionel. 1998. *Hur är samhället möjligt?: om den tidigmoderna naturrättens språkfilosofiska grunder. Brännpunkt: Samuel Pufendorf*. Stockholm: Stockholms universitet.

Shaw, M. 1994. 'Civil Society and Global Politics: Beyond a Social Movements Approach'. *Millennium* 23: 647–67.

Shin, Jong-Hwa. 2000. 'The Limits of Civil Society'. In *European Journal of Social Theory* 3(2): 249–59.

Shiro, Ishi. 1997. 'Zur Anwendung des Feudalismus-Begriff auf die japanische Geschichte'. *Japan Review* 9: 75–85.

Siedentop, Larry. 1994. *Tocqueville*. Oxford and New York: Oxford University Press.

———. 2000. *Democracy in Europe*. London: Penguin.

Silvius, David. 1720. *Påminnelser angående successions-rättigheten i Sweriges rike, samt det så kallade souveraine wäldet, upsatte i januarii månad 1719*. Stockholm: kongliga tryckeriet.

Skidmore, Thomas E. and Peter H. Smith. 1984. *Modern Latin America*. New York: Oxford University Press.

Skinner, Quentin. 1969. 'Meaning and Understanding in the History of Ideas'. *History and Theory* 8.

———. 1998. *Liberty before Liberalism*. Cambridge: Cambridge University Press.

———. 2002. *Visions of Politics*, vol. 1: *Regarding Method*. Cambridge: Cambridge University Press.

Skocpol, Theda. 1992. *Protecting Soldiers and Mothers: the Political Origins of Social Policy in the United States*. Cambridge MA: Belknap Press of Harvard University Press.

Smolar, Aleksander. 1996. 'Civil Society after Communism: From Opposition to Atomisation'. *Journal of Democracy* 7(1): 24.

Souyri, Pierre François 1998. *The World Turned Upside Down: Medieval Japanese Society*. New York: Columbia University Press.

Spegel, Haquin. 1712. *Glossarium-sveo-gothicum eller Swensk-ordabook, inrättat them til en wällmeent anledning, som om thet härliga språket willia begynna någon kunskap inhämta*. Lund: Abraham Habereger.

Staël-Holstein, Germaine de. 1980. *Des circonstances actuelles qui peuvent terminer la Révolution et des principes qui devraient fonder la République en France*. Geneva and Paris: Droz.

Staniszkis, Jadwiga. 1991. *The Dynamics of the Breakthrough in Eastern Europe. The Polish Experience*. Berkeley, Los Angeles: University of California Press.

Steiner, Helmut. 1997. 'Aufbruch, Defizite und Leistungen der DDR-Soziologie: die 60er Jahre'. In Hans Bertram (ed.), *Soziologie und Soziologen im Übergang*. Opladen: Leske und Budrich, pp. 223–62.

Stepan, Alfred. 1985. 'State Power and the Strength of Civil Society in the Southern Cone of Latin America'. In Peter Evans, Dietrich Rueschemeyer, and Theda Skocpol (eds), *Bringing the State Back In*. Cambridge: Cambridge University Press.

Stockholms historiska bibliotek. 1755. (ed. Carl Christoffer Gjörwell), vols. 1–2. Stockholm: Nyström/Gjörwell.

Swedberg, Jesper. 1716. *Schibboleth. Swenska språketz rycht och richtighet*. Skara: Kjellberg.

Sylwan, Otto. 1896. *Svenska pressens historia till statshvälfningen 1772*. Lund: Gleerup.

Tarrow, Sydney. 1996. 'Making Democracy Work across Space and Time'. *American Political Science Review* 90(2): 389–98.

Terrier, Jean. 2001. Pouvoir législatif, opinion publique et participation politique dans la *Philosophie du droit* de Hegel. *Revue francaise d'histoire des idées politiques*, 13.

———. 2002. Culture et types de l'action sociale. *Revue européenne des sciences sociales – Cahiers Vilfredo Pareto*, LX, 122.

———. 2004. *What Nations Are, How They Think. Transformation and Diffusion of the Ideas of 'National Character' and National Traditions of Thought in France, 1860–1920*. Ph.D. thesis, European University Institute, Florence.

Tessin, Carl Gustaf. 1746. *Kårt tal om svenska språkets rykt och upodlande, hållit för kongl. svenska vetenskaps academien, af ... Carl Gustaf Tessin, då han afträdde sit praesidium d. 10. januarii 1746*. Stockholm: Salvius.

Then swänska Argus. 1732–34, no. 1–16. Stockholm: Schneider.

Tidningar om The Lärdas Arbeten. 1742 (edited by Olof Celsius).

Tilly, Charles. 1993. *European Revolution, 1492–1992*. Oxford: Blackwell.

Tismaneanu, Vladimir (ed.). 1995. *Political Culture and Civil Society in Russia and the New States of Eurasia*. New York, London: M.E. Sharpe.

Tocqueville, Alexis de. 1992 [1835–1840]. *De la Démocratie en Amérique*. Paris: Gallimard (Pléïade).

———. 1994 [1835–1840]. *Democracy in America*. London: Fontana Press.

Topalov, Christian, ed. 1999. *Laboratoires du nouveau siècle. La nébuleuse réformatrice et ses réseaux en France, 1880–1914*. Paris: Editions de l'EHESS.

Traitez du gouvernement civil en Anglois. 1690. In *Bibliothèque universelle et historique de l'année 1690*, vol. 19. pp. 559–91.

Troncoso, Moisés Poblete and Burnett, Ben. 1962. *The Rise of the Latin-America Labor Movement*. New Haven CT: College and University Press, New Haven, Conn.

Tuck, Richard. 1979. *Natural Rights Theories: Their Origin and Development*. Cambridge: Cambridge University Press.

———. 1993. *Philosophy and Government 1572–1651*. Cambridge: Cambridge University Press.

Tunander, Ole, Pavel Baev and Victoria Ingrid Einagel. 1997. *Geopolitics in Post-wall Europe: Security, Territory and Identity*. London: Sage.

Valenzuela, Arturo. 1978. *The Breakdown of Democratic Regimes: Chile*. Baltimore: John Hopkins University Press.

Vallier, Ivan. 1970. *Catholicism, Social Control and Modernization in Latin America*. New York: Prentice Hall.

Vegesack, Thomas von. 2001. *Iakttagelser vid gränsen: när skönlitteraturen möter sina vedersakare*. Stockholm: Natur och kultur.

Verhofstadt, Guy. 2001. *Ethical Globalization – Workable Globalization* [online]. UNIDO Publications. Available from: http://www.unido.org/en/doc/4889 (26 November – 2 December 2001).

Viroli, Maurizio. 1990. 'Machiavelli and the Republican Idea of Politics'. In Gisela Bock, Quentin Skinner and Maurizio Viroli (eds), *Machiavelli and Republicanism*. Cambridge: Cambridge University Press.

Wagner, Peter. 1994. *A Sociology of Modernity. Liberty and Discipline*. London: Routledge.

———. 1998. 'Certainty and Order, Liberty and Contingency. The Birth of Social Science as Empirical Political Philosophy'. In Johan Heilbron, Lars Magnusson and Björn Wittrock and Dordrecht: Kluwer (eds), *The Rise of the Social Sciences and the Formation of Modernity*. pp. 241–63.

———. 2001a. *Theorizing Modernity. Inescapability and Unattainability in the Social Sciences*. London: Sage.

———. 2001b. *A History and Theory of the Social Sciences. Not All that is Solid Melts into Air*. London: Sage.

———. 2001c. 'Modernity, Capitalism, and Critique', *Thesis Eleven*. August 2001.

———. 2003a. 'As Intellectual History Meets Historical Sociology. Historical Sociology after the Linguistic Turn'. In Gerard Delanty and Engin Isin (eds), *Handbook of Historical Sociology*. London: Sage, pp. 168–79.

———. 2003b. 'La forma politica dell'Europa – Europa come forma politica'. In Giuseppe Bronzini, Heidrun Friese, Antonio Negri and Peter Wagner (eds), *Europa politica e movimenti sociali*. Roma: Manifestolibri.

———. 2003c. 'Versuch, das Endspiel zu verstehen. Kapitalismusanalyse als Gesellschaftstheorie'. *Vortrag auf der internationalen Adorno–Konferenz*. Frankfurt, September 2003.

——— and Heidrun Friese. 2002. 'The Nascent Political Philosophy of Europe'. *The Journal of Political Philosophy*.

Wakeman, Frederic. 1998. 'Boundaries of the Public Sphere in Ming and Qing China'. *Daedalus* 27(3): 167–89.

Walzer, Michael, ed. 1995. *Toward a Global Civil Society*, vol. 1. Providence: Berghahn Books.

Wargentin, Pehr. 1756. 'Svar, Gifvit på Kongl. Vetensk. Academiens Vägnar, Af Des Secreterare'. In Carl Fredric Mennander, *Tal om bok-handelen i Sverige, hållit för kongl. vetenskaps academien vid praesidii afläggande, den 8 maji, 1756*. Stockholm: Salvius, pp. 27–29.

Weber, Max. 1964. *Wirtschaft und Gesellschaft*, vol. 2. Berlin: Kiepenheuer und Witsch.

———. 1994a [1895]. 'The Nation State and Political Economy'. In *Political Writings*. Cambridge, Cambridge University Press.

———. 1994b [1917]. 'Parliament and Government in Germany under a New Political Order. Towards a Critique of Officialdom and the Party System'. In *Political Writings*. Cambridge: Cambridge University Press.

———. 1994c [1919]. 'Politics as Vocation'. In *Political Writings*. Cambridge: Cambridge University Press.

Wiarda, Howard and Harvey F. Kline (eds). 1985. *Latin American Politics and Development*. Boston: Houghton Mifflin.

Willetts, Peter. 2002. 'Civil Society Networks in Global Governance: Remedying The World Trade Organisation's Deviance from Global Norms'. In *Colloquium on International Governance, 20 September 2002 Palais des Nations*.

Williams, Raymond 1976. *Keywords: A Vocabulary of Culture and Society.* London: Fontana.

Williamson, John, ed. 1994. *The Political Economy of Policy Reform.* Washington, DC: Institute for International Economics.

Wittrock, Björn 1999. 'Social Theory and Intellectual History'. In Fredrik Engelstad and Ragnvald Kalleberg (eds), *Social Time and Social Change: Historical Aspects in the Social Sciences.* Oslo: Scandinavian University Press.

World Bank. 2001. *Attacking Poverty: World Development Report 2000/2001.* New York: Oxford University Press.

Wrede, Hindric Jacob. 1743. *Tal om et borgerligit samhälles eller et land ock rikes rätta styrka, samt sätt ock utvägar at komma där til, hållit för kongl. svenska vetenskaps academien den 26 januarii år 1743.* Stockholm: Salvius.

Yamamoto, Tadashi (ed.). 1995. *Emerging Civil Society in the Asia-Pacific Community.* Tokyo: Japan Centre for International Exchange and Institute of Southeast Asian Studies.

———. 1999. *Deciding the Public Good: Governance and Civil Society in Japan.* Tokyo: Japan Center for International Exchange.

Zimmermann, Bénédicte. 2001. *La constitution du chômage en Allemagne.* Paris: MSH Editions.

Zimmermann, Clemens. 1991. *Von der Wohnungsfrage zur Wohnungspolitik. Die Reformbewegung in Deutschland 1845–1914.* Göttingen: Vandenhoeck and Rupprecht.

INDEX